Borrowed
Earth
Cafe ☺

Borrowed Earth Café ☺

Climbing the Ladder of a Dream

A book for the millions of people who believe in dreams and are ready to climb

BY

DANNY LIVING

iUniverse, Inc.
Bloomington

Borrowed Earth Café ☺
Climbing the Ladder of a Dream

iUniverse books may be ordered through booksellers or by contacting:

iUniverse
1663 Liberty Drive
Bloomington, IN 47403
www.iuniverse.com
1-800-Authors (1-800-288-4677)

ISBN: 978-1-4620-5489-3 (sc)
ISBN: 978-1-4620-5490-9 (hc)
ISBN: 978-1-4620-5491-6 (ebk)

Printed in the United States of America

iUniverse rev. date: 10/27/2011

So, you're like, "Can I write the title, like, on a scrap of paper and not have some lawyer knocking at my door?" And we say, "Lord, tell us you're not copying and pasting chunks into your son's application to get into Harvard or something."

Really, we just ask that you respect our property.

Also, I mean, look at us. Do you want to listen to a couple of Neo-Hippies?

For the record, Danny and Kathy Living are two regular people with no special training who decided, "Let's do it."

All gung-ho. Geez, what were we thinking?

And watching *The Secret* 90 days in a row? Come on, wasn't there something else on TV?

To Kathy, my wife, my girl . . . this book is for you.
I wouldn't take one brick out of the Road behind me.
All of them were necessary because they built the Road that led to you.
You are another Angel who speaks with the Voice and a Vessel of the Electricity that illumines Light Bulbs.
You are the Silence—a Nobody who became a somebody who will someday go back to being Nobody like me and everyone else.
Back from whence you came, I came, and we all came and to where we will all someday all return.
To the Kingdom Within . . .
Which for now is a place inside my chest, the force behind an outward pressure that sometimes leaves me taking slow, deep tearful breaths so I can stand it.
Thank you for encouraging me to share myself, to hug people, to love myself wholly without apology or reservation . . . to write, to sing and live. Really live.
When I was little, I thought my wife would be my best friend—someone who I would spend the entire day with all day long; every day, for the rest of my life.
I thought it was just a silly little-kid notion.
But, there you are, exactly what I saw in the Realm of Dreams all those years ago. In the Catalog.
I love you . . . thank you for loving me back.
Also, I'll always be grateful for all who've encouraged me . . . all of you, the Likers, the Commenters, the Distracted. Careful what you clap for! Next thing you know, some fool has written a book. My parents, Katie and Jim Moran, the ones who did The Work, capital T, capital W, they clapped for me, which filled me with courage, which watered my word-seeds, from which grew a Garden of Words and Laughter that beautified my life. I grew up watching them encourage and help people in the best ways they could. They opened their home . . . to me . . . to everyone. They

shared. *Their home was a gathering place, a place to laugh, to share food and to leave feeling a little better than when you arrived. I blame them for everything good, including Borrowed Earth Café, which is a neo-hippie version of my home growing up. Jim and Katie's love was like sunshine and rain on my soil and a wonderful garden grew inside me. When I could talk and later write, the garden grew and grew and grew until I could tend it myself. But man, people keep appreciating that garden and I feel like the luckiest guy in the world. People like all of you, who keep showing up, encouraging me to keep that garden alive. So, I decided to put my hand to the plow again and write another book. My first book,* Yoga: The Secret *healed my body. This one healed my soul. There's a grateful little kid who feels so loved inside me, smiling, trapped in the body of a 49-year old man clomping up the Ladder of Laughs, up to the top of a Wall somewhere where he imagines he'll eventually just sit with his eyes closed and smile forever. Nothing to see, hear or think about. Nothing to feel but good.*

:)

"Like a silent messenger bearing inward the food stole into my very essence and spoke in a quiet whisper
I love you."
—Danny Living

"He who gives food finds Happiness."—Upanishad

So, Who Are Danny and Kathy Living?

"Mind is the Master power that molds and makes, and Man is Mind, and ever more he takes the Tool of Thought, and shaping what he wills, brings forth a thousand joys, a thousand ills—He thinks in secret and it comes to pass; Environment is but his looking-glass."—James Allen, from "As a Man Thinketh"

~

"We don't inherit the Earth from our ancestors, we borrow it from our children."—Chief Seattle

~

We're the kind of fool people who believe in ourselves.

Modern pioneers not afraid to walk away from what we know, get in a wagon and head West, so to speak. Head into uncharted territory in our lives, maybe a little scared, but willing to keep going West anyway.

Try something new.

See where it takes us.

See who we meet along the way, even if it's a bolder version of who we were before we hit the trail.

See how it *feels*.

Have an adventure.

In December of 2006, we went on a raw food diet following a 30-day detox. At the end of the detox, the booklet that came with the package of herbal supplements suggested eating raw food for three days before going right back to *your normal diet*.

Normal.

We had been eating vegan food for about a year back then, and before that, vegetarian food. But, for most of our lives, we ate what everyone else eats.

Sorry, no hippie dippy, free love, flowers in your hair, Woodstock refugee, tie dye, incense and peppermints, funky monkey, commune story. (Danny could probably invent one, if you're interested.)

Danny is from Westmont, Illinois, a little working class suburb of Chicago.

Me? I'm Kathy. How ya'll doing? I spent the bulk of my life in Tulsa, Oklahoma.

An Okie, if you will.

I'll be your narrator.

THREE DAYS OF
ONLY RAW FOOD

Huh. Where to begin?

How about free? No sense running up a credit card to just try something new like some newbie golf goober.

So, I checked every book out of the library they had that boasted raw food recipes. I sat down at the kitchen table, spread all the books out and picked three days worth of meals from the pages.

I wrote down the ingredients I needed on a shopping list and wrote on a separate piece of paper: *Monday, Tuesday, Wednesday,* or whatever days it was, and then the name of the recipe, the book, page number and the meals for each day under the words *Breakfast, Lunch, Dinner* and *Dessert* beneath each day beneath each day.

Seems all the meal bases were covered.

You're thinking, "Wait, a shopping list, the days of the week, and page numbers?"

It sounds hokey, but if you don't make a plan, you're out of luck, right?

You end up going to the store, throwing things in the cart and coming home and going out to dinner anyway, eating off all the easy quick things while the produce rots in the vegetable drawer ("I ain't cooking . . . I work" or a 100 other reasons) or you eat the same things you ate last week . . .

And the week before.

God, you're starting to be your parents.

Oh no.

Go Back to Your Normal Diet . . . or Keep Going . . . West?

After our three days were up, we were feeling pretty good. Real good in fact. Better than either of us had felt in years.

Was this the food? Or was this the contrail of the detox? All that junk inside us, tossed out, our innards swept and dusted, the drawers re-lined with paper, cleaning out our 40-year old plus bodies.

Since we had the recipe books, we made a decision to stretch the three days out into a week. After all, we wanted to try some other recipes . . .

Heading West . . .

After three weeks, Danny says to me, "I don't want to go back . . ."

And I'm like, "To a corporate job?" And he says, "That too, but I mean I don't want to go back to cooked food."

"I knew what you meant. Me neither," I said.

And so that wagon set out along the trail, leaving something behind. A three-day journey first, now without an endpoint, just an empirical direction.

And no desire to turn around and go back.

To any of it.

And a buzz of something. An excitement, yeah, but something else too. Call it a stirring, an awakening of sorts.

An awakening, which for both of us had begun a few years earlier before we met.

A guy and a girl who'd met at a place they'd done yoga.

Danny and I taught at the same yoga place, but he wasn't at all like anyone else there.

You wouldn't believe him then. At least 30 pounds heavier, hair shaved down to within a half-inch of his scalp. "I do it myself," he shrugged. "Every couple weeks I squat in the basement like a baseball catcher, unfold a single sheet of newspaper on the basement floor, put my palm on the top of my head, and take it off, sides and the back, then, switch to a little longer blade, and do the top—all the little hairs raining down on that paper. Fold it up and toss it out."

I remember looking at his hair, just a little burr on his head, but it all seemed to be there. Just shorn off.

"At your age, hair's like a trophy," I said. "You should let it grow out."

He seemed interested and looked at me as I continued.

"Some people say hair is your spiritual antennae," I continued.

He twisted his mouth into a little smile. "Yeah?"

"Yeah," I said, looking up at all those little nubs. "You should let it grow."

I taught a gentle 5:30am morning class. You don't want to *break* people at that hour, tear something loose. You're kind to half-awake people. No, you get them to relax, get them into a calm meditative place, which is where any yoga will take you if you'll let it.

Danny said I was like a fish tank and he became a frequent figure in the back of the class.

Mr. Basement Buzz Cut.

Danny taught a 90-minute Sunday morning class. Leading people through a challenging Ashtanga Yoga sequence.

Mr. Hard Core yogi.

But nice and laid back about it.

A *guy* who'd *done* a lot of *yoga*.

Guy Dunyoga.

But, a guy who, the more yoga he did, found that his body was this huge storehouse of information.

Information that he had thought he'd buried.

The yoga was waking him up. He was *feeling*.

Maybe waking up to unpleasant facts like, I don't really like my job and, what happened to the happy little kid that made people laugh? The writer in college that the teachers said had what it took. "You could be the next new Chicago writer /poet," said one.

The guy who took pleasure in having people over for dinner, making people laugh with stories and jokes, yeah, have a good time, but also maybe circle around to some deeper, more meaningful conversation, but here, I made you a plate of food . . .

What happened to that guy?

A rude awakening, if you will.

The yoga acting as the catalyst, those poses and the breathing and the relaxing was giving him a sort of *rude awakening*.

Rudy Wakening.

But instead of going back to sleep, rolling over, pulling the covers up, he says he began to *awaken* in *earnest*.

Earnest Wakener.

Back in the wagon, the road stretched out far and unfamiliar before us.

But this feeling: It was like a warm sun. Beckoning.

I think we both thought that clean shiny feeling, the *buzz*, would go away, if we went back.

No one wants the buzz to go away.

Wee!

So, we decided to keep going. Keep eating.

Where we had been was soon out of sight. We stopped glancing over our shoulders and fixed our eyes on the trail and then, at all the scenery, seeing some of the little miracles we'd been overlooking, illuminating things here and there, the wagon rocking gently. No provisions in the back.

Sorry, Pardner. Gonna have to make your own food now.

No problem. As long as this *buzz* sticks around. Whadaya want me to chop?

In January 2007, we joined a raw food Meetup group. The woman who organized the Meetup group was looking for a place to host the next Meetup and we offered our home.

About seven people showed up and we had a great time.

The next month, we said we'd have it at our home again.

About 12 people showed up the next time.

Meanwhile, the organizer kind of lost interest and we asked to be made the assistant organizer, which allowed us to post messages, upload pictures and all the fun stuff an organizer does. We began to use Meetup to correspond with new members and promote our Meetups.

Danny all of a sudden, in little fragments, getting to be the writer again. And I think that was when we started to understand that this was all about a lot more than just food.

We started to discover what color our parachute was, maybe, and the idea was born within us that we were really just sharing ourselves with people.

We were feeling good and we wanted to share. We wanted to pass it around like a plate of food, "Here, we made something."

Try it.

And I think that we became very aware of how much enjoyment we received from having people over, talking to them and serving them food we'd made gave birth to the dream that we might someday do this as our way of living.

We were paying very close attention how we felt when we did things. I think we'd both come from places where working was something you did in exchange for money and hopefully you derived some degree of a sense of accomplishment and satisfaction from the doing of your job.

But this? To really love what you do? To feel really good about it all the way up and down?

This was new.

What were we doing?

Sharing ourselves and our way of *living*. Talking and sharing from our hearts but also from our kitchen, a place where we made food while those same hearts beat a happy rhthym.

We were trying to just concentrate on the business of taking care of ourselves, the yoga, the food, and the excavation of the buried garbage: the food we'd eaten and the feelings we'd stuffed and stored away . . . the toxic things.

Not making a living.

Just living with a capital L.

Our name just another pun, I guess. Maybe we were just two more characters to write about.

Danny and Kathy Living.

No doctor was around to spank this idea of sharing Danny and Kathy Living all the time, not just a couple times a month . . . it was a home birth all the way. It slid out easy, hold the forceps, didn't even hear the stork flapping away, mind you, the stork thinking, Now *That's* a baby . . .

We took a lot of pictures during this time and Danny would write a narrative of the day's trivial silliness and then write captions for all the pictures.

At night, he'd prop himself up in bed, upload pictures and write into the night, or during the day, he'd think of something, tell me, and I'd tell him to share it.

Share.

We'd see something or do something which would make us smile or just plain laugh because we were happy and we felt good and when you're happy and you feel good, you smile more and you see the humor in things.

But then we'd think of those other people who we knew through Meetup and who we could instantly communicate with by simply navigating to a webpage and clicking a button.

Suddenly, you could tell them what just made you smile with words or pictures with captions and they'd write back.

Like little kids saying, "Again!"

It made you feel good, knowing that you were feeling good and, if for even a moment, you might have spread a little happiness somewhere in the world and it felt like you were doing something good with your life.

And, like the same kind of kid, you'd say to yourself, "Again!"

And you'd share some more.

We didn't know it was like some wonderful machine inside you that keeps growing.

There's two states of being, as far as I'm concerned. One you might call War, which is represented by any unrest or mental discomfort.

The other?

Peace.

There's a War Machine that requires more conflict to grow and operate.

The Peace Machine?

Man, all you have to be is nice.

To grow and operate?

You gotta keep being nice.

Nice.

Peace.

The Peace Machine.

But who would have thought after all these years two old people like us would finally ask ourselves what we were doing with our lives?

Me, this person with kids and a house and no job reading all these recipe books and spending all that time making food in my kitchen when I should have been worried about the future and out pounding the pavement looking for another job I didn't really like.

Danny. Writing in the open. Sharing his writing.

Not keeping it all in a box . . . of notebooks full of essays, short stories and 100's of poems written from 1988, the year his son Andy was born, until 2004 when we met. He'd hidden them. Buried them along with the name Danny.

When I met him, he went by Dan, not Danny.

Later putting the Y at the end, like he does.

In his world, words became Wordsy.

And Dan became Danny.

I'm still not sure if those people came to our house for the food or the entertainment or just to have a "safe" friendly place where they could come and try the food and not feel judged.

And the talk . . . sometimes circling around to deep subjects that maybe didn't normally see the light of day but managed to find their way blinking into the light of our living room.

You would be absolutely amazed at the wondrous power of tasty wholesome food and a safe place to talk freely and be yourself unafraid.

In this case our living room.

The Living Room: The red U-shaped couch, the two-story ceiling rising up 20 feet high above us. A half-wall balconey up there, a colorful Mexican blanket, rainbow-striped and folded neatly hangs over the wall on the ledge up there—a ledge around the balconey with some plants on it. The see-through-to-the-next-room fireplace across from that couch and a big World Market wicker basket with a serving tray on top to remind us we're here to serve. A 43-pound amethyst cave on the big gray-slate tiles that wrap around that fireplace and a fragile off-white paper light. You barely see those concentric hoops pushing out to hold the shape, like a finger reaches up 5-feet high right next to "Danny's Spot" on the couch, the furthest leg of the U. Me, if company's not over, I'm laying down on the expanse of plush veloury material on the couch, a hand behind my head and hopefully a foot in Danny's lap. Keep those hands rubbing my feet, Pardner, I say with a smile. (Note: In 2004, I taught Danny to be an amateur reflexologist and have assured him that all that's between him and a certificate of completion is 100,000 hours . . . on my feet.)

But, back to the Meetup—boy, the people did seem to enjoy Danny's writing.

I think they'd read it and laugh and say, "Hey, this is funny. I want to go to their house and try the food."

Sometimes people would stay long after all the others had left and we'd sit on our big U-shaped couch and talk.

And it rarely was about food.

We were making people laugh with the stories and jokes, yeah, having a good time, but also eventually we'd circle around to some deeper, more meaningful conversation, Danny handing them a plate, Here you go, we made some food . . .

And the Danny who he'd hidden away for over 20 years started to emerge, blinking in the sunlight.

There you are.

We'd all sit on that couch laughing and having a good time.

But sometimes we'd sneak serious in there.

Like the food and the laughter was the distraction.

"Write," I'd instruct him, handing him the computer.

My little closeted writer, having a little fun, but always trying to close that door.

Like he was hiding.

I took the door off the hinges.

"You're out now, mister," I informed him.

The next day, we'd have tons of comments from people who'd loved the words and pictures and had gotten a good laugh.

No one was paying us to do this. We felt good and we wanted to share it.

Feel good first, and then share.

This had nothing to do with money.

Whenever we had a get-together, we always tried to serve the best possible food, welcome new members and share what we were learning.

Soon, we had over 30 people coming to our little town home. We decided we'd found our passion.

THE SECRET MARATHON

In the spring, someone brought a copy of the movie *The Secret* to our house and we watched it at a Meetup.

We thought, yeah, you watch it once and you're all motivated, but you've got all those years of being a doubting Thomas working against one 90-minute movie.

So, we decided to do an experiment.

Watch it every day for 30 days in a row.

Which we did.

Then we loaded it on our PC and would play it for the next 60 nights as we were falling asleep, keeping the volume at a level that you could just barely hear if you laid still . . . with the idea that the words were still being recognized and understood by our conscious minds, even if in the background.

It's theorized that everything has a sound vibration signature. Plants that are exposed to soothing classical music tend to grow to be healthier, under the same conditions, as compared to plants grown without music.

Signature, like the sound *writes* that vibration on that which it touches. Signs its name.

Likewise, plants exposed to music with a loud non-soothing sound (like heavy metal for example, but not to pick on heavy metal music, but it just effects the plants differently), tend not to grow as well as other control group plants grown without music, or grown with soothing music.

We thought that as living things, *Livings*, we would try and subject ourselves to soothing sounds as much as possible.

Also, we began to drastically cut and then almost completely eliminate our exposure to news, television and other non-soothing media.

Your body eats more than just food as part of its sustenance: The thoughts you think, the feelings that those thoughts create . . . we think these thoughts and feelings are the very seeds that grow and become the garden of our current reality and circumstances . . . and that these thoughts and feelings are more powerful than we realize.

And maybe with a little tilling, weeding and cultivation . . . plenty of fresh water and sunshine . . .

The same theory that holds that everything vibrates (slower or faster) and therefore produces sound also says that all sound has a measurable vibration or frequency.

Certain frequencies cause relaxation in the body while others can create a tense or stressed response.

Masaru Emoto's book *The Hidden Messages in Water* provides factual evidence that human energy expressed in thoughts, words, feelings, intentions and even music . . . all these have an affect on the molecular structure of water—the same water that makes up more than 70% of the human body and, coincidentally, is the same percentage of water that covers the Earth.

70-some percent of our bodies is water.

70-some percent of the Earth is water.

Here's the product description from Amazon:

The Hidden Messages In Water *explores water's susceptibility to human words, emotions and thoughts. Japanese scientist, Masaru Emoto, has been researching this new field of science by freezing samples of water that have been exposed to either positive or negative words, emotions and music. Through photographs, Dr. Emoto has found that water exposed to positive influences produces beautiful, perfectly formed crystals, while water exposed to negativity produces ugly, malformed crystals. Because the earth and our bodies are both composed of 70 percent water, the power to change the essence of water means that humans have the power to evoke change on a global or personal scale, by way of water.*

Our experiment or story had us trying to expose our bodies to a steady "diet" of daily frequencies that promoted good feelings and a calmness.

In a way, this conscious decision to attune ourselves to these frequencies daily was a form of meditation.

Sound yoga.

These kinds of practices, if pleasurable, cause the body and mind to crave them and desire to repeat them.

The *Buzz.*

So, we had this dream, this vague idea that we wanted to do something where we could be together, and, keep doing what we were doing, and feed not just our stomachs but also something else.

I think the destination to any dream is traveled by means of a balloon that you and other people, captured by your vision, inflate with the air of repeated breaths of life, faith, and hope. But mainly, the journey is fueled by old-fashioned hard work and narrated by your own voice of encouragement. Soon, your basket lifts off the ground, the Wind takes you high in the air and the next thing you know, you are traveling West, over the country, out over the Ocean, slowly descending towards a little cluster of islands that look just like the place on the map you've had in your mind . . .

Yeah, a balloon, and we're like, Hey, forget the wagon, let's go higher . . . and faster. Really see the sights. Maybe high five a bird.

BIRD: "Where are you two love birds headed?"

DANNY: "West."

BIRD: "Don't forget to enjoy the journey. It's what it's all about."

DANNY: "Thanks. Hey, don't poop on the wicker, Buddy."

~

Danny has this fool idea that we have a place in Maui.

Like it's there just waiting for us.

I guess he figures it's about as West as you can go.

Danny says, "Growing up, I remember reading that if my faith was as big as a mustard seed, I could say to the mountain, "Mountain, get yer butt over there . . ."

(I think Danny got this from the King James' Profane Little Brother's Edition of the Bible that his parents kept in the brown, oak glass-doored bookcase that had a slightly musty smell of cedar at the end of the hall. The bookcase, all booky, a breakfront, 3-door affair, an heirloom from his grandfather's attic, his grandfather, the dentist, "Doc," they called him, the house library, sitting topped with photos of the grandkids now. The bookcase, the last sight at the end of the long hall, the house fairway, right before the dogleg turn into his parent's kitchen. That Bible tucked next to a 1973 well-thumbed set of *The World Book Encyclopedia*, above a collector's set of Mark Twain leather-bound books, a tattered *Webster's Dictionary* and his dad's precious National Geographic magazines.)

I believe this to be a paraphrase, in fairness to King James' little brother (the lesser James Jim).

While I've never tried it on a mountain, Borrowed Earth Café was the result of fixing our minds on a vision, working our butts off and seeing the result with a date next to it . . . written clearly in our own hand on a paper stuck to our bathroom mirror.

Yeah, you want the Mountain to move, but usually, faith requires *you* to move, a lot . . . boldly, strongly and with endurance beyond what you're used to.

The Mountain's like, "Yeah, I could up and move over there where you're pointing, but why not climb me? Come on up!"

And, "I think your faith's maybe gonna mean *you're* supposed to move, not me," says the Mountain (maybe just a metaphor for Obstacle).

Underneath the vision for WHAT YOU IMAGINE are words and pictures and emotions . . . and, I think some of those words can express dissatisfaction with the way things are.

Not very Zen, but I consider myself half-awake, which means until I'm all the way out of Consciousness Bed, I can still expect a little unenlightened whining.

I can hide it, or, I can embrace it and use it.

I think, just like the best recipes have sweet, sour, salty and bitter in them, the Way towards moving mountains, climbing mountains or just moving, God, doing something about that niggling feeling that you need to do something, it can also include a little dissatisfaction.

I guess as long as it's not just idle complaining. That's hard to bear. Especially if there's no action. No moving.

Interesting how 'action' is at the end of dissatisfaction.

Otherwise, you just have dissatisf . . .

Like you're dissatisfied, but without any action. Not really motivated to do anything about it.

Man, I can only imagine what long-term dissatisfaction does to the water in a body.

I wonder what the messages in the water of the body of a person who's stuck looks like?

I consider a little dissatisfaction just the right seasoning needed to make a Dream Recipe taste just right.

Also, not on our website, but part of the story, yes, is that Danny copied the entire book *The Secret* (there's a book by Rhonda Byrne with the same name as the movie) in his own hand . . . a trick Danny used to use when studying to help record information in his mind for recall.

THE MAGICAL POWER
OF UNEMPLOYMENT

I had lost my job a few months before we'd started eating raw food all the time and ended up on unemployment for six months.

Then, about the time my unemployment ran out, Danny lost his job. He'd been working as a consultant for a guy who was probably looking for more of a friend. This guy was interested in raw food, but also had a lifestyle that included a lot of alcohol—and, as we've observed, alcohol and raw food can be enemies in some people.

And, *too much* alcohol and raw food definitely don't mix. Eventually, it seems, the person will have to choose one or the other.

But, being unemployed? Turned out to be one of the best things that ever happened to us.

We ended up spending almost six glorious months together, 24/7.

Most couples lives are more like 24 minutes / 7 . . . and here we had gotten a taste of 24/7 and it was like the food we were eating . . . the more we ate, the more we craved it.

The idea of going back and working separately again seemed unfathomable. Danny had worked in IT and I had worked for a custom homebuilder.

As Danny's hair grew out, the idea of cutting it to go to interviews bothered him.

Sometimes I wonder, at least for Danny, if the idea of our own restaurant was partly about keeping his wild head of hair.

Can you see Danny in an interview now? Picture it with me:

Danny's got a tie dye t-shirt on, a baggy pair of cargo shorts and he's slumped a little in the guest chair. He's got a big, size 13, brown Croc, spattered with dried food, propped up on the edge of the guy's desk. His thick wild dreadlocked hair cascades past his shoulders with those three 1-inch in diameter, red, yellow and green wooden beads stacked like a little traffic light tied to the longest dread. Danny looks at the guy across from him, wedged in the dismally grey little cubicle with the guest chair in front of the inexpensive modular desk with the cheap white Formica top. Danny saying, "I don't know, this place looks a little boring. What, you put the pictures of your kids on your desk to remind you not to run?" The guy behind the desk looking at him like, "Who let rasta man in?" and, "Is this guy, what, like some kind of musician?" and finally, the interview ends before it begins, the guy saying one word loud enough to be heard 50 feet away, "Security!"

Meanwhile, all those messages we were putting in our water started having their effect.

Things began to happen. Little things, but things that seemed to be leading us to something.

A friend of ours named Jillmarie (her names all run together, say it like one word) had a little coffee shop in Aurora called *The Greenleaf Café* that she'd opened with her mother and sister . . . their dream . . . and she said she had a lot of customers looking for sugar-free desserts.

We started selling cookies, our truffles really, in her shop.

Pretty soon, we were making $25 a week or so. Not big money, but it was encouraging. We had an inspired thought, decided to take the next step. We took a breath and spent $800 on a little glass door refrigerator.

We had four months left on Danny's unemployment, and it was difficult to imagine how this encouraging, yet tiny sum could support our family. Well, in the movie, they say when you catch yourself doing that kind of monkey math, meaning worrying about money running out or anything else that hasn't happened yet . . . STOP!

It's like all that emotional negative energy that your body generates when you're scared and worried writes on the water of your body and it vibrates.

Just imagine that person up to their neck in a pool of water. You're up above them 20 feet on some observation platform with a clipboard and a camera and hey, there's tiny rippling shakey waves coming out from the person's body and traveling to all the sides of the round pool . . . then they bounce off the wall and come back at the person.

That's how it works.

The vibrations that come out from you, good or bad, happy or sad, kind or cruel, caring or cold, hopeful or doubtful, confident or scared.

These waves that come out from you ripple outward in the moisture bubbles in the air that make the air humid. They travel out and bounce off everything while also striking things that match the sender's frequency. Like two birds calling out for each other in the jungle; each knows that a same-species bird has made communicative contact and they fly toward each other.

If you're feeling badly, you're broadcasting.

If you're feeling good, you're broadcasting.

If a dove lands on you, smile.

If an angry starling swoops at you, ask yourself what you've been thinking about.

Please.

We put more things in that little refrigerator and started to sell more.

One day sitting on the sofa, we heard someone on TV say that Chief Seattle quote:

"We don't inherit the Earth from our ancestors; we borrow it from our children."

And Danny, the word man, looks at me and says, "Borrowed Earth. Wouldn't that be a good name for a business?"

Why not?

We started making labels on our home computer that said, "Borrowed Earth" and stuck those on the boxes we put in that little refrigerator at Jillmarie's (did you say it like one word or are you puttin' a space in there, Pardner?).

HEY KIDS!
WHO WANTS TO OPEN
A RESTAURANT?

Two weeks into *The Secret* marathon, we were driving to the city for a date to eat at a raw food restaurant.

90 minutes on the expressway, looking at brake lights.

I said, "This is crazy. We're driving 90 minutes to eat dinner. We're gonna eat in 45 minutes and then it's like, 90 minutes home. 3 hours driving for dinner. I wish there was some place closer."

Danny said, "Yeah, we should just open our own restaurant . . ."

And then neither of us said anything for five long minutes.

And then Danny said the *Nike* thing, "Let's do it."

So, that night, he wrote on a piece of paper in big bold letters:

"In OCTOBER of 2007, we opened Borrowed Earth Café."

We picked a date a few months in the future, as *The Secret* says, ". . . your goal has to be believable for you."

Not knowing this was extremely aggressive and us, well steeped in ignorance, started believing we could actually do it.

No prior restaurant ownership experience. None. Zero.

I waitressed some in my 20's and Danny, well, he worked at a snack shop one summer with his little brother, serving sweaty people, people smelling of chlorine and summer leisure, dripping on the floor, ordering a quick meal to eat pool side.

No real money.

No real plan.

But no one telling us no.

We were careful to not share our goal with people who had a history of discouragement.

A lot of times you can "talk out" a dream and all that talk energy depletes from your action energy. Only talk about it enough to act again . . . talking can quickly start depleting you, even though it feels exciting and good . . . if you find you're not taking action steps, hush yourself with kindness and start a daily tick list of to-do's.

Or, you tell enough people, especially people who've long since shelved their own dreams, well, you might find yourself getting talked out of it.

"What if it fails?" they'll ask. The one question that has single-handedly killed the dreams of more human beings than any other consideration: "What if . . . ?"

And we say, "What if you die with your song unsung?" and, "Is living under the dictatorship of fear . . . is that really Living?

We taped that paper with our boldly written dream and the date to our bathroom mirror and looked at it every day, and I'll report that it got all curled and flecked with Danny's toothpaste shrapnel.

Tooth Brush Visioning became the morning and evening meditation ritual. Those two-minute automatic shut-off toothbrushes?

Best money I ever spent. All you need is something to look at while you brush.

Something magnificent.

In August of 2007, we got an automatic email from Meetup saying the organizer had dropped and the message asked if we'd like to take over.

We said yes!

In the mean time, our Meetups had grown to 45 plus.

By then, our unemployment was starting to dry up, but we clung to the belief that we could manifest Borrowed Earth Café, if we just believed that it had already been ordered from the catalog of the Universe.

Every morning our imaginations would fly right at the mirror and grab on to that note and cling.

We could cling. We were clinging.

At first, we found a 108-year old farm house a mile from our house that we were going to buy and turn into a bed and breakfast. That half-acre out back? We were going to grow food in a garden and have some of it be part of our food supply.

A business banker, the zoning board, and the county loved our idea, but the nine-month process was too long to wait.

We had kids to feed and we needed an income now, not nine months in the future.

PARTNER

A local restaurant owner, whom we shall refer to as Partner, was interested in our concept and wanted to be our "partner."

"Partner" it turns out, had different ideas about what would work.

Turns out he had a dream.

"It's a place where people come and eat," he said, sweeping his hand in a grand gesture that tried to take in all of the land on our local Community Supported Agriculture (CSA) farm near our home in Naperville, Ilinois, where we had driven with him. We had belonged to the CSA for years and planned on using their food in our restaurant.

"We'll use this little milk house here," he said indicating a small white brick structure the size of a one-car garage. One-car is probably a generous description. I wager you could park a Mini Cooper hatchback in there, the sides scraping the opening as you pull in, maybe with room for two folded lawn chairs.

Chairs folded and squashed up against the grill.

'Cuz you couldn't open the door once you were parked inside. Not an inch.

No sir, climb over the back seat and out the hatch.

He continued.

Borrowed Earth Café ☺

"The people will sit on the lawn here," he indicated a little expanse of grass that sloped up to the barn where the farmer, who we knew, eyed Partner warily.

Apparently, this dream had not occurred to Partner lying in bed.

He was having it right now, right here. Careful, don't step on that squirrel there, *Partner*.

"Uh, outside?" we asked.

"In a big white tent," he said. Like, see? I've thought of everything.

Like the kind you stuff your outside wedding reception under, hope it doesn't rain, man, everyone's shoes gettin' all muddy, the bride and bridesmaids got ugly grey spatters up and down all that lace and taffeta.

A tent.

We were curious now, but had already given each other the signal: the eye roll and finally, the silent Cuckoo Bird, swirling the pointed index finger clockwise, like you're drawing a circle, around your temple.

When Partner wasn't looking, we made faces at each other, me and Danny, riding out the end of the dream.

Get in our car and go home.

Geez, what were we thinking?

We'd worked in this man's place for one absurd day and had seen enough to realize that like this dream, a restaurant owner can make it up as they go, goof ups and all.

It was like another green light, like the Universe was saying, "You can SO do this."

In the mean time, Danny and I kept our arms and legs inside the car as the bar lowered on our laps, the jolt of the car starting it's way down the track on the Milk House Café Rollercoaster Ride.

Wee! Arms up! Big smiles!

Enjoying the comedy of it.

We prompted further details, probably subconsciously wanting more material for this section of the book, not yet written, the movie, not yet available on DVD or some kind of Watch 'Er Now!

"What about in winter?" Danny asked, thinking, Yeah, it's Chicago, it's gonna get a little chilly.

Now we were just messing around.

. . . CLICK CLICK CLICK CLICK the rollercoaster car climbs up that steep hill . . .

"We'll run a cord into the milk house and hook up space heaters there, and there," he said pointing to what would be the future source of juice for the H in the café's HVAC future and then he pushed open a narrow side door that didn't quite close. *clickety-clickety-click-click, almost to the top . . .*

We all glanced inside.

There was an old sink on the wall, a desk and a couple refrigerators.

"See," he said, "There's water and electricity. This will be the kitchen." He pulled the door as closed as it would go.

Whee! Down the big hill and into the first hard turn . . .

31   *Borrowed Earth Café* ☺

It was a glorified, undersized garage.

For a Mini Cooper with the paint scraped off the sides, the two folded chairs mashed up against the grill.

He rubbed his palms like he was warming them.

It's always good when a plan comes together.

Plus, we had water and electricity. And heat in the winter.

We stood next to the future kitchen / milk house and on the grass floor of the future dining terrace / tent.

. . . *car goes through loop-d-loop and starts to climb . . . click, click, click . . .*

Up the hill, the farmer stood leaning with both hands on the top of a long handle of a shovel. He was watching us now.

We waved and he waved back with the hand on top of the shovel without taking his hand off the shovel; a little finger wave. Not putting too much into it.

Partner waved, his arm high. He turned to us, beaming, "See, he likes me."

I was trying to get Danny to laugh now, blow his cool.

"What about the bathroom? Where will the ladies from Naperville pee?" I asked.

Whee!

I swear Danny made a noise like he was choking back smoke, but I refused to look at him, fearful he'd cross his eyes or pull some face and I'd be lost. When it comes to making you laugh, he's dangerous to spar with. Very dangerous. He says, "I always win."

Partner looked at us patiently. "Port-a-potties," he said pointing. "There, and there."

Whee!

He paused, the dream seeming to come to a slow halt and you could almost hear the ball bearings in his brain clicking together, someone forgetting to grease them.

As the Milk House Café ride came to a halt, we kept our arms and legs inside the car and when the bar lifted we got back on solid ground, the terrace / patio, to be precise.

"Let's go to talk to him right now!" Partner said excitedly.

Around the grounds, people were busily preparing for an annual Earth Day festival held on the farm.

"I don't think now's a good time, what with the festival and all," I suggested.

He seemed determined, but we somehow pulled him toward the car, not wanting to subject our friend the farmer to the Milk House Café dream.

We dried our eyes discreetly, composed ourselves, and each shook Partner's hand and went home.

Problem was, how to break the bad news to him?

Sorry, you're a little too Mad Hatter for our Alice in Wonderland.

I had the idea that we could pull a *Fiddler on the Roof.* Say we had a dream. How my dead grandmother appeared and shook her finger at me, "Ach, don't open a restaurant, Bubby. What are you thinking? Oy vey."

We could say it was a Sign.

Appeal to his superstitious side, this Partner and his Milk House Café dream.

But, in the end, we just did the girl thing.

We didn't call him.

Meanwhile, Sean, the commercial realtor who'd shown us the farm said, "I don't want to scare you, but 9 out of 10 restaurants fail within the first year . . . but that means you got people in year one of five-year leases, just looking to hand someone the keys."

We said, "Go on."

It sounded like recycling. Recycling's good.

Sean had met Partner and well, he hadn't been impressed.

We told him about the Milk House Café and he laughed his big laugh, "If you two didn't get away from him, me and *my* partner were talking about doing an intervention."

He continued, "You don't need a partner or investors. You two are all you need."

BORROWED EARTH CAFE

Sean believed in us to the bone and somehow his voice was like our own voices saying, "You can do this, *you're Danny and Kathy Living. You can do anything,*" which became our mantra.

Sean was a big Irish guy that sat in his office with his girlfriend Kathy and actually ate our food. We used to drive to see him, go up to the second floor and we'd sit at this big wooden conference table, his jaws working, enjoying something we brought to share with him. He'd have a big smile on his face.

"I think you got something here," he'd say.

He smoked cigars and liked his steak rare, his beer cold and his whiskey neat, but he loved our food.

He looked just like the actor, George Kennedy. Swear to God. He was built like George Kennedy too. Big, but with a genuine 10,000-gigawatt smile and this big heart.

He'd smile at you and suddenly, you'd stopped worrying.

Sean found this little 30-seater restaurant by the train in downtown Downers Grove, right by the Tivoli Theater. The owner had made it almost four years and had closed down several months earlier.

Sean had helped him find the place and get started more than four years before.

He took us there and we loved it.

It was in a strip mall at the bottom of a tall condo building in the heart of downtown Downers Grove, a small suburb, a 25-minute ride from Union Station in Chicago, on the Burlington Northern Metra train line.

The historical Tivoli Theater was about 200 feet east of the place. Our spot had a large patio with room for five wrought-iron tables and chairs for the warmer months.

There was an expanse of glass windows across the front and a door to the far right.

When you walked in, you took a hard left and you were in the front, a small dining area with three 4-top tables and two smaller tables that fit three people.

There were ceiling fans throughout the place (which Danny eventually took out back and spray-painted each blade a different color: Red, Yellow, Blue, Green and White).

A black Formica counter with a faux brick front stood back about 10 feet from the windows, a two-level deal that acted as the "open office."

Behind that counter but pushed over against the far wall we would eventually park our little glass refrigerator we brought from Jillmarie's, sliding it onto blankets and tenderly into the back of our white Chevy pickup.

Behind the black front counter was a tiny recessed alcove, maybe two-feet deep, and stretching up to the black ceiling tiles. The alcove had a rack of dusty wine glasses, just a decoration now, and above the glasses, a high shelf with some faux plants left behind. Below the plants, a black tiled counter, maybe 2x2 which housed our drinking glasses and the legion of silverware rolled in white cloth napkins like trays of giant white cigars. Below the little 2x2 counter, a wine cooler that we filled will carafes of water.

When people come in, Danny says he counts the clinks of glasses and knows how many people we're seating. Then you hear the clunk of the wine cooler closing, meaning, someone's taking out a carafe of water.

Eating in or taking out: Just the two choices really.

A little doorless opening in the "office" next to the alcove led to the kitchen. There were stainless steel worktables; two lowboy refrigerators and one of them had a mini-salad bar with a lift up metal hood and a little cutting board rail in front. This would become Danny's universe, standing on that little 3x3 black anti-fatigue mat for hours, plating food, a stack of tickets lining the top of the adjacent lowboy. We eventually moved a refrigerator up front so he could grab a plate and have everything he needed to assemble any order within reach.

My universe?

The whole place.

Eventually, I was able to make food all day and wait on as many as (Danny counted once) 41 people in the restaurant at a time. We had no server, dishwasher or chef that day.

He said I was a machine, with a look of admiration I'll never forget.

We were Danny and Kathy Living; we could do anything, right?

A friend worked with us in the kitchen for a few days and proclaimed me the "heart and soul" of Borrowed Earth Café.

"What's Danny then?" I asked.

She chuckled, but didn't answer, like, come on, You know. Like maybe she was thinking of a different part of the anatomy. The Voice, maybe, but, at times, when he's crabby, something else, found somewhere lower. ;)

A regular customer sat at the counter once, Danny on his mat, parked in front of the salad bar and she said (he told me later) that he was a hard worker. She knew the hours we worked and that we once went nine months without a dishwasher, a server and, during the same nine months, God help us, without a chef. A couple year into our venture, we had a string of chefs that didn't work out and we decided (foolishly) that we would fast . . .

The Great Employee Fast.

Try running the place by ourselves.

With no help. Zero.

Me and Danny, by ourselves, running an entire restaurant, well into it's 3rd year, with a steady stream of hundreds of regulars.

One month, we said. We can do it.

Which stretched into two, come on, we can go one more. The next thing you know, we'd gone nine.

'Bout killed us.

We swear our almost 50-year old bodies could never take the punishment we subject them to if it weren't for the food.

We were / are masochists. *No pain, no brain.*

Danny told me he laughed and said that he told that customer who pointed out how hard *he* worked that he'd only met one person in his life who could keep up with him, match his endurance.

"Who?" she had asked.

Then, he said he pointed to me, out at a table, talking to some ladies having lunch.

"Her."

But back to the tour.

There was a 6-foot high rolling baker's rack, which we filled with cups, teapots and ice cream sundae dishes, tucked in a niche behind the dessert fridge in the "office."

Another 6-foot high, 4-shelf, wire rack stored all the plates and serving cups and bowls.

All those worktables had storage areas underneath which were filled with sheet pans, pots, kitchen equipment attachments, parchment paper, food storage film, cheese cake pans, soup turines and mixing bowls as big around as a tire.

The kitchen was open and a 20-foot long curved red quartz countertop (which we found out cost almost half what we paid for the restaurant) spanned the length of the open kitchen, giving 10 people on high-back tall chairs a view into the kitchen. We would spend the next few years listening to astute customers, as they watched us chop and prepare food and say things like, "Is that a carrot?" Maybe just trying to make small talk or show their food knowledge, I'm never sure.

Above the long red counter, on the customer's side, there are two tv monitors, mounted into the walls, and, attached to web cameras. These monitors allow people to see the tops of the worktables, making it perfect for teaching classes.

Behind the tall back chairs at the counter three tall 2-top tables sit along the wall, which leads to a little back hallway. There is a 5x5 area with two doors, a standing hall tree and some hooks on the wall to hang coats on, and a little community bulletin board. The doors led to the men and women's bathrooms. Danny's daughter painted an 18-inch in diameter, red circle on the men's door and painted "Mars" in the center of the circle in white letters and a similar yellow circle on the women's proclaimed you were now entering "Venus," as a John Gray tribute, and allusion to his book *Men Are from Mars, Women Are from Venus: A Practical Guide for Improving Communication and Getting What You Want in Your Relationships.*

Danny's daughter is very artistic and he said, "Go ahead, paint something, anywhere you want." And she twisted her mouth into a familiar grin and said, "Any where?" And he's like, "Yeah, paint anything you want." And she comes back five minutes later. "Done."

It makes people smile, unless they haven't read the Marsy / Venusy book or don't know the allusion, and even though there's a standard sign mounted to the wall by each door that announces each room's gender designation. Occasionally (a man usually), someone will go into that back hall and then peek around the corner, "Venus or Mars?" and Danny will say, "They're the same," meaning, there's no urinal in either, you pick.

Not really helping them decide. Not giving anything away, but having a little fun, offering a little philosophy.

Back in the kitchen, there were two hand-washing sinks at either end and next to an open doorway leading into the dish room, a two-hole vegetable sink sat with a metal shelf above it, that ended up loaded with big gallon containers of spices.

Through the back of the kitchen, you walked into the dish room, a 3-hole sink to the right and a metal work table to the left for drying racks and a place to put clean plates and cups on in drying racks. Another hand sink was at the end of the 3-hole sink and then, a tiny utility room packed with a 25-gallon hot water tank and a wire rack for cleaning supplies, maybe 5x5, just on the other side of the wall from the little hallway leading to Venus and Mars.

Continuing down the way from the dish room, the wall was lined with a double door refrigerator, a single door freezer and a double door freezer.

Around the corner from the dish room, on the back wall of the restaurant, there was a bigger area which housed a large sliding glass front refrigerator,which we would fill with produce and more wire racks for dry storage and the back door, which lead to a common grey concrete hallway with cinder block walls which lead to the back hallway and eventually to the dumpster, the last place we would walk to each night, dragging the big garbage can which tucks under the dish room 3-hole sink.

Sean said it was perfect for what we wanted and he was right. The whole place? Maybe 1200 square feet. 20 x 60ish. Almost the same as our house.

But with a cash register.

It would be our new home, a place to feed Sean and people like him. When someone who just eats a standard diet comes in and loves our food it means something more to us. We wanted to make food for everyone, not just vegans and vegetarians. We wanted to create a "safe" friendly place where they could come in and try the food and not feel judged.

Like at our house.

One of our friends ate at our restaurant and said, "This feels just like your house . . . only there's a cash register," and, "the kitchen's bigger, but there's no couch."

A couch? Good Lord, we'd never get outta there at the end of the night. Just pull a blanket over the last person, shut the lights out and go out the door, but grab those wind chimes Danny's rigged.

The wind chimes hang from the ceiling above the door, but Danny set it up so the little paddle suspended from a string in the middle of those chimes (which attached to the little wooden disk that strikes the chimes) touches the middle of the guide arm at the top of the door. When someone pulls the door open from the outside or pushes it open from the inside, the paddle strikes the guide arm on the door and the chimes sound, signaling and inbound or outbound customer.

You know, it's just food. But it's real. Nothing in a box or can. Food made fresh, by hand, with love, chopped, blended, maybe dehydrated, shaken, not stirred, but not cooked or processed or loaded with chemicals or preservatives.

Just nuts, seeds, fruits, vegetables and spices.

It's just food, but real food. Not changed or tweaked in a laboratory.

Made in a kitchen.

Old school.

But that restaurant, it was perfect.

We Had
the Money
to Open

At the time, we didn't, but you have to say it in the past tense.

It worked.

So now, we needed money.

Danny said, "We need an accountant. Someone to help us figure out how to buy this."

We called Sean.

"I got just the guy," he said. "His name's Frank."

Within hours, we had the number of the accountant guy named Frank who had helped his brother finance a dream of owning a home in Hawaii.

Frank seemed to think that buying a restaurant was about as hard as opening a can of beans, to hear him tell it.

"You just take the thing and you form a corporation . . . and that," his voice trailing off like we all knew what "and that" meant. We put ourselves and our future into his hands, a man who seemed to think what we wanted to happen was a piece of cake, or a can of beans, I have to ask Bobby, he's the metaphor morpher.

Just when we thought that little piece of paper on our mirror and our belief system was a Santa Claus wish, things started to happen fast.

Which meant we had to act.

That's what the movie *The Secret* says. You have to *act*. You go to the Mountain, Danny and Kathy. *Move*. Do something that comes to mind, a phone call, a big ask, a thoughtful gesture.

Stop dismissing your own genius and start hanging around with geniuses or at least singing songs to birds that sing sweeter songs, no sense in bashing beak to beak with another buzzard.

You gotta *move*.

On October 11, 2007, we walked out of an attorney's office with the keys to Borrowed Earth Café and we drove over to 970 Warren Avenue and unlocked the front door.

We had done it! I remember we hugged each other.

I still can't believe we did it.

BEFORE WE START, LET'S FLY TO SEDONA AND TAKE A COOL PICTURE

We locked the door and got on a plane and flew to *Raw Spirit Festival*, a PG-rated *Burning Man* get-together, really, in Sedona, AZ.

We climbed up to *Airport Mesa,* a plateau with a steep incline, dotted with loose Arizona scrub trees, rocks red, red clay soil and an eery electric crackle up top, a Vortex up there. We walked around and at dawn the last day we suddenly felt something powerful and ancient. Danny put his arm around me and held the camera at arm's length.

Click.

Work Versus Worry

Three days later, we were back at the restaurant, the windows all papered over with white butcher paper.

I wrote really big on it: "What do all these people have in common?" and we plastered it with 8 x 11 pictures of celebrity raw foodists we found on Google images. Below the pictures I wrote, "If they were in Downers Grove, they'd eat here."

All day long, while we were cleaning, we'd hear people outside, a little muffled, but we'd hear it:

"What do all these people have in common?"

And then the guessing.

It was fun.

Soon after, the village sent someone by to tell us to take the "sign" down, that we didn't have a permit or some Rule 32, paragraph 5, subsection 7, right there where my finger is pointing, the guy said, read it, sub-sub-sub section 2 article 4, "No Happy Signs That Promote Laughter Will Be Hung By A Future Business With Spools of Butcher Paper and Pictures of Celebrities and a Magic Marker."

Wow, they had us dead to rights.

We took it down, but as a silent winking smiley face with a protruding tongue, we had a professional one made that was within village guidelines, of course. Paragraph 3, subsection 1, right where *my* finger is pointing, ". . . a business is only a value to the village as a source of state sales tax revenue if it can attract and transact with customers."

I want to mention that with all the uncertainty, all the unknowns, all the things that would happen in six weeks, we stayed focused on cleaning.

Six weeks until Danny's unemployment runs dry.

Putting our hearts and souls into the task at hand.

Letting the future happen in it's own time.

Doing our best in the Present.

Not getting hung up worrying about the Future, a future that hadn't happened, a Future, we started to realize, was something we built with our minds.

That worry? It'll 'bout paralyze your soul, your inward eye fixed on something, your imagination, your feelings, your thoughts, like brick and mortar, always building.

Your mind, really, the Architect.

But, nonetheless, we still had practical concerns and questions to answer.

And you're probably wondering, "How much food do you have to buy? Where ya' gonna get everything you need? What do you need? How many people are going to come the first day and the day after? How much food do you make?"

We wondered the same things, so we ordered a seasoned chef from the Catalog of the Universe, that thing, just like a big JC Penney catalog to us now, run your finger down the page and point and say, "Gimme . . . that one!

Gimme One
Super Chef

"We Had a Super Chef."

Stuck it right on the mirror.

Someone who would fill in some of those blanks, but not make us feel stupid.

A while later, we found out, irony of ironies, that Partner's top chef was in the wind.

He *was* a Super Chef.

We'd seen him work and we'd eaten his food. Look up physical confidence online and I bet his picture's there, his apron on, stretched tight across his impressive form. He'll be holding a gleaming 10-inch chef's knife easily in his hand, like an extension of him. Mountains of chopped produce filling bowls all around him, salad campers of food piled on metal worktables surround him.

His mouth twisted into a little grin.

Easy. Done.

Apparently Partner had pushed this guy's buttons a little too hard and insisted, after he clocked out one evening, that he make food for a party that walked in half-hour after close. He ordered him. Super Chef had worked a 13-hour day and when Partner "ordered" him back into the kitchen, Super Chef told him to go fork himself.

Super Chef was a nice guy, but he also had been a champion wrestler. He was still at his wrestling weight, to the pound, and had biceps like softballs, a tiny waist, a broad back, and a thick all-business neck. He'd also been a soldier in the Russian Army, doing a tour in Afghanistan. He was only about 5'8" but he looked bigger. He had a physical presence that was palpable.

He was no one to fork with.

We called a friend who knew people at Partner's.

All we knew was his name and that he lived in Chicago. This Super Chef.

The guy we wanted.

The guy we ordered from the Catalog.

No problem.

Within a day, we had Super Chef's number.

Super Chef, though not a native English speaker, remembered us on the phone immediately and began to jibber excitedly when Danny told him what we wanted.

Turns out his wife had just had a baby and he had delayed going back to work so he could do the dad thing.

The timing, like all the rest of what happened, was perfect.

Someone or Something or maybe No One or Nothing, it seemed, was watching over us.

People kept coming into our lives when we needed them like they were being queued and sent on stage by some Director.

And we were starting to think that the piece of paper on the bathroom mirror we were clinging to, the 90-days of *The Secret*, the food, the media blackout, all of it, it was all starting to change our water.

And our own Borrowed Earth.

Super Chef met us for coffee, took a quick, professional walk through of our soon-to-open restaurant, and loved it.

"When do we start?" he said grinning as we stood outside now on the solid ground of the future patio.

So, a week before we opened, we followed Super Chef's Honda CRV to the city and visited a restaurant supply store and a little Middle Eastern grocery store and loaded up for the Future.

Easy. Done.

Super Chef was a machine that just needed a little grease, a little appreciation really. He taught us plenty and we learned a lot on our own. He stayed with us for nearly two years and we still think of him fondly, living somewhere down south, bringing his wife and two children to live near his mom, which was all his mom had ever wanted.

WE OPENED
BORROWED EARTH CAFE

"Work hard and stay in the Present and everything you need will be provided."—Earnest Wakener.

Six weeks after we'd opened the door, on Monday, December 3rd, the health and fire inspectors stood lingering in the front of the restaurant. The hard wood floors gleamed in four-color alternating stripes of bamboo. The old lady French café wallpaper was replaced by No VOC paint, a soft pebbly yellow we'd rolled on, covering up the little scrap marks and goof ups with a flourish. We hung a blanket up front, a queen-sized Hopi Indian Pendleton-looking thing clipped sideways to a bamboo curtain rod on little bamboo rings, a predominantly kelly green wool beauty with red, blue, yellow and purple triangles along the sides and a golden border and four 12-inch high hands, near the bottom. As if two people were standing in front of it, side by side, putting their palms on the blanket.

The Hopi say the design represents when new people come to a land, they join hands on the land with the people who live there.

Like the Earth and what comes forth from it unite them.

We thought it fitting.

The front door was rigged with bells and wind chimes, and we put a little splashy fountain in the vestibule, slate squares inset with a two-foot in diameter blue and green tiled representation of the Earth based on a watercolor done by Danny's daughter.

Everything was clean and shiny. We even took all the ceiling tiles down and washed them.

All those trips, up and down the ladders, punctuated by trips to answer those sales calls that started rolling in.

It was like restaurant boot camp.

We loved it.

The Borrowed Earth Café Rocket ready to launch in 5, 4, 3,2,1 day until Danny's unemployment runs out.

Whoo-hoo!

As those inspectors stood there milling about, all our inspections and forms signed, the first few people walked in.

"Are you open?" they asked.

We looked the question at the health inspector, who nodded.

We have lift off. Destination to the West Wall at the End of the Universe. Everything we needed to get there in the rocket: Me and Danny.

"Eating in or taking out?" we said, which we would say 10,000 times.

They had just walked into our café and we had just began our first steps on the journey that would take us over 8,000 miles, almost seven a day, according to a pedometer, the distance from Chicago to Afghanistan, the place where Super Chef had done his tour.

The mission: Feed people and let the food do the talking.

Offer a kind word, a joke, and some encouragement, share your experiences.

Oh, and have a lot of fun.

A few months later, Sean and his partner stopped by and had lunch and sat at the big long counter bar that looks directly into the open kitchen.

I remember his big red cheeks, his white curly hair and that smile.

We were packed, front tables, the high, two-tops along the wall. The counter was filled with diners, alone and in pairs, shoulder to shoulder.

Every time I glanced over, Sean was absolutely beaming. Our success was his success.

"I've only lost one. That was the guy you bought the restaurant from. Look at that," he said confidently.

It was the last time we ever saw him.

SEAN

*"We stood on the threshold of our Future
and suddenly, an Angel appeared in the
guise of a common man. He took us by
the hand and led us into the Realm of
Dreams. Then, as quickly as he appeared,
he vanished and returned to Heaven from
whence he came. Now, he lives inside of
us and we only have to touch our hearts
to find him in the place he has always
lived."—Danonymous*

A couple years after we opened, Sean's girlfriend Kathy stopped by and told us he had died, a massive heart attack.

I would gauge Sean was in his mid-50's, give or take. Not much older than us.

I remember her standing next to the counter up front. Danny and I huddled around and she told us quietly about Sean.

Danny and I were up by the cash register and it suddenly felt like all the wind got sucked out of the place.

But then, as we talked about Sean, we all started to smile.

You couldn't help yourself.

And suddenly, we all got a little quiet.

And it was like we all felt him there.

The first time we wrote the story, we had a much shorter version of all the events leading up to the opening of the restaurant.

Sean wasn't in there.

One day, while I was re-reading the introduction to the story, sitting at our kitchen table (*the* Office—the restaurant doesn't have one), reading the "Who are Danny and Kathy Living?" part, reading it and trying to recapture the feeling of movement toward opening the restaurant, and suddenly, Sean (and Partner) came bubbling up from somewhere and before I knew it, he and Partner were there on the computer screen.

So I started typing and it all came tumbling out.

As I wrote the Partner part, I couldn't help it, I started to laugh . . .

And then, I started to write about Sean, and I had to move back from our Macbook.

Because I started to cry.

I had buried them both.

The Partner part, well, that was fun to remember.

Sean? Bitter sweet.

And as Danny read what you just did to me in the car on the way to the café, speeding down 75th Street, no doubt running a little late, Hey, call the cafe and tell them what they already know ("We're gonna be late . . ."), he started to cry softly and something huge bloomed in our chests.

He stopped reading and shook his head.

Borrowed Earth Café ☺

I looked over. No sound, but his lips were pressed together and he closed his eyes squeezed shut and tears leaked out. He shook his head and took in a shuddering breath and let it out.

"Don't say anything," I said.

Sean.

I reached over and put my hand on his chest, where Sean was now and left it there.

The place where Sean lives.

Wait, put your hand on your heart.

Sean.

Sean was the best person to come out of the Catalog of the Universe.

"You two are all you need," he had said.

Yes, Sean. But we had lots of help from people like you.

Thank you.

Danny and I will always be grateful.

Ready?

"What people say you cannot do, you try and find that you can."—Henry David Thoreau

"The past only has the power that we give it. Our vision of the future, like a beautiful sun, beckons, but the only real power is in the Present."—Earnest Wakener

Note to those who are considering a Borrowed Earth Journey and want to read this for ideas, information, and inspiration: by God, you're thinking of doing something, anything, with the hope that it has Meaning and that you might be better for the experience. It's what you've only dreamed of up until now.

That's what we said.

But know this: dreams are the seedlings for your reality if you will let them be and trust that you have everything you need right now, that you're capable of great things, things you can only imagine.

You can do it!

We are just two regular people with no special training in what we do or really, what we ever did. We believe that with a positive attitude and a willingness to do hard work, we can do anything. "We're Danny and Kathy Living," we say to each other. "We can do anything."

And so can you.

You're you and there's never been anyone quite like you. Your brand of wonderful is just what you need to do that thing, that thing you hope has Meaning.

Throughout history, we have heard and been inspired by the Journey, whether it be quietly read as a bed time story, studied in school or read in the words which tow us through the pages of a story gently, our imagination the horse pulling the wagon of our mind and heart and soul along a path traveled by another, a path we travel, through those words, together.

Heading West.

Thank you for reading our words . . .

Now, do this: write your dream on paper, in the past tense, in your own hand. Write it clearly and concisely in one powerful sentence with the bold hand of an explorer, the Hero of your story, setting forth with a song in your heart. Write what you did, like you already did it, in the past tense, as if someone is telling your story 100 years from now.

You did it, it was done, and it was wonderful, because you're wonderful.

Put a date on it and as things come to mind to do, people to talk to, books to read, things to practice, take ACTION!

If the date comes and goes. Don't worry, move the date out a month (no more) and keep going.

If you have your heart and mind set on one thing and there seems to be a lot of resistance, like with our 108-year old farmhouse incident, say, "If not this, then something better."

Don't get so attached to a 108-year old farmhouse that you miss the 30-seater in Downers Grove right by the Tivoli Theater.

The place that ends up being just like your house . . . with a cash register, but minus the couch.

Action is required of you to keep those people, circumstances and opportunities coming.

ACTION or INACTION are the proofs of your own belief in your own beliefs.

Read that again.

Practice and make sure you feel good about what you are doing and you will keep doing it because it feels good.

Read *that* again.

The Joy you are looking for is available right now in the doing of something you love that helps others. Start right now, today. If you desire to make food and serve food to people, make something and serve it to someone you love today, especially if it's yourself. Anyone can do that. Feed someone. Feed yourself first.

The oxygen mask drops first for you . . . and I'm not just talking about your job, Pardner.

You deserve happiness.

Fall in love with what you do now, here, in your current situation . . . if you don't love doing it now, no amount of money you might make can make you love it.

Love doing it now while it's being done for free from your heart . . . everything else will be provided.

And, when the internal prompt comes to make a call, try something new or do something bold, ACT!

It's okay to be scared and do it any way. I want to say something about being scared. This is a Dannyism, but I think it works.

Two people get on a roller coaster (no, not the imaginary Milk House Café kind, a *real* one).

(Don't panic, the two people aren't going in different directions, or away from a common point of origin on a map at different rates of travel. This ain't a word problem. I wouldn't do that to you, Pardner. Math ain't my strong suit.)

So, two people sit down on a roller coaster, the bar comes down over their shoulders and the car jolts to a start.

Each feels something in their stomach from the movement... and their thoughts and that *feeling* following their initial thoughts will trigger more thoughts. Thoughts that are rooted in their histories, their individual stories, their experiences. Things they've been told.

Things they believe.

As the car starts clicking up the big hill, one person starts to get "scared" and apprehensive.

The other person starts to get excited and feels something like happy anticipation.

One person gets scared on the roller coaster.

For the other person, these are the joyous moments they live for.

Then, as the car careens around the track, for those few minutes, each has a totally unique experience, separate and different, but fundamentally, physically, identical as far as the external stimulus, the ride is the same.

But what each does with their mind and the feelings in their body determines whether they experience pleasure and happiness or discomfort and unhappiness.

Same ride.

Danny used to practice the martial arts.

When he first started, he was around 18, and he said he would get scared and didn't enjoy it, the fighting with the other people part. He had been picked on and bullied as a kid and fighting pushed all those old buttons.

Because of his story.

His. Story.

History.

Later, Danny learned that he could harness that "feeling" and use it to energize him during the fight and people used to say he frightened them mostly because he was smiling and they could tell he was enjoying himself.

Weird.

Danny soon loved fighting . . . but only after he learned to harness the feeling and control his head while he was "on the roller coaster" did it become enjoyable.

It took practice.

Likewise, when decisions to do something generate feelings, ask yourself if a stronger and more confident person in the same situation might act differently and then BE THAT STRONG PERSON . . .

It takes practice, but eventually, little victories lead to bigger ones and pretty soon, as the car careens around the track, you're smiling, your arms are up and you're enjoying yourself.

Before the *Whole Foods* supermarket was built out in Naperville, we would drive to the closest one we could find which was 30 minutes away. We have some customers who drive an hour each way to *Whole Foods* because they can't get organic produce by their homes . . . but they drive and make the effort because they're worth it. They are prompted to buy organic food and that means they are taking action to get it.

You're worth it!

Your dream is a metaphor, happiness is always is available Now—this thing you do or plan to do—this is just something to keep a roof over your head. The Joy you're seeking will not be found at the end of your Journey.

No.

Life is too wonderful to withhold such a Gift . . . it is freely available along the Path and is found in each act of service.

It's not until you give that you get.

Write that last sentence on a piece of paper and put it ABOVE your goal with the past-tense construction and the date. It's what the whole ball game is about.

If you want to get, you have to give.

Speaking of get, Get out of your head and start living out from the heart, that silent Portal that watches from your chest, gently guiding you on your Way.

Sean's House.

Trust your gut. Follow your heart.

Be a kid again . . .

The fact that people can feel like a kid again means that the kid in you never dies, we just tuck them away when we grow up.

Which means the kid is still in there.

Why not let the kid play, huh? Maybe have a little say in things once in a while.

People Like Us
on Facebook . . .
All of Us

> *"Most of this is silly, but some of it's serious . . . I sneak serious in while people are laughing . . . when they're not paying attention. See, people think they're just laughing and eating the food, but that's just the distraction, isn't it? "—Danny Living*

KATHY: "Hey, finally, you signed your name to something. Getting tired of hiding behind me and all your characters?"

BOBBY: "Not yet."

KATHY: "Let Danny out."

GUY DUNYOGA: "He's busy."

RUDY WAKENING: "He's left the country with Mr. Bing."

KATHY: "Save it."

EARNEST WAKENER: "Well, you've been on him to write another book."

KATHY: "I wouldn't say I was on him. More like, around him."

BOBBY: "Like a mother blanket."

KATHY: "Your metaphors always come up short, mister. Call me the Coach."

GUY: "Cheering him on?"

EARNEST: "Another Mrs. Winings, his fourth grade teacher?"

BOBBY: "Telling the little kid he's a good writer . . . and he believes her."

KATHY: ". . . but he shanghais my Facebook account. Starts a little side project."

EARNEST: "He does it for you, you know."

KATHY: "What?"

DANNY: "All of it."

KATHY: "There you are."

WAIT, SO WHO'S REALLY WRITING?

When I first got a Facebook account, Danny got one too, but since we share a computer, in order to keep things separate, Person A has to log off Person B's account and log on as themselves.

You can't have two active Facebook sessions with two different accounts in the same browser at the same time.

Or, if Person B (B, as in Bobby) is lazy, he could just start posting stuff as Person A.

Further, Person B could start making up characters out of thin air, philosophers, poets, yogis, dishwashers, a mouse on a motorcycle wearing a pull-up diaper, birds and once, maybe just for the creative challenge, an ant crawling across the floor, mumbling to himself on the way home from work . . .

And, had Person A not enjoyed Person B's writing, you might not be reading this.

Hey, use your own account.

But mine seemed to become the only account.

Question: Why don't you two just use your phones?

Answer: 1) Because we have old, snails-pace-texting-punch-the-number-pad Motorola flip phones, 2) we're together 24/7, 3) we have one computer at home we share and the work one, and D) 'cause we're too cheap to have two additional internet plans—Good Lord, that's

$60 extra a month, Pardner—you really need to have your thumbs working all day, like some kid clicking away on his Nintendo?

Which turned out to be lucky for me.

Aside from some of this up front writing (like this sentence, or this word even, or that comma), a lot of the content of this book was posted to own my account (<u>Kathy Brodsky Living</u>), over a 6-month period, 420 characters at a time (who's the stoner at Facebook who set *that* character limit? 420, ha-ha, we get it) or, in the more expansive Comment boxes below.

Statuses that I didn't write.

The writer was Danny, but he almost never makes an appearance.

Mostly it was this guy Bobby, a dishwasher at our restaurant who has yet to do dish one (I think *I'm* Bobby the Dishwasher, if you want to count clean plates, glasses, forks, knives, spoons, mixing bowls, spatulas, and the rest of the commercial kitchen bric-a-brac).

And then there was a philosopher named Earnest Wakener, a yogi named Guy Dunyoga (please), another philosopher Rudy Wakening (stop). Then, he crossed into the animal kingdom and our pet birds, Rocky and Buddy, they started posting, too.

Arguing like an old married couple.

He wrote out these little short dialogues, like some of the ones you've already read.

People loved them.

Especially the sales calls.

Most of these conversations, stories, phone calls, all of it, they're based on things that really happened. Things at the restaurant, things at home, all of it.

And, some of them, the statuses, the dialogs, these are things that emerged from Danny's mind, from a frightening organic farm barely contained under his dreadlocks, the soil that grows all wordland creatures great and small. Creatures with hopes, dream, aspirations and farcical anecdotes, creatures engaging in Who's On First dialog so bizarre it anyone's guess (including Danny's, truth be told) where it will go.

Creatures who converse, using the dialog format that is normally reserved for plays.

CREATURE 1: "Let's say something silly on Facebook."

CREATURE 2: "And what, get me fired? My boss demands all employees "friend" him so he can keep an eye on us. He tricked me too. Get this, in the interview he sidles up while were talking, brings up the subject of Facebook. Yeah, sure, I'm on there, I say and he gets this little smile like, Sucker."

CREATURE 3: "Will you two shut up? We're watching a ball game."

CREATURE 4: "I wanted to catch the end of *Dancing With the Stars*."

CREATURE 5: "I heard that's fake."

CREATURE 1: "What, like pro wrestling?"

And so on.

No one gets to the point, but you keep reading any way, 'cause *Dancing With the Stars* isn't on for what, 22 minutes?

And those little 420-character or less statuses were a little release valve, a place to capture a moment, to find humor or just share a snippet of a conversation—something we thought was funny or would make people think.

All day long, he'd run up to the computer for a minute, type something and then go back to what he was doing.

And if I heard a certain kind of typing, I'd try and find my way up there, click on the *Firefox* icon and go to my profile.

And there they were.

Sometimes, "Bobby" would take a phone call or something would happen and two minutes later, and there'd be something on Facebook.

Sometimes people would be in the restaurant and see or hear something happen, CLICKETY-CLICKETY-CLICKETY and they'd look up from their phone and laugh, "Ha, I saw what you just posted. Nice!"

Bobby the Dishwasher, in particular, found his way into my reader's hearts.

Bobby, he's like Ralph Cramdon, Homer Simpson, Fred Flintstone . . . all those lovable goof-ups with wonderful patient women on screen with them. We laugh at them, because they remind us that we're humans, lovable, fallible humans.

Sometimes, when I'm away from the computer, I'll come back and, Hello! I've written something poetic.

Or maybe it was Bobby.

Or the Pun Name Brothers: Rudy Wakening, Guy Dunyoga and Earnest Wakener.

And, on rare occasion, Danny.

It's like an illiterary box of chocolates.

You never know who you're gonna get.

One day, I found I'd written this.

"I passed on ambling around the nearly treeless neighborhood of aluminum-clad gray, beige and yellow town homes, an apparent sameness that is sometimes comforting and at others, a symbol of something, homogeneity or a lack of imagination, I can never tell. Instead, I lay on the cool concrete of my morning porch and stared up into the sky and closed my eyes, drinking in the feel of the glorious sun . . ."

Quite a few people wrote to me about it.

~

BOBBY: "Who wrote the poem?"

KATHY: "You mean the neighborhood thing?"

BOBBY: "Yeah, it's like a poem."

KATHY: "It's not a poem."

BOBBY: "It's *so* a poem."

KATHY: "I'm not going to argue with you."

BOBBY: "Because I'm right?"

KATHY: "No. You have dishes to do."

~

"I stopped trying to be a somebody

and became a nobody

nothing left to defend

nothing to prove

no story or plans to distract me from seeing

all the little miracles I had missed each day

they illuminated around me like fire flies

and like a child again on a summer night

I was free."—Earnest Wakener

～

BOBBY: "See? Another poem. Look at you."

KATHY: "I didn't write that. I think you know who wrote it."

BOBBY: "Earnest Wakener?"

KATHY: "You made him up."

BOBBY: "Earnest Wakener or Bobby the Dishwasher?"

KATHY: "Or Guy Dunyoga? Or Rudy Wakening? I bet it was Danny."

BOBBY: "You know he blames everything on me."

KATHY: "Subtle. Ever thought of being just Danny?"

DANNY: "Where's the fun in that?"

~

DANNY'S DICTIONARY:

Dialogorrhea (die-uh-log-uh-REE-uh): noun, a conlink, or edifice of two or more words to form a new, fake, made-up, but hopefully clever, word with an easily discernible definition.

Dialogue + Logorrhea (excessive words) + diarrhea

root, Neo-Hippie Modern English for a tendency to speak or write using the accepted theatrical construction of the dialogue format but with way too many words winding off topic, off track, spiraling out of this world . . .

Good, Better, Best

"Wait, I think way too much of this is silly, and while we might eventually get to serious, since we're still laughing, let's keep it up. What, more Bobby? I thought you'd never ask. I always loved that little guy."—Danny Living

KATHY: "We're good."

BOBBY: "We're better than good . . . we're average."

KATHY: "I thought it was, like, Good, Better, Best."

BOBBY: "And you're thinking, better than Good is Better, but I don't want to say better than Better . . ."

KATHY: ". . . cause better than Better is Best."

BOBBY: "Should we start over?"

KATHY: "You know, we can do anything."

BOBBY: "Like run a restaurant and work like dogs?"

KATHY: "Yeah, that, too. But anything we put our hearts into, I think we can do it and it'll turn out good. For the better. And that's always best. You know why?"

DANNY: "Because, 'We're Danny and Kathy Living and we can do anything?'"

KATHY: "Yeah, but say it without the question mark."

DANNY: "I had a question mark?"

TRUCK STOP LOVE

CUSTOMER: "The food, does it take a long time to make? I mean, is it quick?"

BOBBY: "Like Truck Stop Love."

≈

KATHY: "Truck Stop Love?"

BOBBY: "That quick."

KATHY: "I can't believe you said Truck Stop Love. I'm watchin' you."

BOBBY: "It's a real thing."

KATHY: "Yeah, but there's a thousand analogies you could have picked."

BOBBY: "No one's done Truck Stop Love."

KATHY: "So, you're blazin' a trail."

BOBBY: "In so many words . . ."

BOBBY THE DISHWASHER

> *"If I'm supposed to feel like One, why do I still feel like Two?"—Bobby the Dishwasher, on Meditation*

Meet Bobby, Borrowed Earth's Dishwasher.

When the phone rings, it's good to have a go-to person who can field those annoying sales calls . . . providing answers to questions that even the most imaginative sales script writer could never have dreamed of . . .

He's got a past-the-shoulders batch of dreadlocks and a cocky walk . . . a walk I call clomping. He clomps. He has a collection of tie dye shirts, bleach-spotted cargo shorts and baggy pants and size 13 brown Crocs, the ones with the holes. He has a couple colorful knit rasta hats, but sometimes, he winds all that hair up into this crazy fan that sticks up over his head, looks like a dreadlock Joshua Tree. 6'4" and about a buck sixty, if he's got a wet rock in his back pocket.

With his hair up, he's been taken for a long-lost (and probably for the better) Maasai, an African tribe that allows for men to have multiple wives, who maintain the family home, made from dung.

Bobby only has one wife, but she works her apron off outside the house in a restaurant, which she owns and operates . . .

Their house has aluminum siding and the only dung *near* the house is left on their lawn by their inconsiderate non-Maasai neighbors.

Bobby's entreaties to have their dog's leavings picked up and thrown AT the house, in an effort to eventually live in an improvised traditional Maasai dwelling, are met with frightened stares, which also could be the result of having a 6'4" man with a shock of electrified hair asking you to pick up your dog's poo and throw it at his house—though, a lady with a Great Dane considered it momentarily, deciding finally that her bursitis might be aggravated grievously by trying to throw a 2-pound doggie doo over 18 feet of lawn to the home's nearest external wall.

Maritally, Bobby talked about adding another wife to the mix, but the idea was quickly vetoed by Wife 1, along with the plan to have Wife 1 stay home and tend crops and / or build a house out of dirt and poo, her claiming exemption as a non-Maasai married to a man with wild hair and a vastly diluted Maasai blood line.

"Bobby," I tell people, "may be 25 percent Maasai, but he's 100 percent dufus."

~

Alright, let's clear the air.

Who the heck is this Bobby?

And who put him in charge of the phone?

Good Lord, that boy is a dufus.

It breaks down like this: Danny was born Bobby, but was adopted by people who changed his name to Danny. I met Danny and we got married.

Long story short.

But while we were getting married, someone filled our car with suds, and Danny's like, "Mr. Dilman!" whipping his head around, the soap ruining his shoes when he opened the door.

More on Mr. Dilman later.

Bobby is Danny . . . but Danny is Bobby really, except when he's Danny, then he's Bobby.

If you have questions, you can call the restaurant.

Ask for Bobby.

He'll set you straight.

~

Bobby, our resident telemarketing call handler, plate scrubber, glass rinser, dishwasher emptier / filler, high-box reacher, floor mat wrangler, customer face / name idiot savant, and poet laureate, 1984 Suma Cum Laude graduate and valedictorian of DishU was one of those employment risks that was worth taking.

He was 9 and 1/2 minutes late for the interview.

Danny and I sat patiently, but not up straight behind the counter.

I sat behind the computer, right knee bent, a pink Croc propped on the open second drawer, a make-shift foot stool.

Danny sat slouched in a chiropractically inappropriate position, his right forearm on the counter, spine twisted in a manner that shoots pain into his left hip.

It should be noted that whenever we sit with preposterous posture, our chiropractor, Dr. Smith (not the whiny guy from the TV show Lost in Space, not him—the robot with the swinging arms and him ran off and got married, who knew?) sits in his office and he perks up, like he's hearing a far off alarm bell. And he thinks, "Uh-oh, Subluxation and shakes his head. We can almost see him: he's in his office frowning at an anatomical man's buttocks with his muscular / skeletal structure artfully depicted over his skin above Dr. Smith's head mounted on the wall in a black frame, and him thinking, "I gotta get a Norman Rockwell or something, Lord, I'm tired of looking at that man's butt everyday." And he imagines us off in the café, slouching, Ach! And he says, "Look at those two, Slump and Slumper."

KATHY: "He's late."

DANNY: "Who?"

KATHY: "The dishwasher guy, Bobby."

DANNY: "We have a dishwasher?"

KATHY: "Well yeah, you mean, a machine, duh, but that guy, the one who sent that long email about the job."

DANNY: "The valvidictorium?"

KATHY: "Valedictorian."

DANNY: "Is that how you say it?"

KATHY: "Point is, he's late."

DANNY: "Is he starting today?"

KATHY: "No, come on, keep up. He's got an interview today."

DANNY: "What time was he supposed to be here?"

KATHY: "Well, 9 minutes ago by the computer clock."

DANNY: "Should you be slumped like that? Your foot in the drawer?"

KATHY: "Look at you."

DANNY: "What?"

KATHY: "I'm at least trying to sit up straight. You gave up before you sat down, slid right onto your forearm like you were falling. Your hip's gonna hurt when you stand up."

DANNY: "Yeah, but I'm comfortable now. I'm living for the moment. Not worrying about the future."

KATHY: "And not sitting up straight. I can hear Dr. Smith tisking."

DANNY: "I always just call him Dave. Don't you hate that butt guy picture in his office? Wait, he tisks?"

KATHY: "Like a disapproving teacher. Hey, back to Bobby."

DANNY: "What kind of guy calls himself Bobby. What did it say, he's what, like 50?"

KATHY: "Same as you, 49. It'll be like having two kids instead of one. You're Danny, not Dan."

DANNY: "I thought we had four kids."

KATHY: "You know what I mean."

DANNY: "So, when he gets here, do we say something like, 'Punctuality is important to us, Bobby.'"

KATHY: "No one says punctuality any more. It'll sound fake."

DANNY: "It's a real word."

KATHY: "I don't want to use it. Let's just say late."

DANNY: "But we're late almost everyday, hustling up to the door, arms full of bags and aprons and things, you fumbling out the key,

Hey, lookit all that garbage blowing on the patio, all the neighbors looking at us like, Look at these two, late for class . . ."

KATHY: "Yeah, but we're the owners."

DANNY: "I thought it was Mr. Bing."

KATHY: "Hush."

DANNY: "I'm just saying maybe this Bobby dude being late means he's one of us. One of the Late People, Johnny Come Lately, See You Later Alligator, Catch You Later . . ."

KATHY: "I get it. Party 'til Yer Tardy."

DANNY: "There you go."

KATHY: "But we need to establish boundaries, guidelines, rules . . ."

DANNY: "I thought we agreed that we wouldn't have those things."

KATHY: "No rules."

DANNY: "No guidelines."

KATHY: "No boundaries?"

DANNY: "The way we like it."

KATHY: "Maybe we can get him to answer the phone."

DANNY: "The sales calls?"

KATHY: "Why not?"

DANNY: "Like a personal assistant?"

KATHY: "Something like that."

DANNY: "Give him all the crummy jobs."

KATHY: "The ones we don't want to do."

DANNY: "'Hey Bobby, I think there's gum under this table . . .'"

KATHY: "'Hey Bobby, 1800BUYSTUFF . . .'"

DANNY: "I like him already."

KATHY: "Shhh, here he comes."

DANNY: "Bobby Come Lately. He's tall."

KATHY: "That's kind of a stupid looking hat."

DANNY: "I think it looks good. I like him already."

Back in December of 2007 when we opened Borrowed Earth, we had spent the previous six weeks cleaning the place out, selling off the stove (it used to be a little cooking school / French Bistro, and man, that guy decked the place out for us), putting in bamboo flooring (four colors in alternating stripes—couldn't make up our mind to save our lives, so as not to offend the other colors, we picked them all) and getting the place ready.

Before we even opened for business, that phone started ringing off the hook . . .

Sales calls.

"Is the owner in?"

"Who's in charge of credit card payments, the electric bill, satellite radio, cleaning supplies, kitchen utensils, napkin and towels purchasing, floor mats, meat procurement, taxidermy, table leg trousers?" Etc., etc., etc.

You'd be up on a ladder, scraping the French lady at the café cartoon wallpaper off the top of the wall and RING! RING!

And then one of us would say, "@#$%*&%@!!"

DANNY: "Wait, you said it too."

KATHY: "I said, It?"

DANNY: "You know what I mean."

Then, we'd climb down the ladder and go get the phone, "No the owner's not here!"

Hang up and get back to business.

All day long.

Jeez, they were relentless.

NOTE: To the person at the phone company who freely distributed our number, this book is our revenge. We took the lemons and made lemonade, clipped the lemon wedge to the side of the short tumbler, chucked some ice in it, sat back on the front porch, kicked out feet up and said "Ah!"

You did us a favor.

So, in order to cope, we invented an owner.

We decided to call him Mr. Bing.

A fake character that we rolled down hill like a huge snowball.

And you know what they say, when snow rolls downhill, it collects more snow, if it's winter.

The ball gets bigger.

And starts to roll faster.

Man, pretty soon, we're running along side, cheering, like kids with a go kart.

Whoopee!

Pretty soon, we were fighting to get to that phone.

Danny, however, proved to be the Alpha Liar and the race to the phone now only had one runner.

Then, Danny decided to add another layer of camoflage between him and the sales legion by inventing Bobby.

Bobby the Dishwasher.

From Tennessee.

With the mom that's a witch doctor.

And the football-sized tick on his dog Blue's butt, the golf ball-sized flea on his tail, for God's sake.

The whole nine yards.

Lord, the details.

Go out to the cow farm, fill 'er up, phone rings, back 'er up and lift the bed.

≈

Phone rings and I'm signaling like the New York Yankees' manager for Bobby, a little come here with the chin and an upturned cupped hand, two short backward waves with the fingers together and *the* eye roll.

Sales call.

Bobby comes in and takes the phone like a relief pitcher.

I mouth silently,"Mr. Bing" and Bobby nods, slouches on the stool up front and there, the mischievous smile, but the business voice:

"Mr. Bing speaking . . ."

New employees are required to take a brief half-day workshop, which covers Proper Inbound Telemarketing Call Handling.

The workshop includes scripts, role-playing, voice coaching, as well as fielding a Bobby-supervised live call prior to receiving a Certification of Completion signed by Bobby.

Participants must be able to spin a credible yarn and are given some leeway, after a 30-day break-in period, with embellishment of the Story.

The Story of a business without owners, an all-volunteer staff, solar power, walkie-talkies, out houses, off-the-grid, but with an expansive backyard with a view of Sedona . . . an Absurd Urban Oasis and unlikely candidate for any product or service, a business with a healthy disdain for advertising opportunities . . . and endless source of pitch-foiling confusion.

A good call leaves the solicitor eager to hang up first . . . and fast.

*Ruler move down, close-up of thick red line drawn with an audible sound through BORROWED EARTH CAFÉ, a little asterisk * and the note scrawled in the margin: Call at your own risk!*

Graduates mantra?

WWBS

What Would Bobby Say?

～

Phone rings

DANNY: "Borrowed Earth Café."

800 CALLER: "Is Danny there?"

DANNY: "No."

CALLER: "Do you know when he'll be in?"

DANNY: "Sorry, we had to let him go two weeks ago . . ."

CALLER: "Oh . . . who are you?"

BOBBY: "My name is Bobby. I'm the dishwasher . . ."

Bobby the Dishwasher and Borrowed Earth's Poet Emeritus was quoted in the Dishwashing Monthly Magazine, *SUDS!* saying, "It's not Guess Who's Coming to Dinner?" but, how many. Spencer Tracy and Katharine Hepburn's guests arrive all day long, coming in 1, 2's and 10's, some wanting to sit near the window, others, just take out, please . . . some just wanting to use the bathroom."

～

. BOBBY: "Electricity? No, we've switched to generators . . . we've got a troop of squirrels up on the roof in hundreds of wheels, runnin' their sneakers off day and night to keep the lights on in this place . . . Hello?"

$\sim$

DANNY: "Borrowed Earth Café."

800 CALLER: "I'm Betty from Opinion Survey and I'd . . ."

BOBBY: "Ma'am, you're calling a restaurant on Friday at lunch and you're asking for an opinion? You don't want to hear my opinion right now . . ."

$\sim$

DANNY: "Borrowed Earth Ca-fe."

SECURITYCOMPANY: "Can I speak to the person in charge of security?"

SOUTHERN BOBBY: "Ma'am, we don't need no secure-tee system. We got us a dawg named Sam."

SECOMP: "A dog?"

BOBBY: "Yes, ma'am. He's a big ole German Shepherd 'bout 4 years old. He sits up in the winda'. Don't nobody come in at night they see a big ole dawg in the winda'."

SECOMP: "That's true."

$\sim$

Bobby the Dishwasher has been courted by several fashion hair designers who are keen to help market his latest idea: An attachable men's hair extension which allows someone with a corporate, military or parochial school-regulation hair cut to enjoy a social life that includes a realistic-looking dreadlocked pony tail. The name? The Phony Tail . . . available in four different colors . . .

$\sim$

When Bobby the Dishwasher fields a sales call from Texas, he likes to answer with a drawl that sounds like, "HOWDY! BARD EARTH CA-FE!"

~

KATHY: "Don't the callers ever say something like, 'Hey, when you answered the phone you sounded all midwesty. Soon as I mentioned I wanted the owner or got into my pitch, all a sudden, you're like, all Hee-Haw.'"

BOBBY: "Midwesty? Hey, say, is that a gen-u-ine Tennessee accent, ma'am."

KATHY: "Not even close to Kentucky. I mean, don't they say, 'Wait, you just changed your voice, you got, what, some kind of Southern accent now?'"

BOBBY: "I think they don't care. Would you care, you go up to the table and get an order, the lady sounds like a cultured socialite from the Hamptons? Then, you drop the plate off a couple minutes later, she goes, 'Thank ya' kindly,' all Tennesee Williamsy. "

KATHY: "Why are we putting the Y on the end of these words? Wait, Tennesee Williams, didn't he like choke on the cap of his eye drop bottle? 'Sides, I never waited on anyone from the Hamptons."

BOBBY: "Yeah, God, the eye drop cap. I guess it's better than Elvis. The toilet. Please, drag me out into the hall by the ankles, that happens. You know, we never finish what we start talking about, do we?"

KATHY: "What were we talking about?"

BOBBY: "See?"

~

I asked Bobby if he launched into Area-Code-Centric Accents as a means of bettering communication or enhancing the Sport of Phone Phun.

"I'm hurt that you have to ask," he said with a wink.

～

BOBBY: "BARD EARTH CA-FE!"

800OPINIONRESEARCH: "Hello. Is this Borrowed Earth Café?"

BOBBY: "Yes, ma'am. This here's Bobby. I'm the dishwasher."

800: "Uh, is there an executive chef or owner in?"

BOBBY: "No, ma'am. The owner done left the country. Left me'n my girl t'run the place. Don't know when he's coming back . . . just up'n left us."

～

Bobby's dad stopped in for a little while this afternoon. The phone rang and I saw it was an 800 number and I instinctively handed his dad the phone . . . who began speaking with a thick Irish brogue, launching into a wee tale of a small restaurant operating without electricity or any clear leadership . . . not inclined towards purchases from callers . . . Bobby grinning the whole time, like, Check out my dad.

～

DANNY: "Borrowed Earth Café!"

INSURANCE CALLER: "Yes, I'd like to talk to someone about your insurance . . ."

BOBBY: "Well, we got lucky there. My uncle is an insherns agent and he gives it to us at cost . . ."

CALLER: "Sounds like you've got it all taken care of."

BOBBY: "You wouldn't believe it."

~

In our continuing sojourn, our dance, cheek to cheek, with the Legion of Telemarketers, Danny and I talked about a possible new move, a change of step, an uptempo cha-cha-cha . . . maybe drop the fiction . . . 86 the Story. Or do we continue to follow the perils of Bobby and his girl, mindin' the store? Mr. Bing, on the lam, all that Co-op, No Utility, Rolling Snowball Story?

KATHY: "What say we try answering the phone truthfully."

DANNY: "You mean, 'Is the owner or manager there?' and we say, 'Yes, I'm the owner/manager, how can I help?'"

KATHY: "Be up front, Drop all the owner's out of the country, Tennessee Bobby camoflage."

DANNY: "No more lies."

KATHY: "Face 'em head on. No thank you, we like our Credit Merchant Services vendor, Utility company, Internet provider, Soap Dispenser company, Napkin / Bar Towel distributor, blah, blah, blah. Now hang up. I've got people in here who want to eat. Call the next number. Scratch this one out. Game Over. I wish you well in your job, but I need to do mine and well, you're tying up the house phone. Fine then, we ain't buying what you're selling . . ."

DANNY: "..have a nice life, goodbye. What about Bobby?"

KATHY: What about him?"

DANNY: "Can he still answer the phone?"

KATHY: "Keep him in our back pocket?"

DANNY: "Call it a Get Out of Phone Call Free card."

KATHY: "Like Monopoly."

DANNY: "I didn't really like that game."

KATHY: "Me neither. My brother was like Napoleon. Eight years old and swollen with power, grinning at everyone, like an idiot there on the floor in his footie pajamas, 'Lookit me, I got Park Place and Boardwalk and you owe me $500 dollars, pay up.' Lookin' at me like he's taking my kidney out and feeling good about it."

DANNY: "I always picked the Shoe."

KATHY: "Little Dog."

DANNY: "Maybe if we don't recognize the number, we dish it off to Bobby."

KATHY: "Let him talk."

DANNY: "Leave us to run the restaurant."

KATHY: "He ties them in a quick sailor's knot and then, back to the dish room."

DANNY: "I heard we're getting a door."

KATHY: "Who told you that?"

DANNY: "I think it was you."

Dish Room Door

Bobby got some fool new hat . . . a bright red, yellow, green big-stitch rasta affair, knit together with a little drawstring at the bottom . . . cinch that thing up, gonna corral all that hair. He stacked and cordoned off his hair up into a big beehive, stuck the hat on and grinned, like some Dr. Seuss goofball character . . .

Dishwasher in the Hat—

I eyed his hat, a good foot over his head and decided to have The Talk . . .

KATHY: "I'm thinking about putting a door between the dish room and the dining room, maybe get one of those swinging metal kind, got one of those portholes, give you a peek on the other side, 'case some waiter's plowing through, got his arm bent, palm up, 30 cups of soup balanced on one of those trays big as a tire."

BOBBY: "We have a waiter?"

KATHY: "Listen, point is, we muffle some of that dish room noise . . ."

BOBBY: "I haven't clinked a plate since 3:00 . . . well, I broke that glass, but you said the plate noise . . ."

KATHY: "You broke a glass?"

BOBBY: "So, people will just see my head through the hole?"

Kathy eyes hat and looks back at Bobby

KATHY: "Well, yeah, they can check out your hat."

BOBBY: "But we keep the dish noise down. You probably won't even hear if one breaks."

KATHY: "Like you're not even doing dishes."

BOBBY: "But the little window. People look over, Hey, look, there's a guy in there, I can see him moving, looks like maybe he's doing dishes, I can't tell, you can't hear anything."

KATHY: "Like an exhibit."

BOBBY: "Cool."

Mr. Dillman

Bobby's high school counselor predicted that Bobby "wouldn't amount to anything."

At age 49, Bobby made an appointment with the school, identifying himself as an alumni and he asked if Mr. Dilman still worked there. Two days later, he sat in the chair across from Mr. Dilman and said, "Remember me? Well, I'm doing dishes at some restaurant now, got it real good." Mr. Dilman, he says, was impressed.

MR. DILMAN: "Bobby, geez, look at you all hairy now. Is that real?"

BOBBY: "My hair? Yeah, it's real. Wanna feel it?"

MR. DILMAN: "Ew, uh, no. What can I do for you?"

BOBBY: "Well, I wanted to come back and tell you how I'm doing."

MR. DILMAN: "Yeah, how'd you turn out? You some kind of musician?"

BOBBY: "No, I work in some restaurant in Downers Grove."

MR. DILMAN: "So, you're like, the owner?"

BOBBY: "Hey, someone calls looking for the owner, who do they give the phone to?"

MR. DILMAN: "You come up take the phone, all business, 'Bobby here.'"

BOBBY: "Yeah, but sometimes I'll tell 'em other stuff too. I mean, we get a lot of sales calls, but I handle 'em, because . . ."

MR. DILMAN: " . . . you're the owner?"

BOBBY: "On the phone, yeah. See Mr. Dilman? We're getting along now, just talking. I'm sorry about your car."

MR. DILMAN: "That was a long time ago, Bobby."

BOBBY: "Yeah, but I poured dish soap in the crack in your sunroof and got that big hose from over on the wall over by the teacher's lot . . ."

MR. DILMAN: "It looked all white inside, and I'm thinking, 'Is that my car?'"

BOBBY: "And you opened the door . . ."

MR. DILMAN: "And all those suds and water come tumbling out . . ."

Bobby and Mr. Dilman, in singsong unison say

"And ruined my wing tip shoes, the one's my father left me, God rest his soul."

BOBBY: "I can't believe they read that in court."

MR. DILMAN: "The judge . . ."

BOBBY: "He hated me too."

MR. DILMAN: "I think he was more upset about the shoes than the upholstery."

BOBBY: "It was soap . . ."

MR. DILMAN: "Which put the hurt on . . ."

BOBBY: "' . . . the genuine leather inserts.' I remember that part too."

MR. DILMAN: "They read that too."

BOBBY: "It seemed all about the shoes. I'm sorry, Mr. Dilman."

MR. DILMAN: "It's okay, Bobby. Litigation and time heal all wounds."

BOBBY: "The judge said that, yeah. Hey, it was good seeing you again. Good bye, Mr. Dilman."

MR. DILMAN: "Good bye, Bobby. I'm happy for your success."

BOBBY: "Thanks, Mr. Dilman. Let's just say you inspired me to be better."

MR. DILMAN: "People like you remind me of why I do this, Bobby."

BOBBY: "Stop by some time, Mr. Dilman. Say, what kind of car you drive now?"

MR. DILMAN: "Ford Mustang convertible. Bright yellow with a black top."

BOBBY: "Look at you. I bet it's real nice."

MR. DILMAN: "It's parked out back, take a look on your way out to your car. She's a real beauty."

GUY DUNYOGA

> *"One hand clapping, without illumi-*
> *nation, can sound a lot like one hand*
> *slapping."*—*Guy Dunyoga*

Obscure modern mystical writer Guy Dunyoga, an occasional waiter at Borrowed Earth Café, said that when he worked in the corporate world, he used to wear spongy earplugs as an "aural contraceptive sponge," protecting his mind from being impregnated with unwanted mental corporate seeds. "Attenuation first . . . then attention," he intones enigmatically, a finger raised.

In a rare BBC interview, Guy Dunyoga said that he also wore headphones while he worked on his computer, though he wasn't listening to music. He said people used to "pop in" to his office to chat, but by carefully avoiding eye contact and making a theatrical production of pulling one giant cup off his ear and saying loudly, "Huh? Did you say something . . . sorry," without looking away from the monitor, he noticed that the headphones worked like a visual taser to discourage interruptions.

His co-workers, he remembers fondly, found other people to talk to about their yards, kids, wives and dreams of escape.

"Tune in, turn on . . . and tune out the world," he said with a Learian certainty.

"Modern mystics needn't go to a remote cave to navel gaze and to find Oneness through Aloneness, when Oneness is preferable in a world of Twoness," he said, referring, by Twoness, I believe, to the Bathroom Code.

Borrowed Earth Café ☺

"Headphones, ear plugs . . . these are merely modern, portable caves that we can enter during our daily lives."

BOBBY'S MAMMY

Bobby's mammy Ethel was the daughter of a poor Tennessee coal mining family. Her father had worked in the mines for some 30 years and had an old dented helmet with a light fixed to the front that, when switched on, illuminated a bright foot-candle swath in even the darkest dark and Ethel and her siblings used to play with it when their father, Bobby Sr. wasn't working or answering sales calls.

Bobby said, as the eldest, Ethel was handed the helmet solemnly by her mother when Bobby Sr. passed away from complications from the black lung and an incident involving a rolled up TV Guide, a faulty reclining mechanism on a Lazy Boy and *The Ed Sullivan Show*, an incident that I don't want to clutter this page with, but, it should be noted, an incident which Bobby recalls with a mixture of pride, sadness and nostalgia.

She kept that dented helmet in the back of her and Bobby's father's closet.

Ethel loved that helmet as much as the name Bobby, deliberately passing up an opportunity to marry a fine young man named Earl to marry a boy named Bobby, a n'er do well, a plodder, a low brow, a spectacular underachiever, but a kind man who loved Ethel and followed her around like a Golden Retriever, an apt dog choice, as the man was always either preparing food for her, handing her a beverage or washing dishes, a sub task he later farmed out to Bobby-Bobby, who loved washing dishes, as the window over the kitchen sink gave him a good vantage of the interstate, just 35 feet from that very window, measuring from the screen to the white line.

Borrowed Earth Café ☺

All those cars whizzing by and Bobby could see the people in the cars, those people looking like, Hey, I see a guy doing dishes in there.

Moreover, Ethel liked the name Bobby so much she decided, forget convention, and named all 12 of Bobby's siblings, boy or girl, she didn't care, Bobby, much to the consternation of the teachers in Tennessee PS 135. Bobby's siblings thought that the name Bobby was, to use the description shared by all Bobby-Bobby's brothers and sisters (The Bobby Collective), *The Bobby Curse.*

Bobby said that in her dotage, neighborhood children used to come after dark and look into the windows, long after Bobby-Bobby had set off on foot (in those big Crocs) for Chicago to wash dishes at Borrowed Earth. The Bobby Collective had scattered like dropped marbles to all points on the globe, and Bobby Sr. had gone off to the Big Telemarketing Cubicle in the sky, dying from complications resulting from an incident involving a rolled People Magazine, a faulty mechanism on a Barcalounger and *Jeopardy!* Ethel just had plain bad luck when it came to important men in her life, rolled magazines, reclining furniture and television frivolty.

Those neighborhood kids stood on tip toes and looked from the darkened night into the windows at Ethel, that miner's hat on, light blazing, sitting in a rocking chair, gently tapping her curled left palm with a rolled magazine, humming softly to herself.

Full Disclosure

Under Employment Disclosure, Bobby gave a full accounting of the incident in 2nd grade when the teacher asked what the three R's were and Bobby, the linguaphile, pointed out that only one actually began with an R, the other two, a W and A, respectively. Though it happened 39 years ago, to hear him tell it, you'd think he just came back from the principal's office, ears ringing from Ms. Doolin's tongue's cat o' 9 tails feature.

I listened with fascination as he told the story, rich with detail and augmented with a flair for the dramatic that I secretly found to be, well, intoxicating.

The teacher, well, she sounded like the mean kind of teacher that doesn't like kids but teaches so she can feel powerful, making them feel bad about themselves, chipping away at their self-esteem one critical remark at a time, one red unhappy smiley face at a time, one big red check mark at a time—the big red check marks, WRONG! The kind that makes your heart sink because you can tell she pressed hard and made it with a thick red marker whose fumes should be illegal.

No doubt the big lanky clown sitting across from me applying for the dishwasher job had been a handful then, just 10 years old and already causing problems, particularly when an Authority Figure was involved.

I can see him at the back of the room, looking out the window, drawing cartoons, anything to pass the time, Uh, it's only 10:30, he's thinking, looking at the big clock on the wall over her desk, high above her tight bun that framed the permanent scowl of disapproval on her face.

I remember at the beginning of the interview, him sliding the folder full of photos across the table. I'm thinking, Pictures? Glancing through them quickly:

—Bobby looking pensive, his hand on his chin like he's thinking (ha!).

—Bobby in front of a stack of gleaming plates, a blue ribbon or medal around his neck, proclaiming sadly, "Dishwasher of the Year."

—Bobby petting a little green bird while typing?

I closed the folder on his pensive shot and looked at him.

Look at him. Kinda hokey, but serious.

And then all those character references.

"He's a character," the last one I called said laughing. "Ask him to tell you about riding his bike in his underwear . . . after he gets the job, though."

So, I took a chance.

Call him a Project. My Pygmalion.

I asked him about the biking in his underwear story and he nodded to himself and smiled and patted my arm and walked off to stick his arms in the sudsy water and splash water all over the front of himself, his head dangerously close to the metal shelf over the sink . . .

I'll keep asking, maybe see if he can work the bike underwear story into one of his phone calls . . . maybe the owner can ride around in his underwear on a bike, a red one-speed cruiser. Mr. Bing on a Bike in his Briefs . . . sales people afraid they're gonna come by and see some guy in his skivvies, his hands on his hips, shaking his head in the classic exaggerated No, saying, "We don't want any." Then they imagine spending the rest of the day trying to get the image outa their mind:

The guy, standing there in his underwear, the bike leaned against the windows out front . . .

And 2:15am? Hey, they weren't that hard up for a commission.

BOBBY AND THE PSYCHIC

A storefront along our way home has a big yellow neon sign that says, "PSYCHIC!" and a smaller neon blue and red sign below it that perpetually says, "OPEN!" Last night, on impulse, I pulled in and reached over and opened Bobby's door, "Go get your fortune read," I instructed. He grinned, saying, "I'll be right back." He came out $15 poorer, but with two free Energy Stones, a white one and a black one, which he said were "Concretium" and "Asphaltia," respectively.

~

KATHY: "So, what'd she say?"

BOBBY: "How do you know it wasn't a guy?"

KATHY: "Call it a hunch."

BOBBY: "She says I've got great potential . . ."

KATHY: " . . . but you haven't reached it yet. You tell her you're a dishwasher?"

BOBBY: "No, I didn't give anything away, see if she figures that out."

KATHY: "$15, you keep your tarot cards close to the vest?"

BOBBY: "Exactly."

KATHY: "So, you've got great potential, but . . ."

BOBBY: " . . . but, she sees something happening soon."

KATHY: "Cards or crystal ball?"

BOBBY: "No, check it out, she's using an application on her iPhone."

KATHY: "Nice. Modern."

BOBBY: "She thought that in a past life I might have been a general . . ."

KATHY: ". . . pain in the neck?"

BOBBY: "She didn't say it that way, but she said I had been a leader."

KATHY: "And now you're the king of the dishes."

BOBBY: "It's good to be king. She mentioned you."

KATHY: "Do tell."

BOBBY: "She said that you're good for me and that I'm lucky in love."

KATHY: "Tell me that you knew that $15 ago."

BOBBY: "No, that one was a shocker . . . . OW!"

BOBBY THE WAITER

Lately, I've been giving Bobby a little more waiter time on the floor.

Taking off the training wheels.

Letting a little line out . . .

Call it a calculated risk.

～

He had this table of women laughing at lunch this week and I worried about what he was saying.

Everyone all buddy-buddy at the end . . . they left him a 40% tip.

Okay.

～

I heard him "help" this older woman. Her and her companions had finished eating, a little left over dessert in little square eco-friendly sugarcane boxes. This woman was unashamedly eating her take out cheese cake right out of the box, finishing off the whole thing, the other people at the table heckling her, Hey, look at her, can't even wait to get in the car, for God's sake.

Bobby rides up to the table, Sir Bobby to the rescue and leads with his mouth, like a fighter. Not a rightie or a southpaw. More of a mouthpaw. He drawls, all Tennessee now:

"If God didn't want us to overeat every once in a while, He wouldn't have made our stomachs all stretchy and stuff to account for the holidays and what not . . ."

She grinned at him, "That's right."

∽

BOBBY: "Hello! Eating in or taking out?"

KATHY: "What are you doing?"

BOBBY: "Practicing."

KATHY: "In the mirror?"

BOBBY: "I wanna see how I look when I say it."

KATHY: "You're self-assured . . . that's it . . . chin up . . . back straight."

BOBBY: "Ow."

KATHY: "Don't hurt yourself."

BOBBY: "Can I seat the next people?"

KATHY: "Maybe you should stretch first."

∽

BOBBY: "This lady told me, 'I can run, swim, hike, play tennis . . .'"

KATHY: "What was she talking about?"

BOBBY: "She has more energy from her raw food diet."

KATHY: "Sounds like a tampon commercial."

BOBBY: "I know, I'm thinking, She says the T word, I'm gettin' Kathy."

~

CUSTOMER: "That man's sitting in my seat."

BOBBY: "There's 20 other open seats."

CUSTOMER: "But that's *my* seat."

BOBBY: "So? Sit right next to him. Make him uncomfortable."

CUSTOMER: "Like when you're in the men's room alone and that guy comes and stands at the one right next to you? All those empty ones and he's right next to you."

BOBBY: "Yeah, don't be *that* guy . . ."

1 minute later

KATHY: "What are you doing?"

BOBBY: "Helping someone decide."

~

CUSTOMER: "You mind me asking what the tattoos mean?"

Bobby spreads his hands, palms up, arms extended

BOBBY: "These? The spirals?"

CUSTOMER: "Yeah. Do they mean something?"

BOBBY: "Everything moving in an outward circle away from the center and then spiraling back from whence it came. Or something. Like the Universe. Which line do you see?"

CUSTOMER: "Which line?"

BOBBY: "White one or the black one?"

CUSTOMER: "Yeah. I see. Hey, I like that."

BOBBY: "See?"

～

CUSTOMER: "I'm looking for a restaurant that'll make a dessert."

BOBBY: "I'm the executive chef's assistant. What kind of dessert?"

CUSTOMER: "It's made with oatmeal, peanut butter, Nutella and Marshmallow Fluff."

BOBBY: "How about that."

CUSTOMER: "I'm actually trying to put on 20 lbs."

BOBBY: "Awesome."

CUSTOMER: "20 lbs of fat. Not muscle. Pure fat. 20 lbs."

BOBBY: "It's good to have goals."

～

Last week, we met a lady who was trying to gain 20 lbs of "pure fat," she had said, grinning.

She came back today and was chewing the fat with Bobby, our dishwasher, who was out on the patio busing a table.

She told him about Project Fat and Bobby says, "Lady, I don't wanna gain fat or muscle . . . I'm just trying not to get dumber."

∾

Two sales people walk into the café and I notice how Bobby's face lifts into the most beatific smile: Bobby the Sales Killer. "Packaging for our take outs?" he repeats to the two with the briefcases, looking at him. He whispers, sotto voce, "My uncle gives them to us at cost . . ." They want to know who Bobby's uncle is, but he shakes his head and assures them that if his uncle finds out he's talked . . . and draws a finger across his throat and shoots me a look and gives me that idiot grin I love.

∾

LITTLE GIRL: "Mommy, what's the man doing?"

MOM: "Ask him."

GIRL: "Mister, what are you doing?"

BOBBY: "Moving food from the containers onto the plates . . . I used to just wash dishes, but now they're giving me more responsibilities."

∾

Phone rings

KATHY: "Borrowed Earth Café."

CALLER: "Do you have food for my picky vegetarian daughter?"

KATHY: "Uh . . ."

CALLER: "And what is there for me? I don't like nuts . . . or salad. I'm kind of picky too."

1 minute later

BOBBY: "Who was that?"

KATHY: "A picky mother with a picky daughter."

BOBBY: "Maybe picky's hereditary . . ."

~

A man walks in. It's the middle of the dinner rush and he's holding a little plastic cup in one hand, his other hand covering the top, "Do you have any milk?" I said no and he turned around and stalked out.

Bobby's father told him to never trust a person carrying a cup with a covered hand, "Son, there's something they don't want you to see and it could be a live animal . . ."

~

A mother-daughter 2-top walks in and stands up by the front . . .

BOBBY: "Hi! Eating in or taking out?"

MOTHER: "In."

BOBBY: "Okay, you can sit wherever you like . . ."

They hesitate

BOBBY: "Or, I can pick for you. But, I tend to seat people back there right by the bathroom."

MOTHER: "We'll sit at *this* table here."

BOBBY: "There you go."

KATHY: "Helping people decide?"

BOBBY: "I'm here to serve."

∼

KATHY: "Go see if T2 is ready for their check."

BOBBY: "What's my motivation?"

KATHY: "Motivation? Like, are they ready to pay?"

BOBBY: "No, I mean, am I aloof, distraught . . . ?"

KATHY: "You mean like in a play?"

BOBBY: "Yeah. I'm a waiter and I'm feeling . . ."

KATHY: "You're somber and alert, but polite. All business now . . ."

Bobby puts a serious look on face

BOBBY: "Like this?"

KATHY: "Off you go."

∼

DANNY: "Borrowed Earth Café."

CALLER: "Yes, is this Borrowed Earth Café?"

BOBBY: "Yes it is."

CALLER: "What time do you close?"

BOBBY: "9:03."

CALLER: "9:03? Why don't you just close at 9?"

BOBBY: "Just drop the 03?"

CALLER: "Close at 9."

BOBBY: "That's a good idea! I'm going to change it right now . . ."

∼　ı

BOBBY: "Hi, come on in. Eating in or taking out?"

Customer looks around, then looks up, then down, then straight ahead, narrowing the eyes, frowning now

BOBBY: "Don't over think it."

PHONE PHUN

Turns out the 2005 landmark Do Not Call Registry doesn't apply to business phones. Turns out you're still staked out like a goat. So rather than get turned out, you turn the tables, all eight of them, plus the five outside.

So, you get yourself a hired hand. A dishwasher, a ne'r do well named Bobby who you have to watch like a hawk, but is like an idiot savant (or at least an idiot) when it comes to "handling" sales calls.

Don't get mad.

Get Bobby.

A man who answers the phone with a Tennessee accent so poor, people from Tennessee have written and complained.

"It ain't Tennessee," they write.

"That boy watched Hee-Haw, 'bout all we reckon," says another.

But he's mine and he answers the phone:

"Bard Earth Ca-fe!"

. . . and says things like, "The owner ain't here. No, ma'am. Me? My name's Bobby. Yes, ma'am. Three B's like flibbertigibbet. What? Four B's? No, three, like Flibbertigibbet! Hello?"

∼

BOBBY: "Bard Earth Ca-fe."

800SERVICEINFO AUTOMATED VOICE: "Your credit card service provider could be charging you too much money. Push 1 for . . ."

Bobby quickly punches in 3825968

KATHY: "What are you doing?"

BOBBY: "Sending a text message . . ."

KATHY: "Using the cordless work phone?"

❧

BOBBY: "Bard Earth Ca-fe."

OUT OF AREA: "Yes, is the owner or manager in?"

BOBBY: "No sir. This here's Bobby. I'm the dishwasher."

OOA: "Well, I'm the dish-patcher. Ha-ha. Do you know when the owner will be back?"

BOBBY: "I don't rightly know. He'n his wife's on a train going to Mexico. They send us pitchers on Facebook."

OOA: "Well, then, I'll call back."

BOBBY: "You do that."

❧

CUSTOMER ON PHONE: "I was the one who ate there last week."

BOBBY: "Sure, you had the plate, I can see it, there was salad on it . . . and you sat at that table."

1 minute later

KATHY: "Who was that?"

BOBBY: "Got me."

KATHY: "It sounded like you remembered her."

BOBBY: "It did, didn't it?"

∾

Phone rings

DANNY: "Yes! Sales call!"

BOBBY: "Bard Earth Ca-fe."

MEDICALINSUR: "May I have someone call you with a quote for medical insurance?"

BOBBY: "No ma'am. My mammy's a witch doctor . . ."

MEDICALINSUR: "Thank you."

BOBBY: "No, thank *you*."

∾

CALLER: "Wait, is this Kathy?"

KATHY: "Uh, yeah, as a matter of fact, it is."

CALLER: "I don't think you're Kathy."

KATHY: "Fine. It's Danny."

CALLER: "Who is this?"

Phone fumbling noise, muffled talking, then Bobby, imitating Kathy perfectly saying

"Hello. This is Kathy."

CALLER: "Finally. What kinda people you got workin' there?"

Bobby switches to Tennessee Bobby voice

BOBBY: "Ma'am, we got us all kinds."

~

In Bobby's words, when I asked where all those words come from:

"Okay, it breaks down like this. Everyone has that voice in their head that says clever things, but your mouth is like, 'Hey, that's kinda strange, doncha think, Earl?' and you suppress the voice, say something nice or nothin' t'all, as the saying goes.

What about taking off the muzzle, jeez, let Earl out, man, that dude can totally handle this.

Sometimes your Inner Earl has a time delay. You're walking away from some jerk you just hung up on someone who practically underhanded you a perfect straight man line and suddenly, you know the perfect thing to say!

'Cept it's too late.

Moment's passed.

Train's left the station.

The dog's already out the yard.

You replay it in your mind, here it comes, the straight man line and your line, like a bat pulled back, BAM! Right over the wall, I think it broke a windshield in the parking lot.

You take a lap around the bases, the umpire patting your shoulder, 'Nice hit.'

You turn and curtsy and the whole stadium comes to its feet and there's a thunderous applause.

But no, it's five minutes later.

No going back.

So, that means you've got an Earl, fact that you can come up with the right thing to say, if Nice and Nothin' T'all options are gonna gnaw at you . . .

You're saying, Whadaya mean, like, lay some fiction on 'em?

And I say tell 'em you had a dog named Blue that had a tick as big as a football hanging off his butt, your dad chasing it around the yard, 'Here Blue!' Man, he's got a lawn dart he's gonna pop that thing with, all the neighbors hanging over the white picket fence watching, a robin chirping away excitedly in the branches above the yard in a gnarly oak tree, Blue running around practically laughing, like, Hey, I got a flea on my tail looks like a golf ball, who's got a 9 iron?

Say it rapid fire with no pause, the sales person holding the phone on the other end thinking, Good God, a lawn dart, and he's forgotten why he's called.

The more you exercise Earl, the less the delay, and pretty soon, you're Bobby.

What do you need a Bobby for?

We're *all* Bobby.

We just point at him and laugh.

Inside, our Earl is going, '*That's* what I'm talking about.'"

~

Nothing's sadder than getting the sales calls that are 100% machine. The recordings are frustrating. All we do, we hear that robot lady (I think her sister is the one who says, "IF YOU'D LIKE TO MAKE A CALL PLEASE HANG UP!") and we click off.

Frustrating because, there's no person to screw with.

After a machine call, Bobby practically mopes, especially if there's no press number option . . . totally non-interactive.

Where's the opportunity for creativity?

~

CALLER: "May I speak to Bobby the Dishwasher?"

BOBBY: "Speakin."

CALLER: "We'd like to lure you away from there, maybe wash some dishes at *our* place."

BOBBY: "I dunno, see, I'm sleeping with the owner here. I got it purdy good . . ."

~

KATHY: "Borrowed Earth Café."

CALLER: "Is this Borrowed Earth Café?"

KATHY: "Yes."

CALLER: "Thank you."

Kathy hangs up and says

"Confirmation at last."

Happy Birthday Bobby!

Bobby the Dishwasher was born just a little after 10 in the morning.

His mother, a 17-year old immigrant girl, named him Robert.

Robert Porter.

He showed me the adoption papers and the ones that showed how his adoptive parents had to change his name legally from Robert Porter to a name they picked.

Not Baby Boy, like some papers other adoptees had showed him.

She gave him a first and last name and he always wondered if it wasn't some kind of breadcrumb for him to follow, wondering if maybe she didn't want to be found, when he was ready.

It was a fortuitous day, I told him . . . lucky for everyone, especially me, when I think about it.

It could have gone another way, the Cosmic Curtains could have flapped in some other window and it could have turned out different.

I remember telling him how lucky the whole thing turned out to be after he told me about his birth, about the 17-year old girl who couldn't keep him and the people who raised him.

His *real* parents.

The ones who put their hearts and souls into loving him for the 18-some years he was under their roof.

You know, the ones who did all the work . . .

The Work, with a capital W.

We all eventually, unless by some accident of birth, wealth or lack of health, find that we have to work.

Pay the bills.

Take care of ourselves independently of our parents.

Our *real* parents. The ones who do The Work.

The *real* Work.

Whether you have kids or not . . .

. . . or maybe, you *had* a kid and, because you were just too darn young, the ink not quite dry on your driver's license, you had to give that kid away.

And then you had to trust that someone else would do The Work.

A kid that maybe you never get to see again, but a kid that you think about late at night, when everyone's sleeping and you're lying awake in bed or when you look around and see someone else's kid, a kid who would be *that* kid's age, or you spot some grown up kid clomping around in big shoes that touch the Earth attached to a pair of long skinny legs, and you look and think, that could be *that* kid, all grown up now.

A kid that you think about every year when you remember those emotionally charged weeks leading up to the Day, the day you went into a hospital with a bump under the shirt and and came home empty handed, a hollow inside that's more than just empty of baby.

Those weeks before the Day that felt like you were on some Emotional Rollercoaster, arms and legs inside the car, the bar down in your lap, banging around inside the car of the body, the ups and downs and twists that knotted your guts . . .

Then, the car coming to a halt and you get out on a solid ground, ground that doesn't feel the same as it did before . . .

Ground that you walk on and somewhere else, some kid clomps around on . . . and if you really stop and close your eyes, you can almost feel those tiny shudders the Earth makes with each of his first tottering steps, maybe taking longer to walk than most kids, spending extra time crawling, maybe that extra crawling doing a little extra work up in his brain, his real mom not worried too much, like, Yeah, he's not walking yet, but, man, listen to him talk.

Maybe that kid being able to say big words before he's even walking, big four-syllable things, like *Bretzigheimer*, the name of another woman maybe who's also adopted a kid around the same time, a woman the real mom talks to on the phone. She hands the kid the phone, the kind with the cord, I mean, it's almost 50 years ago, the cordless kind not invented yet, the cordless kind you can't send a text message on. That real mom clapping for him, trooping him around to all the relatives and friends like a tiny kid playing a violin, him saying, "Hello, Mrs. Bretzigheimer!" clearly and perfectly. And so she claps and that kid looks into his mom's eyes and performs that trick over and over and maybe, later, sits up front at the dining room table and his mom and dad let him tell jokes, even dirty ones and he becomes a story teller, a writer . . .

. . . you never can tell how a story's gonna end . . .

But, if you're the birth mother, when the anniversary of the Day comes around each year, which you don't talk about, when *that* kid's birthday rolls around, that little blue steals over your soul, a little shadow cast over your otherwise sunny dispositions and you tip toe around, draw inward.

And you think about the little tiny shadow at your side, somewhere else, growing up, then, you think about *that* kid, probably all grown up.

Nearly 50 now.

But still just a big kid.

Maybe a big funny kid.

Someone who can tell a joke, make people laugh, sometimes sneakin' serious in when people are distracted.

A kid maybe, not good at team sports when he's little, gets picked on in school, all gangly and awkward, turns to books to escape the pain of feeling like he doesn't quite fit in with the other kids. A kid that reads so much he ends up with a high vocabulary, still playing the big word violin all these years later, and still later, when the books aren't enough, a kid who starts drinking and taking drugs to escape. Maybe a kid who has an older sister he loves but doesn't always get along with, two grumpy peas in a pod, them, she's adopted too, and a little brother he loves, a little brother who spends the time the kid you gave away spends reading bouncing a ball off the front steps or shooting baskets in the backyard in the dark, a little brother who becomes a real athlete, the kind that holds the high school record for some distance or another . . . but maybe who hurts his ankle and later, settles in and stops moving around so much, changing places. Then, the kid you gave away suddenly putting the books and drugs down and the kid you only can imagine and send love and good wishes to suddenly starts to run.

A lot.

But *that* kid, the one you gave away, he's someone you still feel connected to and maybe, somewhere out there, your feelings so powerful, they reach out across the Earth . . . . you can almost feel his big feet now and those shudders on the Earth traveling around the world and you press your bare feet to the cool kitchen floor in the middle of the night as you sit there and type and you can almost feel him running or walking in the middle of the night somewhere . . . he's just walking now and he's limping a little like his back hurts and he's holding a red leash attached to a big Collie named Laddie maybe and the dog's walking along side that dark sidewalk in a neighborhood slowly alongside that kid. And that kid limping along is thinking about some girl out there somewhere . . . a girl who would always be 17 years older than him, he thinks . . .

. . . because there's no where in the Universe to hide from a mother's love, not even if she's sitting up on top of the wall at the end of the Universe, a ladder leaned against that wall, *CLUNK!*, sitting up there with her eyes closed, smiling, sending her love which she can never contain, it almost hurts to try, it's so huge, an overwhelming feeling that she had to breathe slowly and deeply through so she could stand it when she was back on Earth, when she was a Somebody, or after she died, that last breath fluttering from her lips, fluttering some Cosmic Curtains in some window somewhere. But now, back to being Nobody, not in bad way, this Nobodyness, because there's no history or future, just a big wide beautiful Now that has no words or thoughts, just the one Feeling, the biggest one; she's now in a place in which she no longer breathes to adjust the faucet on that feeling, the Biggest Feeling, capital B and F, the One without words or thoughts that put that huge outward pressure on her chest at times when she was on Earth, and now, so she can stand it, she doesn't work the faucet any more with her breathing, she just sends it to her family and friends, to everyone really, but especially *that* kid, maybe *because* of the sacrifice she made . . . the forgotten memory of that sacrifice somehow having left her forever a little partial to *that* kid . . . at least if you're *that* kid, it feels like you're getting a whole lot of something from somewhere else, something you learn to breathe slowly and deeply through with lips pressed together, eyes squeezed shut, little tears leaking out, happy, happy, happy tears . . .

If you're *that* kid, you feel lucky.

Borrowed Earth Café ☺

Maybe, if you're *that* kid, you might call them Lucky tears . . .

. . . capital L . . .

Tears that take you, even if you're still a Somebody, to that place, that seat up on the wall out at the end of Universe, the ladder behind you on the wall you climbed hand over hand after you leaned it against that wall with a CLUNK! or maybe, if you're really lucky, you discovered the place purely by accident, imagining what it would be like to be Nobody, just try it on, or that place you found yourself suddenly after sending up a flare into the night to ask for help.

A place you forgot about for nearly 30 years, but that you found again by accident, wondering what happens after you die, when you're not in your body any more, when you have no history any more, when you don't have a past to look back at or a future to worry over or look forward to that distracts you from seeing all the tiny miracles that illuminate like fireflies around you on a summer night, the ones, if you simply watch and don't think, you appreciate and are grateful for.

Things you missed when you were distracted by the past or the future . . . .

Or maybe you find you're in that place, seated up on top of that wall, your ankles crossed, maybe holding hands with some woman, a mother, maybe even the mother of *that* kid's wife, someone sending her kid love . . . Big Love, capital B, capital L, that huge overwhelming wonderful thing that we feel and call love that floods the entire Universe, in the space between everything, the canvas that everything's painted on, that existed in the Void, spiraling outward, inexorably outward, then back from whence it came, the spiral of Love, the white line that touches the black one in that spiral we draw on a piece of paper and, sometimes even, tattoo on our arms to remind yourself what's really important, this love spiraling out from the Void that fills you so big you can only give it away, you have to, because you simply can't breathe slowly and deeply through it any more to work the faucet, you have to send it on . . .

We send that big love, the white line spiraling next to the black line out from the Void that fills us 'til our eyes fill with tears and we send it on, give it away.

The best things, maybe, not the things we get to keep but the ones we give away.

The sacrifices we make.

Maybe the stuff of the *real* Work.

If we're really lucky, like I've been, you find yourself doing something you think has Meaning. You have to do something, yeah, because you need enough to keep a modest, non-leaking roof over your head, pay for groceries and have a little in the bank in case the car needs to be fixed. But, you focus on doing what you love, this something, which for you has Meaning, and somehow, if you work hard, it provides just enough money to tinkle on any problem that comes along.

But you're doing something you feel good about.

And it's something that provides enough.

Something that you do because you love doing it and so you keep doing it and hey, somehow, like your efforts are attached to a kitchen at some Karmic Bakery, you keep getting a serving of your daily bread.

Just enough for today. The only day we really get.

Enough so you can focus on serving other people, maybe a little of their daily bread, even if it came out of a dehydrator, without being worried or distracted, distracted so you're unable to see those fireflies, those tiny miracles that illuminate around us each day, if we watch and stop thinking . . .

Enough so you learn to trust that the daily bread will show up if you keep doing what feels right and true for yourself in your situation.

That something you do, and it can be almost anything, with the hope that it has Meaning and that you might be better for the experience.

Enough about Enough.

Let's get back to the real parents, the one who change the diapers, who hold the bottle, later the spoon and then, look, the kid does it without help . . . the ones who do the cleaning, the worrying . . . and eventually see those little ones flap their wings, more bird than butterfly, and go off and build their own nests . . .

People who maybe can't have their own kids, maybe the wife's Fallopian Tubes are blocked and she can't have her own, but that doesn't mean she doesn't have a maternal itch, a tickle inside her, someone who maybe felt a lot of love growing up and has a lot to give away, has to so she can stand it, the breathing slowly and the pressed lips and leaky tears, God, that just doesn't work the faucet enough so you can stand it so you decide you want kids and you see that maybe there might be someone out there who has a kid and, maybe that someone's ink isn't quite dry on her driver's license and she just can't do the Work, so you make yourself available to help. Signing up for the Work.

So, lucky for you, lucky for everyone, especially for both kids: *that* kid, the one you'll clap for when he says, "Hello, Mrs. Bretzigheimer!" and also, lucky for the other kid, the one too young to do the Work.

So, the kid with the newly minted license sits on her bed, decides to ignore her own maternal itch and do what's best, she sends up a flare and some curtains flutter in her window and then that woman who can't have her own children, she's sitting on some other bed and her curtains flutter with the same breeze and that Big Love starts to put things in order.

That Big Love that paints the canvas, that *is* the canvas, the paint and the brush and the eyes that step back and watch and say, "That's beautiful" and the heart that beats and stops and goes and sits back up on top of that wall.

All of it somehow coming out of the Void and then returning from whence it came.

The white line and the black one forming one outward, then inward spiraling line with no separation between the two.

For Bobby, it could have gone the other way. Maybe there might have been no breeze that afternoon to flutter the Cosmic Curtains, no butterfly in South America farting or flapping it's wings, maybe that 17-year old girl sitting on the edge of her bed in Chicago somewhere, maybe in some home for Wayward Girls or something, decides to keep *that* kid against all logic, only clinging to some maternal instinct tickling at her from inside a body full of a baby she didn't plan on having.

Maybe that woman with the unpassable tubes sitting on her bed decides they'll just get a dog, shrug, and call it a day.

Maybe call the dog Mrs. Bretzigheimer, let the kid behind the desk at the vet's count out all those syllables on his fingers . . .

But, lucky for me, for everyone, maybe a million different people Bobby will never know, a million people who read about him and a little restaurant just outside Chicago that two fools with no business opening opened, two people who got on that provisonless wagon, then, heck with the wagon, the balloon, traveling toward the beckoning Westward sun . . . then faster, faster, getting in the Rocket . . .

A lucky day, a fortuitous day.

~

BOBBY: "Say that again."

KATHY: "Fortuitous."

BOBBY: "What's that mean? For, for, for who?"

KATHY: "Lucky. Fortuitous."

BOBBY: "For who?"

KATHY: "For everyone."

~

So, Bobby's 17-year old mother named him Robert Porter at birth.

I saw the papers.

Not Baby Boy.

Two names, first and last.

Like a breadcrumb maybe.

The first pass reading through this and I thought, "Put that name in there, Robert Porter, who knows? Maybe if a million people read this, one of them might go, Hey . . ."

Maybe pick up a cold trail.

Maybe that girl who will always be 17 years older than Bobby, or someone who knows that nearly 50-year old story, will read this.

Maybe putting that name in here, like sending up a flare.

Get some curtains fluttering.

You never know.

So, his mother gave him a name, first and last.

Maybe the firm counsel of Bobby's mother's parents and some nuns at school and maybe a nagging sense that this was not her time to be a mom despite the maternal twitch she felt and the feeling that they were right, it was just not her time to do the mom thing; maybe all that resulted in her putting Robert up for adoption.

A moment after Robert was born, he was weighed and measured. Say Pardner, someone saying, Count all those fingers and toes. Then, confirmation, finally, Okay, I got 10, the OB at St. Joseph's hospital said, checking again using his own fingers as a make-shift abacus to make sure, math never being his strong suit.

. . . no, not his strong suit, more like a cheap leisure suit in the closet, a ghastly powder blue affair with lapels that spread out like shameful, oversized wings.

His math, like the suit, an embarrassment. Good Lord, a monkey taking random guesses could probably outscore him on a test, that monkey with the number 2 pencil and one of those rubber grips, keep your fingers curled the right way, the monkey got a nervous eye on the teacher, looks like a gnarly old nun walking spryly around the room looking at the monkeys with their pencils, the knuckle of her middle finger sticking out like a hammer . . .

That OB's math "skills" something to hide and not show in public, keep that in the closet, that weak suit, the finger abacus math and lifetime's worth of arithmetic miscalculations.

I imagine the moment after he emerged, little Robert crying, maybe looking around the tiled room, all decked out in 1962 birth room gear, a lady over there looking at her watch as she recorded the time and date which would be transferred to a birth certificate that would have blackouts on it; a crinkly folded grayish hand-typed document. Somewhere under those black marks that paper held a truth that someone decided Robert should not know. That woman with the pencil, writing those birth facts thinking, Hey, I might get something good while it's still hot for lunch in the cafeteria.

Little 10-second old Robert thinking maybe that everything was still all blurry, Jeez, get that light outa my eye and get this goo off my face and comb my wispy hair and get a diaper on me, I gotta pee.

Before that official document went to Robert's adoptive parents, someone else would take a thick black magic marker or something and make those deliberate blackouts, like drawing a dark curtain between the future Robert and this 17-year old girl. A curtain neither would be able to see through, relying solely on feelings to reach out and touch each other through, across the years, usually around Robert's birthday, when that shadow stole over his heart.

He said it was like he had his hand up against that dark curtain and he felt another hand pressing back from the other side.

Neither making a sound—each sitting in the Silence.

Feeling something akin to a pressure, big and powerful, in the place inside each other's chest.

Sean's house.

If his mother was awake (and she probably wasn't), she'd have seen little Robert taken out of the room and down the hall to the nursery and given his first taste of man-made processed food, a few swigs out of a bottle made from powdered formula, no breast milk for Robert, some nun holding him and cooing in his face, the hooded habit making her look like a penguin, little Robert already forming a joke in his mind about a lady with a funny hat, thinking he'll write it down when he learns to hold the darn pencil without the rubber thing to keep his fingers from curling the wrong way, that Sister Mathilda, his ancient gnarled second grade teacher tried unsuccessfully to force his hand around. A woman, who despite her slightly bent frame and terrifying eyes bugging from behind thick spectacles, would travel the room spryly and crook her middle knuckle, not willing to give eight year olds getting outa line the full finger, as per Vatican regulations, but apparently free to crash the same finger's middle knuckle down savagely on the skulls of miscreant children and exclaim, "Coconut Head!" like some percussive punctuation mark. Later, Robert said he learned a similar move from his 24-year old martial arts instructor, who substituted Sister Mathilda's cry of "Coconut Head!" for "Ki-ya!" But, fundamentally, from a martial arts' perspective, other than the verbal accompaniment, it was the same strike. Robert says Sister Mathilda hit harder, his skull's visceral memory assured him.

Probably within a day or two, a young couple in Chicago with a little adopted girl already, a girl named Marie, would be called, some voice over the phone saying, "Hey, the package arrived safe. Come and get him."

Marie, who would be almost two years ahead of Robert in school, would sleep in alone in a room next to his, the room up by the front hall, a little step up from the sunken front hall, next to the room he shared with his little brother PJ. Robert and PJ's room was located in the heart of the house, right in the middle. A room with a view of the living room tv, which contributed to Robert's lifelong battle with insomnia, all those late nights watching tv over his toes, looking through the wrought iron bars into the living room, at first, a black and white tv and then a series of color tv's, each one better than the last. A room he'd read hundreds of books in while everyone else stayed out and played, avoiding sports that he couldn't quite get the hang of, mostly, preferring to escape into the Realm of Dreams, allowing the words to tow him through the pages of a story gently, his imagination the horse, pulling the wagon of his mind and heart and soul along a path traveled by another, a path he traveled, through those words. After lights out, Robert would tuck his head under the covers, prop his knees up and put the non-business end of a flashlight powered by two D batteries under his chin and keep reading.

All those words. When he was around eight, he started to pick up books his father, an avid reader himself, had finished.

And like some idiot savant, all that high, adult-sized vocabulary started to fill his head and came spilling out his mouth.

～

Robert's parents allowed for 'in-house' swearing but just asked the children to learn to "turn it off" in school, church or similar places where certain words were generally frowned on.

Parents: Be careful what you clap for . . .

When Robert was little, someone made the mistake of saying, "You're funny!"

Then, when Robert was 9 years old, he would tell his first "dirty" joke at the dining room table. He got a big laugh. No one laughed harder than his father—his 9-year old son telling a joke at the Big Table and everyone was laughing.

Robert remembered to knit his brows and lower his voice and sound angry when he was the cop and then to raise his eyebrows and sound innocent when he was $#@%*@! Hour and then the outrage when he's $#@%*@! Hour's boss or whoever answers the call. He remembered to let the people laugh and let it die down a little before resuming in between the three parts of that joke to build the tension: the pullover, the call, then the punchline. He remembered to pause before the punch line . . . and to raise his voice a little at the end and sit up straight when he was telling it and to look at everyone, like he was telling it to only them.

He'd watched his father tell jokes to small groups of people his whole life. His father was the undisputed master. Funnier than any of his uncles, cousins or anyone else Robert had ever met. 20 years later and Robert would hear a good joke and pick up the phone . . ."Dad, I heard a good one," and then launch into the joke.

While Robert's little brother excelled at sports and his sister at school, Robert was reading books that had nothing to do with school and learning to be funny.

Sports and school, unless you're a pro athlete or a teacher, are cast off garments of youth.

Making people laugh?

You can do that all the way up to your dying breath.

You can tell a million jokes and make a million people laugh over your lifetime and while there's no trophies or diplomas, there's plenty of good feelings.

Robert learned that telling a joke, making someone laugh, was like saying, "Hey, I love you."

You just silently sneak the I Love You in the joke, the joke being the distraction.

Robert remembers after his $#@%*@! Hour Family Dining Room Debut, he walked back to the living room where all the kids were watching tv and suddenly feeling strangely grown up.

Like he'd just walked through some door.

He liked it.

You're funny!

He remembers pondering these magical words . . . savoring them, testing them out, liking how they sounded.

You're funny. You. Are. Funny.

Which quickly turned into, I'm funny.

A belief: I'm funny. Repeated over and over.

Robert was funny.

It was like some plant, a perennial I'm Funny plant, call it, watered over and over and over with the repetition of those words, repeating them inside (he learned he was his most available and reliable coach) and shined on with the glorious sunshine of gratitude from the feeling he felt, the feeling of being able to make someone smile, the compost from those other plants, the annuals, Sports, School (he thought, I got lucky, had I been good at the annuals, I might have lost the perennials) dying off without water or sun, becoming compost and making the perennial I'm Funny grow, which helped the perennial I'm Smart plant grow, which helped the perennial I Want to Do Things to Help People Feel Happy plant thrive.

Parents: Be careful what you clap for.

Humans: Pay attention to the internal gardens and take care when you tend your own and other people's. What's growing . . . annuals or perennials? Anything which is nourished with compost, water and sunlight will grow. Annuals die off and become compost. Perennials eventually require the least maintenance . . . they keep coming back and getting bigger. Annuals, like Sports, School and any other thing we can say our kid does and put it on a sticker on the bumper of our car.

In particular, beware those annuals of the Competitus genus, not that playing and learning are bad, no, I love them both, but when they separate, divide and conquer us, cause some of us to feel greater only when we have bested another, humiliated, defeated, trounced, killed, stomped, murdered, beat, creamed, pulverized another or a team of others? We use these violent words to describe our victories that leave us on top, a foot on the back of another.

Hummel Statue Number 666: Competitive Climber, a little boy in a football uniform, a trophy in one hand, held at the end of his arm upthrust arm in victory, the ball tucked under his other arm, a cleated foot on the back of a tall, kid, with long arms and legs who is lying face down, his head turned to the side and you see the pain on his face, he's holding a book in his hand that's pressed to the ground . . . he wanted to play and the other kid didn't want to do anything but play too, but football. Emblazoned on the base: WINNER! The jersey of the tall kid on the ground, above the 0 (zero) on his back, has his named stenciled on for all to see: LOSER.

So Robert practiced his art whenever he could.

While his parents cautioned against combining swearing with school or church or situations with people less enlightened as to the medicinal value of swearing, no similar prohibition or caution or warning label was placed on making people laugh.

Which Robert took to be a green light from the Universe.

Here he was, 9 years old and he as allowed the liberty of saying "$#@%*@!" in front of the audience as long as it was in the telling of a joke.

He remembered his aunts and uncles and cousins all staring at him as he told the joke and when he dropped the $#@%*@! bomb in the punch line, well, he says he can still hear them all laughing.

Later, while this book was being written, a startling realization.

$#@%*@! wasn't funny.

Not at all. Hearing it made people laugh, only to relieve tension. That word or any like it, rippling a negative wave out and that laugh, a cough, more, which helped relieve the tension.

Not a laugh from a joke.

Maybe the joke he told when he was 9 wasn't that funny. But hearing a 9-year old boy say $#@%*@! was shocking, shocking in a way that creates tension, and to relieve tension, you laugh.

Which could easily be interpreted, if you're not listening closely, as being funny.

But, if you're not really looking or listening to your own body's reaction, you think you're laughing because of the joke and hopefully it's cleverness, insight or twist on things.

Bill Cosby didn't swear.

Seinfeld: No swearing.

The Simpsons: No swearing.

Funny, funny, funny, but clean. And smart.

Clean humor is water everyone can drink.

Dirty humor is water that adults keep from their children . . . and maybe they don't drink it themselves.

So, with the last draft of this book ready for print, all those swear words scattered in the pages like dog poo, I wondered, Would *everyone* read this book or just adults and more specifically, adults who, like Bobby, thought up until the last chapter was read and the proofreading done that swearing was funny? And then, suddenly I realized this: the audience was being narrowed by virtue of the presence of *Those Words*.

Words that people laughed at, a nervous laugh, to relieve tension.

Those words actually a crutch, a fake, a cheat.

Not really funny at all.

Those Words make people uncomfortable, so they laugh, then, as a release and you might mistake that laugh for funny.

Not really.

Try again. Admit you were wrong.

Without changing the story and in *every single case*, it seemed, actually improving the quality of the writing. Unless it was in reference to someone swearing (but without spelling it *almost* all the way out, but using a symbol in an obvious place, substituted for one letter—which, at that point, you might as well go all the way), every bit of profanity was removed from the book.

The awakened Robert now understood the degree of profane pollution he'd caused, a repentant guy responsible for a Humor British Petroleum disaster. His whole life, he'd been spilling toxicity into the gulf waters of his body and the bodies of those who heard his words.

Time to clean up the spill, or at least cap the leak.

So, words were changed or shown as $#@%*@! only if the idea of swearing needed to be touched on. It happens, it's part of the language, like French fries and soda are part of our diet.

But, like French fries and soda, just 'cause we can eat them, does that mean we should?

Do I want to make organic raw food word meals for myself and others or do I want to put junk in there?

Are they good for us?

Do they write something ugly on our water and the listener's?

The answer was clear as clean water.

After the words we removed, Robert tried to go the whole day with out swearing.

He did it. Can o' beans.

When he heard other people swear all day long that day, it was like, when those words were said, he listened to the change in their tone.

Their frequency.

It lowered.

They would be talking all happy, the phone would ring, something would fall down, anything, someone would do something dumb in traffic and $#@%*@! they'd say, and then, you'd see they were not as happy as they'd been a minute before.

That word, like a label for a feeling inside them.

It didn't just release some thought / feeling that had just inflated inside them. The guy cuts them off in traffic, they have a choice. They can realize they're scared and breathe to release tension or they can stuff scared and have it bloom into anger and then, $#@%*@! Or realize they've driven too fast, too busy on the phone or just impatient for a myriad of reasons; we've all done it. And so when we see someone else doing it, we get mad . . . because we're looking in the mirror and we bark at them because we are angry, which means we're afraid, we've just stuffed scared, which really means we're afraid of what we've become. And fear really just means a feeling of loss . . . loss of safety. Feeling safe and secure tucked in under the Mother Blanket. When, with our definitions and perceptions and preferences, we throw off that blanket, and we suffer.

We've lost something.

Stuff loss after you let go of the Hand, you feel afraid. Stuff afraid and you feel angry. Stuff angry, and you get sick.

Stuff, stuff, stuff.

The stuff that kills us.

Scared was okay to feel . . . and breathe through. The ancient survival mechanism, the thrill of fear that kept us one step ahead of the pursuing beasts, that filled our veins with chemicals to speed our legs and flood our torso to fuel the fight, if it catches us.

But Robert realized that whenever he felt afraid, not safe, he only had to reach inside and hold the Hand to feel safe again. He was the one letting go. And when he let go, he felt separate. A priest told him once that sin meant without.

With or without. His choice.

Let's see. With felt good, without felt bad.

Easy.

Stuffed down, sitting in the car or over years in an unhappy situation, denied, yeah, $#@%*@!

You ending "hating" everyone around you and especially yourself.

That inward hate like napalm to your body and soul, sometimes burning at an aching heart, the feeling denied in your guts . . .

Robert wanted to be *pure funny*. Observational, insightful, clever, unique, delightful.

Feel good and share it. Period.

Not cheapening the art with a fake release of tension.

He made it two whole days.

And he noticed other people's swearing and paid attention to the dynamics.

Did he want to make other people smile or feed them junk food words?

If words nourished me, he thought, he needed to stop poisoning himself and the people around him.

Maybe Robert hadn't inherited Life from his Past, he was borrowing it from the Present.

That meant he had to treat it kindly. Which meant no more junk food words, no more word pollution.

So, after the words were substituted or removed, he had this realization that maybe those words weren't funny at all. They were toxic. Did he want kids to read about this funny kid and decide to be the next George Carlin? Because of Robert?

He decided the $#@%*@! stops here.

Well into the end of the third day and he thought, "I get it."

Thank you.

49 and he's still in School and being hit on the head with a Big Knuckle, but now, the knuckle's not hitting, but knocking gently, politely, like, Take your time, but also asking, Can I come in?

And play?

Teach you what's really funny. How you can make a million people laugh?

You asked and I'm answering, that flare of yours not even out of your pocket yet, hold the match, I see what you want before you ask and I've been waiting, but I'm glad we are talking again.

I miss you when you forget.

I love you, you know.

You're wonderful and you're just now getting that, aren't you?

It's okay, those are happy tears.

Breathe, breathe.

There you go.

It's okay, I'm always here.

You just forgot.

I was waiting for you to remember.

But take your time.

I don't own a watch.

They're just for keeping you on time.

Why not try being off time for a while?

It's just us any way.

It'll be fun.

Promise.

You'll get your million laughs.

Just keep it clean.

Trust me. Have I steered you wrong so far?

∾

"You're funny!" his cousin Lisa said, grinning.

Robert's adoptive parents' humble home was a gathering place extraordinaire.

When Robert was five, they moved from their neighborhood in Chicago to a house in Westmont just a few miles his Aunt Theresa. They moved to a home the previous owner, Mr. Peterson, had customized himself. Mr. Peterson, with his penchant for humor himself, a tall man, we heard, put the house over a basement with a ceiling so low, you had to duck and occasionally said $#@%*@! if you hit your head on the rafters. Robert's tall dad, the joke master, spent many frustrating commulative hours banging his head on those support beams. Robert's childhood punctuated by a subterranean drum that sounded like this:

THUMP!

Then, wait for it:

$#@%*@!

I imagine Mr. Peterson, tall himself, must be up on top of the wall laughing (gotta relieve the tension), probably hear the *THUMP!* $#@%*@! all the way out there, but while he was here, he had tricked out the modest home with a sunken living connected to a raised dining room equipped with a table that easily seated 10. A common vaulted ceiling fifteen feet above both rooms, the center cross beam up over the railing separating those two rooms, a black wrought iron railing not unlike the kind you'd see buttressing the front porch of a bungalow with tea-cup shaped evergreen hedges. When they first moved there in 1967, there was no railing between the two rooms, but his cousin Katie needed a place to stick her 4-year old head so they could call the fire department to free her from between the bars, so the railing was installed.

The railing acted as a sort of division between the world of the children, sprawled on bean bag chairs, couches or curled on the floor watching tv and the grown-ups, who after dinner, drank, swore, played board games like Pollyanna that included noisy quarter-a-bump pots and plenty of good-natured swearing.

But, the best part was, for Robert, when Robert's father told jokes.

Oh, he could tell a joke!

He did all the different voices, the accents, especially the Irish brogue, the gestures, and exaggerated expressions.

"Uncle Jim is funny," everyone, including Robert, agreed.

And he was Robert's father.

Robert watched him hold a room with his voice and his stories and his jokes and decided that making people laugh was a Noble Calling.

Robert recalls taking the seat at the head of the table and carefully avoiding his father's eyes as he told jokes, except when he'd tell the punch line. Then, he'd shift his gaze to his father's momentarily and would see the absolute delight in his father's eyes.

His father would laugh with the rest of them.

Laughing, thinking of things that were funny and telling them in the hopes that people would laugh became Robert's world.

Something to be good at.

A Noble Calling.

And having a teacher right there under the same roof, no need to go away to some college for that, the master living right there, get to watch him, study the craft first hand up close . . . and as Robert got older, his repetoire larger, his memory and recall, despite the

Borrowed Earth Café ☺

later ravages of drugs and alcohol on young Robert's brain, his father slowly allowing Robert more and more time at the head of the table.

In the spotlight.

Years later, when the kids were grown and cousin Katie's head grew too large to fit between the bars, the railing was taken down and the barrier between the two rooms was removed. The floor was puttied and stained to hide the marks the three-inch square footings on the railing left at 6-foot intervals across the wooden floors.

If you look close, you can still see the slight squarish depressions.

If you listen closely, you can still hear people laughing.

$\sim$

All those books, those jokes, those glorious words, they filled up some giant repository in Robert's mind, assembling themselves, with a little associative nudge from something he saw or heard or thought, assembling into jokes, stories, dialogs, some things serious, sometimes the serious sneaking in with the funny things, the funny things greasing the skids.

Robert said his sister Marie was the smart one, book-wise, straight A's, the Student in the family and shared Robert's love for books, he and Marie sometimes laying on the floor and book racing, seeing who could zoom through a Hardy Boys book or something the fastest, later swapping books over the dining room when they both had young kids.

She also shared Robert's love for movies and music.

Robert learned to play drums, but in the summer between 8th grade and the beginning of high school, he spent $15 and bought a cheap Harmony guiter. After college, his mom and dad bought him a nice Yamaha acoustic, then, after his son was born, a 12-string

Martin knockoff. Me? I sent him off one day to buy himself a Gibson. "Buy the expensive one," I instructed, Mr. $15 guitar, torn t-shirt, frayed shorts and spotty Crocs, looking at him like, "I mean it." Robert would play and sing for me, sitting on the edge of our bed with his eyes closed, singing and playing from his heart. "I never sang to anyone before," he said.

He says guitars have always come to him at high points in his life, like the Universe, dressed like a roadie, clomping up to him in a worn pair of brown Earth shoes, untailored jeans with a rip in the knee, this classic black t-shirt that says BORN TO ROCK, a pair of wrap around Ray Bans and a head of hair out to here poking out of a sunbleached faded red ball cap turned backwards. The guitar roadie Universe girl is always a welcome sight!

It's always a she. A young girl at a store two blocks from his home hands him a $15 Harmony after the lady at the front desk at the tuxedo store he'll later get high at hands him his first honest-to-God, taxes out, social security-set-at-zero paycheck. Then, a lady at the store near his Aunt Patsy's house hands him the six-string Yamaha Martin knock-off (his mom handing him cash to go get it after he graduated college, the guy who I would later encourage to go public with his writing). Then, a woman at a music store ½ mile from our restaurant in Downers Grove, little place decked out inside by a barrel maker, a little barrel of guitars you could short putt across, that woman sells him a 12-string after his daughter is born, a Martin knock-off again (that man loves a Martin, but buys knock-offs)—his mom standing right next to him and she takes it home and then hands it to him on Christmas Eve, that daughter, just about 6 months and some change old, and he plays it to her and his son that night for the first time, nearly cried, it sounded so beautiful.

And after the children stopped napping, their mother thought playing and singing were a waste of Robert's time, so to avoid conflict and keep them from being set ablaze on the growing fire of discontent in his marriage, he tucked them under the bed where they gathered dust for nearly 20 years.

When he first showed up with those two cases (the Harmony long gone, that $15 got him about 15 years, a warped neck, a curled sunlight-heated pick guard and 240 broken string sets), I heard him play, quietly at first. I said one word: More.

And then, he began to sing.

And I said one word: More.

Three years later, he played in front of 40 people with our friend Jimmy, a professional musician and Robert's long-lost brother, you'd think. He played on a used Gibson with a pretty sunburst body that I told him to buy at that same barrel-looking place just down the road.

A guy from a tv show was taping the whole thing for some commercial spot they did on Borrowed Earth on *Check Please!*

He didn't sing, but he played.

Now, he gets together with his son, who plays just about any instrument he wants to. Unlike Robert, he reads music.

They sit on the front porch or even meet up with their instruments and they play.

Finally allowing himself to be himself now.

Marie played in the Holy Trinity School band with Robert. She played the flute. Later, while Robert was playing his guitar, sitting on the edge of his bed, Marie would play in the marching band at high school.

But through all her life, mostly, she sang.

She could sing.

She sang with a beautiful voice that brought tears to Robert's eye when she sang to her husband in the church in Chicago where the two were married.

Her voice rang out powerfully through the whole church.

He'd seen her sing in chorus, but never had heard her alone. She sang to someone she loved.

Robert remembers hugging her briefly, probably for the first time in his life, that afternoon in the vestibule after the ceremony was over.

She looked absolutely beautiful.

Later, when their kids were young, he watched her in a play she performed in at their old high school. His sister, belting out *Abba* music and more.

The former thespian still having fun.

Go Marie!

But, in the family, more than anything, Marie was the one who was good at school.

On the other hand, Robert was the class clown, the cartoonist, the goof off, a distracting element; the kid who could close his eyes and see the words, all he had to do was write them down in his own hand and it was like he could see them on the page, but he never really applied himself until his junior year at Columbia College when his class schedule, his dream, was all reading and writing. Forget the math-related subjects. Not his strong suit.

He'd gone to take his ACT test early on a Saturday morning his junior year, driving the family car to a high school just about a mile up the road from Borrowed Earth Café. He had gotten high on the way, the window down on the Pontiac Catalina and the radio up, feeling just fine.

While he did well in the language categories, he closed the book after a few pages of the math section and ended up getting a 7 in math.

"A monkey taking random guesses on the ACT will get an 8 in any category," his high school counselor had told him, looking at Robert's overall score and, that math score, like a torpedo, sank Robert's college-bound ship's chances at docking at any schools but ones with lowered admission standards.

Lucky for me.

That deliberate act of defiance closed a door, but opened a window.

And the curtains start fluttering.

Robert says while class was going on, Robert, not particularly interested in anything but reading and writing, forget the math, found himself terribly bored by the whole institutional madness, the oppressive dullness of school.

As Marie excelled at school, Robert, a B student with no real motivation, skittered along from grade to grade, dreaming of the day when he'd be done with the whole sordid business of school.

Growing up, Marie was stronger, and as the tendency in any pack of child dogs, acted as the alpha in the house, picking on the weaker dogs . . . until Robert was around 10. He says he picked her up and banged her against the bedroom wall. She collapsed to the floor and lay there, Robert and PJ staring at her form, suddenly worried that the burst of testosterone had killed her . . . and with her eyes closed still, her shoulders started shaking.

To Robert's relief, she was laughing. Probably glad her reign of terror was over, truth be told.

Marie always laughed at Robert's jokes too . . . unless they were directed at her. Theirs would be a tenuous relationship that held a mysterious hidden gulf that widened as Robert got older and eventually was so wide it seemed to Robert it might be impossible to cross.

When they were little, Robert's cousin had called Marie some Italian expression, but he said it like he meant fat. Robert and PJ changed it to a sound-alike nonsense word and they teased her with that word, an unkind nickname that hurt Marie, as readily as if Marie and PJ had teased Robert about his failings as an athlete, both Marie and PJ having more athletic prowess in their pinkie fingers than Robert could summon in his whole uncoordinated nose-in-a-book body.

But it was never said outside the house.

The power that name would have over Marie.

When they were all playing soft ball at the park when they were in grade school one summer, PJ told one of the boys in Marie's class the name. The boy started yelling it out and Marie shot them a look. Robert never told Marie who spilled the beans.

The teasing got so bad that Marie had to transfer to the public school her last bit of grammar school. Robert felt horrible, but let Marie think it had been him, thinking in some ways that he was taking a bullet for his careless little brother.

That afternoon, his mom asked him who had said it and he said nothing and let her think it had been him too.

He told me about that bullet after we met and said he always wondered if that was why he and Marie never got along as they grew.

She blamed Robert.

I always said he should tell her, but his face would twist in pain and he'd say no, at this point, it didn't matter.

But I think it does.

PJ was just being a stupid kid, just as stupid and careless as Robert and maybe Robert was trying to atone for all the teasing he'd done inside the house, the teasing about his sister's weight or PJ's eyebrows or a thousand sins of the tongue, him and PJ teaming up against her, in a team of two against one that was lead by Robert.

Three is a terrible number for children. Two always pair up and one is left out.

The one in the front bedroom.

The only one in the house who slept alone.

Robert's mom said just a few weeks after Robert was brought home, Marie expressed her opinion quite clearly in her 2-year old voice, "Take it back."

It.

Robert wishes he could take that name back.

But what might Marie or PJ's world have been like if it, he, had gone back from whence he came?

"Take it back."

And what if she'd gotten her wish. Got her request fulfilled like she's sittin' in some restaurant. Like, "Waitress, I don't think I like that. Take it away."

Or, back up.

Hey, in 1962, not every 17-year old in a family way gave their kid up for adoption.

There was always the Other option.

Maybe little Robert only lives about eight weeks and they, hey, he goes back Home, the manager keeps him in the bull pen, saying, "Keep loosening that arm, kid. I'll let you throw the next game. Sit this one out."

No Robert. No two against one.

Maybe Marie and PJ gettin' along just fine.

Everybody better off.

Darn that butterfly.

He wishes he could have hushed his little brother, and maybe, not pretended he'd told that kid in Marie's class the name to cover for PJ.

How can you undo a wrong so big?

Sorry's too small a word for when you don't see your sister in your school all of a sudden because she's transferred somewhere else because the teasing got so bad.

His big sister, the National Honor Society kid, the flute player, the physical therapist, a mom with two good kids and a husband with a sense of humor and a love for books, music and movies.

The one who invited him out twice when she was at school: first to Augustana and then later at Northwestern. He had a good time both times. Marie always had nice friends. At one point, he remembers she loosely conspired to drink him under the table. He feigned ignorance of the drinking game quarters he was secretly adept at. Each time he "luckily" bounced a quarter in the glass he pushed it over to his big sister, "Here you go, I pick you." At the end of the night, he chatted away with two of her friends at a high table at a bar. Marie had gone to the floor in search of the quarter and was resting her head against the table leg, eyes crossing. He helped her up and they stumbled back to her dorm room and slept on the floor in her room, talking a little before bed, thinking, I wish she could have somehow fit in the room where he and PJ slept.

It must have been lonely all alone in that front bedroom. No one to talk softly to before falling asleep.

Marie.

Out there.

When Robert lost his job, when his son Andy was not yet one year old, Marie's husband, the man whom she'd sung to, brought those tears up to Robert's eyes, geez, listen, that's my sister singing, a guy who looked out for family, gave Robert a job with his moving company.

One morning he picked up Robert to go move a house and smiled shyly and shared his own happy news: He and Marie were gonna have their first baby.

Robert took the news silently.

He thought about a line from a movie. Stallone and Burt Young are sitting on a couch in Burt Young's living room, Burt Young gettin' a little protective, this butcher trying to take a shot at the heavy weight title is dating his sister, Adrienne, the mousey girl with the glasses, a girl that likes Stallone's turtles, Cuff and Link, and Burt Young says, "Are you [*bad word for sleeping with*] my sister?"

So Robert looked across at Marie's husband and said with a little growl in his voice, "Are you [*bad word for sleeping with*] with my sister?"

Marie's husband looked nervous and opened his mouth and no words came out.

Robert grinned, "I'm kidding."

Gotcha, Bro.

And they both laughed. Maybe a little relief in her husband's laugh there around the edges.

Marie and Robert: Two grumpy peas in a pod.

His sister.

Marie was the good student.

Growing up though, Robert's little brother PJ was the one person Robert loved more than anyone else. No competition. They'd lay in their twins beds in that room they shared and talk late at night. Laughing quietly, but sometimes talking about serious things too. PJ would come to be Robert's early Ed McMahon, a straight man, a kid to make laugh in church, their dad shooting PJ the Look.

Robert looking straight ahead like, *Gotcha, Bro.*

Robert would grow to be 6'4" and was always a head taller than anyone in his little world except his dad, who stood a little over 6 feet. PJ, on the other hand, was from shorter stock, a little athletic kid, but small, compared to Robert.

PJ could run, you can be sure. Fast enough to eventually get a plaque on the wall at the high school they all went to. He was good at basketball, baseball and he was fast. All the pictures of PJ as a kid? He's got a ball in his hand. He'd bounce a ball off the steps for hours or play basketball in the backyard in the dark, right in front of the place Robert would later have his first real conversation with God.

PJ would toss a ball in the house or anything else he could get his hands on. Once he was playing catch inside with a piece of bologna and it stuck high up on the wall near the peak of the vaulted ceiling.

Robert got it down, using a chair and a broom, but that greasy circle stayed up there, a shadowy thing, really, for years until the room was repainted.

PJ loved to sing and had a melodious voice that could belt out an operatic note, his mouth open, and hold it, if he wanted. He'd jump off the furniture and flip on his back like a little stunt man.

But he could sing.

He later used his pipes and his love of sports to try his hand as a sportscaster at a local cable tv show and had worked as a stringer reporter for Taylor Bell, a sports reporter for the Chicago Sun Times, a man who sent PJ off to cover and write copy for local high school games.

In high school, PJ turned his ankle savagely and his sports career, albeit brief and glorious, was over.

A few years later, when Robert had logged a few years of hard long distance running under his belt, he invited PJ to join him at a local road race and couldn't believe it: for the first time in his life, PJ ran slower than Robert, the reformed (but occasional recidivist) clomper. That ankle hobbling PJ for life. Later, PJ developed arthritic hips and the former Mercury, the fast little kid, was forever sidelined.

That picture on the wall in the high school, a memory of what had once been someone to watch run.

PJ was good at sports, but was careful never to say anything to his big awkward brother about Robert's being bad at sports.

Maybe his love for his big funny brother was stronger than those little kid tendencies: the comparing, the criticizing, the teasing that hurts. PJ maybe developing compassion in that crucible of love or, probably heartache, knowing his big brother wanted to keep up but born with a body made for distance, not speed.

They had one season together, Robert's last year playing baseball, on the same little league team. PJ was the shortstop and got plenty of hits, quick with the glove and fast, a base stealer, almost every time he was on.

Robert? The coach hid him in either right field or at second base. Out of offensive harm's way. He only got one hit that year after a summer's humiliating turns at bat that he dreaded.

When Robert was 13, a year before he started smoking pot and drinking regularly (looking forward to it) his parents and Larry's parents took all the kids to Disney World in Florida, but they also made a stop at the White Sox training camp down in Sarasota.

Robert remembers they all stayed at the little motel right next to the ballpark, the motel overrun with players they'd only seen from far away in the bleachers. Now they were up close, right there.

Although he didn't care much for baseball, his little brother treated the game reverently, so Robert walked around with the family camera and asked all the players if he could take their picture, building a collection of snapshots of players he was taking for PJ, his little brother way too shy to ask himself.

Robert? He'd walk right up to them, all smiles, Can we get yer pitcher? This big guy with a Fu Manchu moustache invited both families back to his room, and spent hours talking to them, telling about his adventures as a kid trying to make it in the big leagues.

His name was Pete Vuckovich.

PJ had found a hero.

Over the years, as Pete went from the Sox to the Blue Jays to the Cardinals, whenever he could, he would leave tickets for Robert's dad and PJ at the box office if he was in town. PJ would wait in the aisle above the box seats, and before the game, he'd run down to the wall and wave. Pete would come over and talk to the quick little kid who threw bologna up against the living room wall. Once PJ said, "Nice glove," just making conversation and Pete handed it to him.

Vuckovich was a clown.

And, like Robert, he had a big soft spot for PJ. PJ had a clown at home to make him laugh, and this bigger than life pro-baseball icon, almost as heavy as two Roberts, this major league clown.

He clomped around on the mound when he pitched, made faces at the batters, crossed his eyes, spit and his 6'4" frame and 220 lb body made for an intimidating presence but the fans loved him. He invited PJ to come and see him get the Cy Young Award. Robert remembers all of the family sitting around the tv in the family room watching Pete, who played the big lug first baseman in the movie *Major League*.

PJ was the athlete.

PJ and their cousin Larry (another adopted kid Robert's age, who, growing up, was Robert's closest friend) were both small and fast.

Robert? Well, that big gangly kid wasn't a runner. Not 'til college where he found the race he was better suited for: Distance.

But, as a kid he was awkward.

But always quick with the joke.

Robert was the comedian . . . the excessive reader . . . and much later . . . the writer who learned that his words, like the food he served himself and others, must be chosen carefully. He was himself garden and gardener.

A steward of the land he was borrowing from his children.

He wanted to leave it better than before and atone for his past by making the most of his present but without violence to himelf.

One of his martial arts teachers had a sign that said:

"If there's beauty in the character, there's harmony in the home, and if there's harmony in the home, then there's peace in the nation, and if there's peace in the nation, then there will be peace in the world."

Like something on a Hallmark card but to Robert, it meant something to shoot for.

Robert, as a child was funny, but he still wanted to play with kids and it seemed like all the games were competitive. Before the game began, bearing the stigma of his sports history, he would almost always be last to be picked for teams. Last in the race. He didn't run back then so much as he clomped and sometimes he forgets himself, and a little bit of that awkward kid will come out in his walk, forgetting for a moment the 1000's of miles logged on the road, whittled down to 145 lbs of stringy arms and legs, as many as 26 miles in one day, not some marathon. "Just wanted to see if I could do it," he says. No real water stops, just determination and a thin pair of Nike Waffle Trainers, light blue with the yellow swoosh, thinking, what, it's only 3 or 4 hours, if I hussle, right? No sense in carrying all that water.

This was back in 1981, no number pinned to his shirt or watches or finish line to cross. 13 miles and change out and back, mapped out and ran to run it.

Period. The only one pushing Robert was Robert.

He forgets the 20 years in the martial arts, working out the ghosts of all the bullying he endured as a kid, being pinned to the ground and beaten more than once, too slow to get away, so he eventually learned to stand his ground and fight.

Fight against people who were victims of victims of victims. People who hadn't forgiven the people who hurt them and so in order to understand their tormentors, they had unconsciously become them.

By the time Robert walked unafraid in the physical world, he found that the world had changed, the rules a little different as an adult and the bullying had moved to the emotional plane, you're not paying attention, sending out that weak beacon. Though he was too late to fend off the physical bullies, some how he healed something that had been beaten out of him, that something he'd slowly handed over, a little at a time, but slowly called back and reassembled inside himself as he helped some of those little kids at a martial arts school he'd dreamed of opening a few months after he started, still a white belt.

Kids like him, but getting picked on right now, telling him in his little office at the front of his school, a little ashamed.

And Robert would tell his story and they'd look at him different.

He wasn't some guy with a black belt.

He was one of them.

An awkward kid.

A clomper.

A turtle.

He's says back when he was a white belt, he got that idea, What do I wanna do when I grow up? What color's my parachute? And he rememberd how he'd memorized all those chunks of things, things he could close his eyes and see in his mind, as clear as they were right in front of him. He looked at his martial arts teachers, young guys just a couple years ahead of him and fell in love with the idea of someday having his own school. He thought all that he had to do was push himself. So, he wrote that goal on a piece of paper and kept it, but was very specific. He read in some self help book or another that a person should imagine writing their own eulogy, so, accidentally, he discovered something extremely powerful. He wrote the goal in the past tense, like he had already done it, like he was telling someone, not what he would do, but what he had done.

The brain, he reasoned, processes a historical fact with an unemotional acceptance, differently than a futuristic goal, something that had not yet happened, constructed in the conditional tense, a conditional goal as in, If the conditions are right this will happen, your mind already entertaining the possibility of the outcome less desired.

So instead of writing, "I will open my own martial arts school someday," using the standard construction, he decided, forget convention, and he used the past tense. And he put a date on it.

"By my 30th birthday, I opened my own martial arts school. I was a 2nd degree black belt."

He says that he told people about the goal, but kept the piece of paper and the specific date to himself.

Robert pursued that goal with a fierce determination, an obsessive energy, that surpised him. The lazy kid who could lie in bed and could read away a whole summer was now hyper kinetic. He pushed himself past his limits of endurance and sought new levels. He went to classes six days a week and practiced extra at home in his parent's basement on what he'd learned. He bought an 80 lb Everlast canvas heavy bag and used to shake the house. He tried to hit it 500 times each day with each hand, wearing an old worn out pair of work gloves. He did 1000 situps every day, hooking his legs under a barbell on the floor under the ping-pong table. He looked at the physiques of boxers and decided that if he was gonna do this, he was going to go all the way.

He began to cut down his hours of sleep and once stayed awake for four days, secretly, just to see if he could do it.

By the fourth day, he was dozing while he was driving.

Stupid. Stupid. Stupid. Dangerous. Dangerous. Dangerous.

A Horatio Algier Idiot Tale of a kid who thought if he just became tough enough physically, able enough, fast enough, that he could finally be able to play with the other kids and not end up feeling bad about himself, leaving a place for someone else to feel good. So, in order to build himself up, he starts whittling himself down. All the way down. In a self-destructive manner. A self-inflicted punishment.

Thoses waves he sent out, still coming out, but now starting to come back. Back from whence they came.

Inside Robert.

Heisman Trophy winner Herschel Walker, a martial artist himself said in a Sports Illustrated article, "My body is the army; my mind the general."

And this became Robert's mantra.

All that energy he'd saved up as a kid, like it had been saved up in some Karmic Bank, was now being spent freely. Like a longshoreman on payday.

"Only thing different between me and you," he'd tell those scared little kids in his school later, "is 10,000 hours."

He walked away from everything he'd known, starting with the drugs that he'd started taking as a 14-year old suburban kid smoking a joint behind a little tuxedo rental place he worked at shining shoes with a kid years years older.

He tells me after that first time, he got on that black Schwinn Speedster, barely 14, the summer between 8th grade and high school, he rode home high as a kite for the first time, not up with the high-five wicker poopin' birds, but with his young head up in clouds that obscured a lot of the pain of his childhood demons, his dad who he'd failed to impress by his clumsy attempts at sports, the bullying, being picked last, the abuse and the pain and the shame that he attached to it in his mind, a funny kid who maybe laughed to help ease his own pain. He'd dropped acid, snorted cocaine, taken strong pain prescription meds, (someone else's prescription) ate hallucenogenic mushrooms, swallowed tablets of speed and smoked enough pot to send everyone in Tennessee (including all Bobby's out-of-state relations) to the Quik Trip for Twinkies twice.

He rode home that Saturday and attended church with his parents and siblings, secretly up in the clouds.

Enjoying the buzz.

Then, after that little piece of past tense wishing paper was written, he stopped all of it like someone had put the brakes on a car going 75 miles per hour, throwing him clear, landing safely and relatively unscathed, by some miracle, unharmed and with a sense of purpose.

Next, he stopped drinking.

As a little kid, Robert, PJ and his cousin Larry used to sneak beers and sip them out in the alley or in the basement when all the grown ups where upstairs. He had his first full beer when he was 10 and his last one when he was 20.

At the end of his second year in college, those last two months, he tells me he drank before he'd even had a shower. Then after morning class . . . at lunch time, before dinner and then into the night . . . Larry pulling him in a dorm room once, locking the door and staring at him, dead serious. An intervention, he says. "Head," Larry said, short for pot head, using his personal nick name for Robert, "I'm worried about you."

Larry could outrun Robert as a child and could out drink him as a teenager. Larry had taken Robert out one day and the two of them had steadily each drank 24 bottles of beer in just shy of 24 hours, never eating too much ("Don't wreck your buzz with food," Larry warned and irony of ironies, all those years later, Robert found that honest to goodness food, as Nature handed it to you, unprocessed, unheated, organic, clean loaded with something he didn't understand, that food Larry had warned him would wreck the buzz actually contained some miraculous something in it, another rude awakener, this food, culinary yoga . . . this food now giving him *The* Buzz.).

That day though, the two of them soldiering through those 48 bottles of beer like longshoremen.

Robert left it all in pursuit of a dream, not wanting to be weighed down by vices. Anything that doesn't take you closer to your dream is taking you farther, he reasoned.

He decided that continuing on the path he'd been on and that most of those he knew stayed on, the square job, drinking on the weekends, all that high school and college shananigan stuff, to him, like a boat anchor.

He cut the chain and headed out to sea. Alone.

He set a course across open waters for 10 years in the future, just shy of his 30th birthday, setting the navigational instruments like some crazy *Back to the Future* thing.

"Who would want to learn martial arts from someone with all that baggage?" he said to himself, maybe starting to see what he'd become, and decided that his goal was worth the sacrifice, never looking back, leaving it all behind, including friends who found a sober Robert difficult to be around, not because he said word one about their drinking or getting high or snorting cocaine, dropping acid, popping tabs of speed, mushrooms or any dozen ways to leave the ground and get your head up in the clouds. No, he wondered if maybe his not drinking made them think about their drinking. He wondered, if in some way, Robert became a hard look in the mirror.

No one wants that.

Maybe his silence being more powerful a thing than a million things he could have said but did not. He understood them because he had been them.

He said one night in his backyard, still the white belt, the newbie, he looked up in the sky and said, "God, if you want me to do this, you have to take away the desire to drink and get high."

And God, according to Robert, made good.

Maybe Robert really talking to Nobody that night at all, but Nobody sometimes is the most reliable deity in a life we largely navigate alone, in a sea of circumstances with other people, happiness, sadness, disappointment, defeat, failure and laughter. Our own humbled counsel.

The power, in Robert's case, had been in The Ask.

The Ask for Help.

I need help.

He couldn't do it alone but knowing he needed help was an admission in itself. An admission: the real cost to get in. Get in to a life he dreamed of and out of one, that had 'til now, resembled that cloud he'd rode his stoned 14-year old head home in on his black Schwinn Speedster.

In order to stop yourself, you had to pedal back, hold on, and steer straight.

He told me he cried in the backyard after sending that flare up into the night, the distress call, the Bat Signal, a beacon of light which shot all the way out to the end of the Universe and shined on the wall, the wall on which he later rested a ladder against, *CLUNK*! and climbed to the top of. Swung his legs up and over the top, took a seat and looked out into Nothingness and found an unspeakable Joy.

He cried, not because he was sad, that he would miss the drinking and the drugs, the friends . . . no, he says he cried because the answer was immediate. A wordless reply in the form of a feeling of being in a safe embrace of something powerful that enveloped him like a mother's blanket. A contented joy, like being hugged. A feeling he hadn't had since as a young boy lying in bed, he imagined what it would be like to be hugged by an Angel. The Angel his mom used to sit on the side of his bed and pray to with him . . .

Angel of God, my guardian dear, to whom God's love commits me here, ever this day, be at my side to light and guard, to rule and guide.

And then Robert would say, "Amen. Good night, dear God. I love you." And his mom would lean over and kiss his forehead.

His mom told him that everyone has a guardian angel assigned to watch over them.

Like a Guard Dog.

Robert says he remembers that night in the summer of 1981, in his parent's backyard, he looked up in the sky, standing on the mound of gravel and grass at the end of the driveway, right behind the basketball net set up high on a 4x4 pole. And he suddenly felt this overwhelming pressure in his chest.

A pressure that didn't press down on the sternum from the outside, but swelled from Within.

The Kingdom of Heaven is within you, someone said once.

Maybe not a place to go to later, but right here, right now.

Put your hand on your chest and close your eyes. Don't say anthing. Don't think anything. Smile, no teeth.

There's really nothing to say or do.

It's a feeling, minus the words.

A joy you feel, sometimes, when you think you're seeing something else.

Here Robert was looking up for help, like a sign he had to tack on the wall at the end of the Universe, like God lived off a million miles away, watching yeah, but like he'd have to wait 'til after he died to meet Him.

～

GOD: "That was the first time you realized I was real, not just some word or idea."

ROBERT: "I was just personifying you, making you out to be some old man, wise, but watching, catching me messing up, maybe not really approving of everything I did, like I was poking around in the dark, trying to live my life but not disappoint you so much, drop below some passing grade, close the book on the *real* math, score so low I can't get over the wall at the end of the Universe. My ladder, too short. No soup for Bobby."

GOD: "You're funny."

ROBERT: [*putting a palm on his chest*] "You were right here the whole time, weren't you?"

GOD: "Keep your hand on your chest and close your eyes. Smile, no teeth. Don't say anthing. Don't think anything. There's really nothing to say or do. I'm the feeling, minus the words. Later, I'm just a fixed peace without that overwhelming feeling you only feel in the meat suit, but it's still being registered in your awareness . . . like PJ holding that opera note, singing it always, just the one note, holding it in a timeless eternity of only Now, forget the watch, they don't work up on the Wall. I'm the joy you feel, sometimes, when you think you're seeing something else. Everything else is just a distraction."

ROBERT: [*eyes closed, a little smile on his face, no teeth, talking softly*] "Yeah, there You are."

GOD: "See, I'm always with you. You were never alone."

ROBERT: "Is this Heaven? Oh my God, not so much, oh, that's too huge!"

GOD: "That's love or whatever you want to call it. Breathe deeply in and slowly out. That's the faucet. You're still in the meat suit. Go ahead and adjust the faucet 'til you can stand it. My boy. My little boy. My wonderful little funny boy. Now don't talk or think. Just feel. I'm right here. I've always been right here. I'll always be right here. Long before you were born to that 17-year old girl and long after your last breath flutters from your lips, fluttering the Cosmic Curtains in some other window somewhere. I Am. My boy, my boy, my wonderful little funny boy."

That unthinking, unspeakable Joy, a feeling with real substance, that wonderful gentle outward pressure, a feeling without words, thoughts or any history, call it what you want, that wordless joy, a silent messenger bearing inward, stealing into your very essence and speaking in a quiet whisper, "I love you."

So Robert left all the substances behind, legal and illegal and eventually walked away from puzzled high school friends because, in Robert's words, "A monk doesn't stay a monk long in the brothel."

So he left it all.

And everyone from that other life.

"The only ones that I wanted to stay close to was Larry and PJ," he says. His bond with Larry had started before they traded the bottles of processed formula for bottles of beer secreted out into the alley when they were still just little kids, and then traded up for bottles of beer, as many as 24 in under 24 hours, as two kids sharing a dorm in an old building just up the hill from the Mississippi.

But as Robert moved farther from the bottles, he moved farther away from Larry, something that still makes him sad.

And, for some reason, PJ, who had never been a big drinker but maybe he didn't understand the Horatio Algier Idiot his big brother had become.

Didn't know him.

Wondered what happened to the other guy.

"He'll always be my brother," Robert says with a sadness that I think is deeper than even he knows, meaning both of PJ *and* Larry. "I miss Larry and he works 10 minutes from where I live."

His mom saw all this.

His mom—not the one 17 years older than him—not her, his Real Mom, the one who did The Work—the diapers, the feeding, the cleaning, the worrying. The one who told him he was smart and funny and tells other people that he's just going through a phase, don't worry, he'll be just fine. The one who teaches Robert to love people through acts of kindness, not just the empty words without actions. The one who teaches him to put love in the food. The one who teaches Robert, wordlessly, to love having people over for dinner.

That mom.

Not the one off somewhere 17 years ahead of him, the faceless angel who's soul stared back at him in son's eyes, in his daughter's eyes, in his own eyes.

And who maybe breathed into the hearts of people who helped Robert.

Angel of God, my guardian dear . . .

People who watered his seeds. People who told him he was smart, funny, a good listener, a good writer, a good father, a hard worker, a compassionate soul, a wonderful teacher, a beautiful plate presenter, an artist, a poet.

The Legion of Encouragement.

And that girl, the one 17 years older than him, her love and wishes for him lived in all of them, wishing the best for the little swaddled baby she'd never know, those wishes somehow banding together and distributing themselves in a 1000 moments Robert would live through. Her wishes vibrating in her body's water, traveling across the air, the world, the Universe, not big enough to hide Robert from her love, sent from 10 miles away, 30 or from the other side of the world or even from a seat on top of the wall at the end of the Universe, the place Robert goes when he meditates now, letting some of that hard yoga go, giving way to the gentle. It didn't matter, maybe she's already traveled out there, put her own ladder against the wall. *CLUNK!* Climbed to the top, swung her legs over, sat down and stared out into the Void, had her own dialog. Sits with eyes closed, smiling, feeling good.

Maybe swinging her legs and talking to my mom, Meryl, both of them enjoying seeing me and Robert eventually cross paths, almost 42 years after Robert's first day on Earth.

Say, would you look at those two.

~

MERYL: "He's tall."

MOTHER: "Yeah, he got big."

MERYL: "Look at their hair. They'll about kill each other with all that love."

MOTHER: "My little Robert and your little Kathy. It's why they're always together. What did the Partner guy say, 'I gotta separate you two, together, you both make this incredible force?'"

MERYL: "They call Robert Danny now. Danny Living. Yeah, the Mad Hatter. Yeah, he did them another favor there. Telling them that together, they made this force. Like the poem about the two angels, each with one wing. They hold on to each other so they can fly. Kathy found that on a card and framed it in this cool purple cloth frame."

MOTHER: "He spotted that two minutes after he moved in. Later maybe, thinking that he'd found his other wing."

MERYL: "Yeah, they've got so much they'll have to share it so they can stand it. Happy?"

MOTHER: "Absolutely. We did good, didn't we? I wasn't always sure but now I am. I wouldn't take one brick out of the road behind me . . . the road you walk when you're alive. All of those bricks were necessary."

MERYL: "Amen. It feels good, doesn't it? It's so huge. No regrets?"

MOTHER: "None. We both made our sacrifices. And we made those sacrifices for our kids."

MERYL: "Funny, she didn't care much for school and back then, I was a teacher. I didn't understand yet."

MOTHER: "But she did. Maybe that's why you two fought. She understood, that little kid with the hair and the glasses. Your arm around her, she's looking up at you. She still has the picture. She's looked at it 100's of times. And so has he. All the real lessons aren't in school."

MERYL: "Yeah, they both had a feeling that school was the distraction."

MOTHER: "And they trusted it. They somehow knew that everything would okay and they'd be okay, 'long as they worked hard and shared themselves. Let's close our eyes now."

MERYL: "Wow, that's so huge. There, I can stand it now."

MOTHER: "Yeah, you don't breathe to work the faucet after you come back, what'd he say about Sean and the angels that appear in the form of people? Oh yeah, 'from whence they came.'"

MERYL: "Yeah, now I just share it because now it's always huge, all the time. I don't have any distractions any more, so I just spend all my time sending, sharing, passing it on. I don't need to hold on to it. I never did. It's not meant to be held, only passed and shared, like the food she makes and the food he plates. Her and I didn't always get along . . . I send a lot of it to her."

MOTHER: "Sure, you know she always understood what was real and so you knew she'd pass it right on. Share it. You and her didn't always get along, but your love for her was fierce. A fierce love because of the other things maybe . . . like you were trying to make up for what you couldn't do then. And now, you spend all the time sending her love."

They pause, their legs crossed, and swing their feet slightly, sitting up on the top of the wall at the end of the Universe, two ladders leaned up against the side and we see them from the back, all the clear beautiful Silent Nothing stretched out Forever in front of them. We see a close up now and we see they're easily holding hands, looking up with closed eyes, still talking, and smiling.

MERYL: "And you couldn't be his real mom, but you longed to hold him and so you did it from afar. A longing love . . . like you were trying make up for what you couldn't do. And you spent some time, when you thought about him, sending him love."

MOTHER: "Like he does with his kids. 'You two do what you have to do to survive,' he said after he left that house, the hardest thing he ever did in his life. He laid in bed and cried quietly next to Kathy for almost two years on and off, a sense of grief and loss that ate at him finally giving way to a realization: that huge feeling that pushed out in a hot ball in his chest, caught his breath in his throat, made his lips press together, then the exhale through the mouth, then the tears, stop calling it loss, grief or sadness when it welled up inside and know what it really was—love. He could skip the sharp, flat stone of his attention with an easy sidearm throw across the top of the sea of memories, that stone skip, skip, skipping across the still surface and he touched the very place on his chest where this same feeling bloomed in a steady outward pressure at times when he was overwhelmed with Joy to the point of tears. There it was. It was the identical feeling, physically, but depending on which way you were thinking, happy or sad thoughts, it either felt good to have this feeling and cry or it felt bad. But, the physical feeling was the same. An outward swell in the chest that moves up into the throat, the exhale and the tears. Love. So, for his kids, he makes a sacrifice, for the only two people who he could look at and see me, the physical me, and maybe most, in his own eyes. Then, he tells them don't call me or see me if it makes home harder and he's back with just his own eyes, but now they have tears right there, ready to leak out if he even so much as thinks about them. But now, they're happy tears and he's thinking, 'I'm sending you love, little girl who wore those overalls over and over, who yelped when I brushed your long beautiful hair, my little well-read reader and smart writer, I'm thinking about you right now and sending my love, those big waves of feeling rippling out across the moisture in the air. And you, little boy, both of you all grown up, Fireball and Skateboard kid. Yeah, there's a stepmom now, you two knew all along there would be, worked into the script when you were not even in school, your high little voices were the best music I ever heard. I love you both and I know that there's nowhere you can hide from my love. I'm just doing what I can, and I'm here and you're there but when I think of you or touch my heart, you are there . . ."

MERYL: "He does love them. Maybe more because he left. I know that I felt the love the strongest when I left. And I think they did too, they just called it grief."

MOTHER: "It's like everyone is like a lightbulb, and the electricity is the love we feel. The more electricity we let ourselves feel when we forget our sense of who think we are based on our history, the more that we feel . . . and at times, the feeling is so huge, it feels like we're 10,000-gigawatt bulbs . . ."

"MERYL: "Just like Sean's smile."

Another person is on top of the wall with them; a big man who looks like George Kennedy. His smile is like the sun.

SEAN: "I liked the George Kennedy part. You two did good."

MERYL: "Thank you, Sean. And thank you for letting us borrow you."

SEAN: "My pleasure. I volunteered for the assignment. I liked them both, but I mostly talked to Danny. I enjoyed every minute with them. He took it really hard when he found out I was not in the meat suit any more."

MOTHER: "He didn't understand yet, still thinking we're the name and the body. We all do it. You know, you about killed Robert with love. He can hardly even type your name without feeling overwhelmed."

SEAN: "All he has to do when it gets too huge is breathe deeply in and out slow. That's the faucet. Adjust the faucet 'til he can stand it. Besides, he knows it's not sad now."

MERYL: "I think he can do what we do. Instead of just the faucet, he can he send it to everyone, 'til he can stand it. Write, talk, plate food, smile, let someone in in traffic, give encouragement, and share it. I keep whispering that to Kathy, 'Keep encouraging him to write.'"

Another woman is there now, up on top of the wall, an older woman, somewhere in her 70's. She's got her eyes closed and she's smiling too.

MRS: WININGS: "That Kathy of yours picked right up where I left off. He must have recognized the Voice. I had a Southern accent back when he was in 4th grade. It was the last year I taught. My swan song. I was 72. The last day of school, I hugged him. He was hiding behind his mom's leg. I kissed him too. It was the last time he saw me."

MERYL: "A teacher like me with a Southern accent. Nice touch. She's a teacher, but a yoga teacher. A teacher with a Southern accent who tells him he's a good writer. Hey, who's writing this? He told her all about you, Mrs. Winings. You're in the yoga book."

MRS. WININGS: "Call me Mary, we're not in school. That book was as much about yoga as this is about a restaurant."

MOTHER: "Everyone always told him that you were the best part of that book. Mr. Distraction."

MERYL: "So then when he writes this book he makes sure to sweep most of the crumbs of the restaurant off the table. You think you're reading a book about a restaurant . . ."

All say together

"'But that's just the distraction, isn't it?'"

MOTHER: "Let's keep encouraging them to share."

MERYL: "Sure. We keep sending them our love so we can stand it, they overflow and they have to pass it on, so they can stand it. The breathing won't work with all of us on this."

SEAN: "Count me in."

MOTHER: "That's right."

MERYL: "I can only imagne what they'll do."

SEAN: "I think that's *their* job. We just send them love."

MRS. WININGS: "I just love happy endings."

∾

GOD: "My little children, my little children, my wonderful, wonderful little children."

∾

Two weeks before Robert's 30th birthday, right on schedule, he still had the piece of paper he'd hand-written 10 years earlier, he got the key and drove to the little strip mall 30 minutes from his house to his karate school.

There was no one to hug, except that little kid inside himself, but it was enough. He was a 2nd degree black belt, just like the paper had said he'd be. The time table spot on, the landing stuck, like he'd ordered the whole idea from some catalog, his finger on the idea, the big book open in front of him . . . there, Gimme . . . *that* one.

10 years after that running and fighting for Robert, because when he was little, Robert was picked on, the slow, awkward kid.

A turtle.

Robert, the turtle, the clomper, but the funny guy, had never really thought what he wanted to do with his life, and instead focused on having a lot of laughs. Back at college, he and Larry confessing that they had no idea what they were going to be when they grew up.

Maybe no one knows what they're going to be. Maybe we focus too much on what we're going to be and not enough on who we are now.

Now Robert had spent 10 hard years not just knowing what he wanted to do, but certain that he would do it. That he had already had done it, his body just catching up with his mind, his mind which had visited his future in the Realm of Dreams.

Had pointed to his future in the Catalog and had been willing to work his butt off.

Quite willing.

The only one pushing Robert was Robert.

Larry had always laughed at all Robert's jokes and told him a million times, "You're funny."

Robert hopes Larry reads this.

≈

LARRY: "What's this 'Head?"

ROBERT: "It's a book. I wrote it for me and my wife and a million people, but I wrote it for you too. You weren't in there at first but then one day, as I was reading through the *Happy Birthday Bobby!* part and all of a sudden there you were on the computer screen. Larry."

LARRY: "I don't know what to say."

ROBERT: "You don't have to say anthing, Bro."

∿

And then Marie.

And PJ.

The *smart one* and *the athlete*.

His brother and sister.

Maybe a book saying something you can't shout across some mysterious gulf.

In the Realm of Dreams, Robert pictures that the gulf has disappeared and once again being able to reach out to touch his brother and his sister.

People he never remembers hugging.

Maybe see if he can't make them laugh.

Gotcha, Bro. Gotcha, Sis.

Once again, maybe pass a book across the table to his sister.

Here, this is a good one, Marie.

Robert would later tell his kids he had a million jokes, "I got a million of 'em," he'd say and he told his children that it was his plan to tell them over the course of his time here on Earth, maybe with that last breath, gentle as a butterfly's fart, fluttered from his lips, a little scrap of fake dialog he'd invented, some exchange between him and a nun with the big brimmed habit, a prank phone call, a one-liner, or just some silly observation on life, laughing at the whole thing, those silly and serious things that bubbled up in his head and out his mouth mostly, but sometimes, written down and shared, notes passed in class, emails to co-workers, the work stuff nearly lost in all that funny text, one woman saying she kept "everything he'd ever sent" who said, " . . . Shucks, Earl you're funny," her nickname for Bobby, both of them faking these Southern accents for a laugh. Maybe he'd use that last exhale to say some words, words that he'd put in dog-earred notebooks and a worn Bell Laboratories journal, then, with some prompting from me, posted on Meetup, then Facebook, then books. Robert, his time in Time now over, going back to the big Clear Everlasting Nothingness of Pure Happy Thoughtless Feeling, Nobody to Somebody and Back to Nobody, the real Robert, that sticky moment looking around the birth room, everything all blurry, and everything that followed up to now, the fluttering breath flapping those Cosmic Curtains, the whole thing going by like *that*.

Growing up, Robert watched over PJ like a guard dog. Larry too, but Larry was scrappy. Robert may have been a guard dog, but Larry was a pit bull.

Robert loved them both and thought of Larry as much his brother as PJ, his Aunt Jeannette showing pictures of the two of them in diapers, for God's sake, the home movies, there they are, Robert and Larry.

After two years of school, Larry took some time off to work and figure out what was next, eventually finishing school back in his home state and became a butcher like his father.

He and Robert and PJ, the three musketeers, all drifted apart, some mysterious gulf. None of them probably, least of all Robert, could tell you why specifically.

Back in 1980, PJ came to visit Robert at Robert's first year off at school. Before he was dropped off outside the dorm, a 100+ old building on a steep hill up the way from the Mississippi in Dubuque, Iowa, some kid on the floor joked about getting Robert's little brother drunk, watch him throw up. Robert's little brother, in that kid's mind, just some lightweight kid. Thinking, this PJ, a junior in high school, all scrunched over the toilet. PJ, just a little guy a head smaller than Robert.

Robert pushed the big talker up against the wall, twisted the t-shirt in his hand under his little brother's malevolent future bartender's neck and rolled his bony forearm into the guy's windpipe with a violence that frightened both of them.

"Nobody touches him. Let him drink as much as he wants. But nobody touches him. Understand?"

He said it like he was telling the guy the time.

Calmly.

Which frightened Robert. Not the violence, but the calm.

When PJ was too little still to keep up on the 2-wheel bikes with the kids in the neighborhood, Robert on his black Schwinn no-speed cruiser with a big seat, let him ride on the seat, PJ hanging on to Robert as he rode him everywhere. Standing up the whole time. Getting off and holding the bike to let PJ off. Didn't want his little brother left at home, so he took him with.

He kept that bike for nearly 40 years before donating to a charity bike sale, saying, Here, take it, but looking back at it, getting a little misty.

Maybe seeing his little brother still hanging on, his small hands holding on to him.

Maybe giving away more than a bike that couldn't carry him and his brother any more.

Robert thinking now, even without the bike, I can still feel him.

Not on the bike. But I can still feel him out there.

His little brother, thinking about his big brother.

And he feels his sister, thinking about her little brother.

And Larry, thinking about his cousin.

Robert can feel all of them out there.

Nobody really able to hide from anybody.

It's 1962.

Robert's still inside, waiting to be born. Not ready for the gooey trip out into the light, ready to go from being Nobody to being a Somebody with a story.

His story.

I'm keeping an eye on him.

I'm not even a year old, but I feel he needs someone to watch him.

Watch him like a hawk.

Make sure he's not in trouble.

Robert's mother, that barely 17-year old immigrant girl, after feeble promises to raise Robert herself, finally succumbed to her parent's insistence that he be given to "people who would love him and take of him," a promise that young Chicago couple made good on. So, she signed the papers, left school during her last trimester to go live in the Wayward Girls home or some such, doing chores and going to makeshift school with the other "sinners," the other "withouts."

All of them young girls in various stages of pregnancy. Robert later met a woman who'd stayed in the same Wayward Girls Home around the same time, a woman Robert met at an adoptee support group, a woman who's own daughter had found and re-connected with 20 years after she was given up for adoption. This woman he met said all the girls endured the hisses of "Slut!" and other things some of the hardened nuns would say to the girls who found themselves there.

So, the three-week old Robert was sent home to grow up with the Morans, a young Chicago suburban couple named Jim and Katie that longed for a baby.

Lucky for them and really, for Robert's mother too.

She'd be happy how things turned out.

Robert dreams of finding her someday and saying, "You absolutely gave me life, but these people were everything you wished for and more."

∾

ROBERT: "I found you. I always knew I would. I pictured it."

MOTHER: "You used the Catalog."

ROBERT: "Yeah, but all these people kept showing up to help me when I needed it. Good things kept happening. People kept telling me I was good at things that you could take with you. They were like angels. They'd show up and help me and then go back from whence they came."

MOTHER: "They live inside you. They appear when you call for help."

ROBERT: "Did you do all that? With your wishes for me? Wishes for me to be okay, wishes that I would turn out okay?"

MOTHER: "You did it. All those angels are just aspects of you. The Voice of Encouragement has many faces, but it's all the same Voice really."

ROBERT: "Like Mrs. Winings?"

MOTHER: "An angel?"

ROBERT: "An angel. My fourth grade teacher. She told me I was a good writer . . . the real magic happened when her voice became my voice. When I started saying it . . . that's when things started to change."

MOTHER: "She watered your writing seed. After that, it was all up to you."

ROBERT: "Thank you."

MOTHER: "For the wishes?"

ROBERT: "For giving me away."

MOTHER: "I knew what you meant."

ROBERT: "You're joking. Nice. That's one. Did I get the million from you?"

MOTHER: "Maybe, but mostly you got it from the books, all that listening, the tv, the adults, sitting around listening to your dad tell jokes, doin' all the voices. All those words, they're just different sounds for the Voice."

ROBERT: "So it's not really me, is it?"

MOTHER: "It doesn't have a name. Nobody. Get it? No *body*. Somebody. Some *body*. Nobody. No *body*. Nobody. Captial N. No name."

ROBERT: "Tell me yours. I tried so hard to find you."

MOTHER: "And when you were ready, there I was. You thought I was far away but I was right there the whole time. You were attached to the idea of me, but it was the love you wanted and you got plenty."

ROBERT: "That was you? The love?"

MOTHER: "Let's just say that all those people who came into your life and loved you were the lightbulbs."

ROBERT: "So who's the electricity?"

MOTHER: "Nobody. With a capital N. It doesn't have a name. Don't try and personify it. It's just a feeling. A feeling so huge, sometimes you have to breathe or it overwhelms you, then you share it, 'til you can stand it."

NOBODY: "Listen to her."

ROBERT: "Are you gonna tell me your name?"

MOTHER: "Why don't you tell me your's first?"

ROBERT: "It's not important is it?

MOTHER: "My boy. My wonderful, wonderful, funny boy."

ROBERT: "The whole thing, that butterfly down in South America or whatever, changed things at the last minute. It did us a favor; it was lucky for everybody, you too. Being a 17-year old mom woulda been tough. You woulda missed a lot of life and maybe resented me. Who knows? That's a lot of pressure to put on yourself. Heck, the ink was still drying on your driver's license. Give yourself a break."

MOTHER: "I always hoped if we met you'd say that."

ROBERT: "About the butterfly?"

MOTHER: "About it being best for everyone including me."

ROBERT: "I knew what you meant."

MOTHER: "Good one. That's one."

∼

It's 1962.

Robert is only 3 weeks old.

His mother has gone home.

To heal and grow the rest of the way up and maybe, once a year, on May 18th, a little dark blue cloud would steal over her soul about a month before his birthday . . . a little dark spot on an otherwise sunny disposition.

"A tiny shadow growing by her side, the life she'd made, Nobody had given for her to weep for, someone she would maybe never know, connected by a memory, being filled, then emptied, feeling a loss that never leaves, it only comes and goes."—Danonymous

KATHY: "Who wrote *that*?"

ROBERT: "I think she did."

~

It's a lucky day for everyone.

Especially me.

They had already chosen a name. Kevin. But, at the last minute, Katie Moran decided to switch from Kevin to Daniel.

But everyone called him Danny.

Which was lucky for me.

Had circumstances been different, that butterfly, maybe, somewhere near the rainforest floor in the Amazon, flitting delicately like two tiny yellow and black speckled flower petals, then, *THFFFT!* it lets out a little puff of gas, some Lepidopteran flatulence, a fart, a butterfly silent but lively, fluttering the Cosmic Curtains up in Chicago in the window in that neighborhood where a 17-year old, a baby growing inside her, faces an impossibly huge decision. An almost imperceptible stirring of the breeze, but there it is, and maybe that girl keeps the kid, and Danny would have remained Robert.

His mom, grandparents, the kids growing up, his buddies in grade school, high school, maybe college even, his wife, maybe the husband and wife at the little neighborhood grocery store he part-timed at as a stockboy, sometimes goin' behind the counter at the deli and slice some cheese and lunchmeat, wrap it neatly in paper, hand it over the top, handwrite the price with one of those black grease pencils with the fat round end he tucks behind his ear, $1.95 for the ladies up front . . . his wife, a cute girl he meets at the city college, has a couple kids with then divorces 20 long years later, finally admitting to himself what he and the girl knew but don't admit outloud . . . that the love left when the kids were small, that they'd become two people without hopes or dreams, two people who didn't get along and spilled that hopelessness into the thick tense air in the house and that the children knew, everyone knew and finally he could no longer deny it. And that knowing made living like this not really living at all. It felt more like slow dying . . .

All those people would have called him Bobby.

Bobby.

And I, all the butterflies aside, likely would never have met Danny.

And you wouldn't be reading this.

Danny loves the story of the last-minute name switch, like when someone puts in their order for lunch, then, while the waitress is going 'round the table, and the index finger goes up, "Wait, I changed my mind."

Like someone who answers the phone as Danny, but decides to change to Bobby.

At some level, a nod to the power of a name and yet, laughing at how little a name matters.

What matters is what's on the inside.

The Nobody part.

The part with no thoughts, no history, no opinions, worries, judgment or even hopes and dreams.

The part that prods your guts when someone calls you a name, or when you feel the sting of a loss of something that was never permanent in the first place—that feeling, it's not pain. It starts low in your stomach, it travels up your body and changes your face . . . and if you're happy the feeling feels good and if you're sad, it feels bad.

A feeling that makes you feel strong and alive or weaker and less than alive.

A positive charge or a negative one.

Good. Bad.

The black line or the white one?

Fix your attention on the one you want to see.

Which one do you see?

Look away and look at the one that makes you feel good.

Your body is votes with feelings.

You don't need to swing a pendulum or check your astrology chart. You live in a pendulum and your wearing an astrology chart with no guaranteed life span, but proven accurate, like a Timex. It doesn't tell time.

But it does tell.

Two people can travel through the same experience under the same cirumstances but their unique story becomes the camera they point at the experience, which determines whether the story is happy or sad or just experienced, free of backwards analysis.

Like seeing something new.

Just drinking in the details with nothing to compare them to.

The part of our brain that can pick out all the sounds around us, but right before we identify the sound.

The Data Gatherer.

The Witness.

The Silent Portal.

The Observer.

The Watcher.

The part of our brain which we can train our attention on, concentrating our brain down to a fine unmoving point, like when we perform a fine motor skill like moving the tip of our thumb and forefinger together so they almost touch.

Try it and stare at the tiny gap. This pinpoint focus is possible to atune to the part of us that is the first line of each sense: the Information Gatherer.

Interpretation is a secondary focus. Interpretation requires backwards analysis, research, opinions, judgments and preferences.

All impediments to just drinking in an experiences.

Silent, but speaking in a plain, honest, uplifting way when required.

Always willing to be a happy, humble servant.

Getting, by giving.

Not the channel undeservedly graced by wisdom, kindness, contentment, joy, peace, forgiveness and love at times.

Not the lightbulb.

Not the meatsuit.

Maybe.

Or maybe not.

But it's something to think about, isn't it?

Maybe the Muse's Muse.

The *real* Writer: *Danonymous.*

The *Voice.*

Danny imagines Jim and Katie driving to St. Vincent's orphanage in the city in what would have been the second week of June.

It would have been hot and his dad and mom would have been driving their pale green Studebaker, the one Danny's dad crashed gently to a stop into the car dealer's wall where he traded it up for a green-blue '65 Chevy 2-door Belair, he thinks, a car they would drive across the country to Disney Land when Danny was 8 years old, a car his mom handed the keys to, 100,000-some miles later, to Danny's cousin David, her sister Helen's son, David's mouth open, he couldn't believe it.

And like any kid can do if they think for a moment, he can trace the cars that carried him through his life, from his first ride to his last ride with his parents before leaving home. Anyone who knows Danny knows his ability to recall, so he can bring back those cars: their colors, makes, models, quirks, dents, secrets, sorrows, joys and the thousands of moments to which any family car can bear silent testimony.

Next came the dark brown Chevy wagon with electronic rear hatch with a pivot arm pad that could crush your hand. That car that got a dismal six miles per gallon, coasting.

The wagon was traded for the ghastly yellow AMC Matador ("you got a *Nash*," his Uncle Johnny said, grinning at a car the color of the golden arches, Uncle Johnny driving a white Lincoln with a license plate that said TACOS that year, probably, a nod to his Mexican restaurant, the car whose horn did the melody for La Cucaracha). A kid in Danny's class laughed a belly laugh and pointed to the car and proclaimed it the "MacDonald's Box."

The yellow Matador was traded for the blue and white landau-topped Pontiac Catalina with the light blue velour interior that was an unforgiving landing strip for a hot seed popping from a joint but carried Danny to the place he was arrested, to prom and in a careening controlled skid around the high school parking lot, his dad hitting the breaks and that car whirling around crazily, his dad talking to him like he's telling him the score of a ball game, working the wheel in a circle, righting that skid, telling Danny that this could save his bacon some day—Danny repeating that wonderful lesson with his kids, when he could.

With three kids driving, they added the tiny yellow Honda Civic to the driveway. A 4-speed manual that was the training ground for the three newly minted manual transmission terminators, that third gear always sounding like you were killing something under the hood.

Then, the stalwart Catalina still in the driveway, the yellow Honda was replaced by a new light brown Ford Escort.

Which stayed behind with the Catalina in the driveway when Danny drove off in his $300 blue AMC Hornet, which was sold off and replaced with a silver Oldsmobile Cutlas, which he drove off to park in the lot behind his first apartment.

But his first ride was in the pale green Studebaker.

But while he was wrapped and ready for that first ride, Jim and Kathie were driving to the orphanage to pick up Danny, the windows down, each working that last smoke, maybe give it a couple blocks to air out before picking up the kid, those nuns catching a whiff of Winston reds on their clothes, maybe give them that disapproving nun look.

Then, Danny's mom flicking her cigarette out the window, a little orange spark as it hits the pavement and skitters to a halt in the street, that car driving off and his mom looking over at Jim Moran, still got his hair, the short sleeve shirt, arm out the window, and she says, "I'm leaning away from Kevin . . ."

And far, far away from *Bobby* . . .

I think the prevailing philosophy on pets and 3-week old babies is that a moniker doesn't really have a chance to sink its teeth into the newly minted's mind until about one month for humans and 7 months for dogs, using the standard accepted comparative inter-species multiplier.

Which allows the adoptive parents some leeway with naming, particularly if they had their hearts set on a boy named Danny versus one named Bobby.

Bobby maybe sounding a little low-lifish.

Bobby.

A man who rises to accomplish not the great, but to toil at the menial.

The kind of guy with dried out skin on his hands from doing dishes.

A lot of dishes.

Maybe a guy who is about finding meaning in the menial, but that's another story.

When Danny's son Andy was born two weeks after Danny's 26th birthday, Danny found himself staring into the face of the first person in his life he'd ever seen that was related to him by blood.

He said Andy emerged all slick and covered with "birth goo," not bothering to use the proper terminology. Andy's eyes were open and he was howling, like, geez, I hope it gets better than *that*.

And Danny admits he cried, he was so happy. All that was out at that point was Andy's head, the foreceps pulled away and Danny said it was the most beautiful person he'd ever seen in his life.

And then, he says, a shadow stole over his heart unexpectedly and for the first time in his life, he thought about a 17-year old girl, someone out there who he ws still connected to, that tug on his heart as real as the little face looking at him.

He and Andy's mom had been awake for nearly 24 hours and Danny said he sat down on the floor of the delivery room after Andy was all the way out, weighed, measured, fingers and toes, yes, I got 10, the OB said.

Sitting on that cool tile, he thought about his little boy, who he had started loving when he was just a bump under a shirt.

And he thought about some immigrant girl, 26 years earlier.

Knocked up in high school, Danny, or Robert, as she named him, just a bump under a shirt. A kid with a locker and hopes and dreams.

And a baby on the way.

When the baby was wrapped, he held Andy and looked into those eyes staring back at him.

Maybe looking for someone else in those eyes and in the tiny upturned face.

Maybe looking for Bobby.

Which got Danny to thinking about something he'd never really cared about up to that point. Now, it starting to take shape and grow, something to think about.

For years, Danny hunted for that someone who would always be 17 years older than him.

Just some lady out there who gave up a kid when she was still in high school.

A girl just 10 years off the boat from Germany. Her parents living over maybe in an ethnic neighborhood or somewhere else in the city, maybe with the other people who spoke their language. 2 papers on every corner: The Tribune and the other paper, the one with the words that only people in the 'hood can read or cut pictures out of and send to their families still across the pond, those papers, the English one and the other, right next to each other in the boxes.

After about five tough years of dead ends, Danny put Bobby away in a dusty box in the attic . . .

And a little blue would steal over Danny's soul about a month before his birthday . . . a little dark spot on an otherwise sunny disposition.

You know, a few years ago, he decided to make a writing project called:

"Let's Get to the Bottom of My Annual Emotional Bottom."

His initial drafts, which were more angsty and Sylvia Plathishly dismal, though they did garner got some style points from the teacher, lacked the real substantive words that you read back over and something inside goes, "Wait, I get it!" . . .

But, something happened.

In Danny's words:

"..a cool calm settles over you that feels like you're staring at the sunset of something, a little fleeting feeling of sadness rippling over you that sinks slowly to a small glowing point on the horizon and disappears into the coming dark . . . a calm that feels ancient and familiar and a little smile forms at the corners of your mouth like someone's just told you the answer to a problem you've worried over for years . . ."

(Though he admits this is a copy and paste from one of his Plath knock offs . . .)

The timer on his particular "Aha!" dinged in the form of a short story, just a few pages in a journal, clips from some of those poems from way back when all this originally got stirred up, a well-worn Bell Laboratories journal being particularly fermented with material, which all got shoveled in here and strung together there, the rest of it coming out, like he says it does, like someone turning on a faucet somewhere, you step back and all these words come out, Danny never really sure who's hand's doing the turning.

Read it aloud to me and the whole sunset thing happened . . .

Happy Birthday, Danny!

Yes, a happy day for Robert and his birth mom, inescapably always to be 17 years older than him somewhere and his real mom and dad, the Morans.

And for me.

May 18th, 1962, a little after 10 in the morning, by the hospital clock and recorded by that lady, looking at her watch, gonna just make lunch in the cafeteria, get this little guy on his way.

He still leaves it off his Facebook page, his birthday . . . but, people find out it's his birthday . . . and some cards and texts and emails, little waves of well-wishes that roll like the steady surf against his shore . . . arrive.

It's just another day really.

And everything feels fine.

Danny said he's glad he's alive and maybe this is a day that we get to feel *that* a little more.

And he thanks everbody for the birthday wishes . . .

. . . especially Nobody.

Some Girls Just Go for Dumb

Several of my female Facebook friends have shared they have a crush on Bobby, obviously hoping to hook up with a low brow, a plodder, someone who's trainable, chews with their mouth closed, but can move heavy boxes and furniture, take out the trash, etc.

A useful man.

Someone who'll go bounding off to fetch you something and bring it back like a big happy dog.

Sit.

Stay.

Heel.

Bobby.

$\sim$

Someone commented that Bobby should run, next thing he knows, he's gonna be puttin' the seat down, my word.

Bobby had questions.

BOBBY: "What's he mean, lowerin' the toilet seat?"

KATHY: "He means that guys should lift the lid of the toilet to pee standing up and should then lower it as a courtesy to the women who may use the toilet after.

BOBBY: "But you tole me to pee sittin' down, 'count of the, whadya call it?"

KATHY: "Splash factor. And then?"

BOBBY: "Flush."

KATHY: "Good boy. And?"

BOBBY: "Wash my hands?"

KATHY: "Without the question mark."

BOBBY: "Wash my hands."

KATHY: "Wash my hands, who?"

BOBBY: "Wash my hands, ma'am."

KATHY: "Good boy. Sit. Stay."

So Like, Who's Really Writing?

Bobby can write. I'll give him that.

It's like the stories and things he weaves with his mouth, he can some how translate onto paper.

But occasionally, I'll say, "Write something. Something funny."

And he'll bunch up.

Get creatively constipated.

"What I need's a little fiber," he says.

"Where do you get your fiber?" I ask.

"Bard Earth Ca-fe," he says with that grin.

∽

BOBBY: "I'm blocked."

KATHY: "You know what Walt Whitman did when he was blocked?"

BOBBY: "He a dishwasher too?"

KATHY: "He was."

BOBBY: "Did more dishes, wait for the creative juices to flow?"

KATHY: "I think you're getting smarter."

BOBBY: "Scary, huh?"

HOME HOLIDAY

"don't we all hide behind walls of industrious importance? faces set in masks of concentration when in fact the mind is languishing over cool green home longing for family faces and the sounds of every night and escape-work-for-now if each morning all the wishes to stay home banded together and shouted in one silent voice perhaps one day we would remain warm in bed all rolling over with closed-eyed smiles having somehow received an answer yes, don't go don't go today you may stay home"—Danonymous

KATHY: "Danonymous? Clever."

DANNY: "I just put on a D at the beginning, see it? Can o' beans."

~

Occasionally, I need to run an errand or, if I've got the stomach for it, stay home.

Leaving Bobby/Danny (one of my friends called him Danby) to mind the store. Leaving the dynamic duo alone with people.

Something that scares the shitaki mushrooms out of me.

The idea of those two big, unpredictable lunkheads clomping around the restaurant.

Not knowing what they might say.

And worse, not being around to hear it.

God, there's nothin' worse than missing a phone call.

They're funny when you read them.

But Good Lord, you should hear that man.

I begged the girls, Jane and Lynn to watch him. They're two local girls that each live in homes not a mile from ours and who started coming to the restaurant a few years back and ended up working with us, God, passing up real careers to chop endless vegetables, slather pasty flax seed goo on dehydrator sheets by the yard and, keep an eye on Danby.

~

KATHY: "Full report. Jane?"

JANE: "1 broken glass, 1 denial. He said flibbertigibbet 14 times, 13 out front. He curtsied to a woman with a pink sweater . . ."

LYNN: "It was more flowery . . . I only got 12 flibbertigibbets."

JANE: "What does that even mean?"

KATHY: "Flibbertigibbet. He's pretending to be smart. It's a Middle English word for a flighty or whimsical person. Now it means 'a gossipy or overly talkative person.' Chatty Kathy, but in this case Gabby Bobby. He's making fun of himself, he just doesn't know it. He says, My name is Bobby, three B' as in flibbertgibbet . . ."

LYNN: "I got four."

KATHY: "And four minus one equals Bobby."

JANE: "Oh, he was barking on the patio."

LYNN: "But at curtsy lady. Like they were playing a game."

KATHY: "Did she bark back? Never mind. They're, like, friends at that point. Sales calls?"

LYNN: "Four of 'em."

KATHY: "Details."

LYNN: "Let's see, let me find my notes, at 11:32am, we got a telemarketing call from what the display said was MEDICALINSUR, so, since it wasn't a customer, I called Bobby, like you said . . ."

KATHY: "I saw it on Facebook, the witch doctor mammy thing. That was good."

JANE: "I have one at 1:32pm . . ."

KATHY: "Still during lunch? 'Hey, let's call the restaurant during lunch and ask for the owner' like they do."

LYNN: "You'd think we'd be on the DO NOT CALL list."

KATHY: "You mean, not the registry, more like a warning to the telemarketer."

LYNN: "Yeah, wait, was that the electricity reseller?"

JANE: "Yeah, remember, he started talking about the generator?"

LYNN: "Yeah, and the monkeys. God, where does he come up with it?"

KATHY: "Monkeys? Never mind. What else?"

LYNN: "5:37pm . . ."

KATHY: "Dinner. Right, 'Hey, the owner isn't there at lunch, maybe he stepped out to get a sandwich. I'll try back during dinner."

JANE: "5:37pm, MARKETRESEARCH . . ."

KATHY: "Uh-oh, owner left the country?"

JANE: "Hopped on a freight train, ran along side, pulled himself up by the ladder thing and climbed into a box car."

KATHY: "He's got a back pack . . ."

JANE: "And his travel ukelele . . ."

KATHY: "Not the banjo?"

JANE: "He mentioned the banjo. Said he traded it for the ukelele . . ."

LYNN: "I can see that. Learning a new stringed instrument."

KATHY: "The man is talented."

JANE: "And perpetually unavailable."

KATHY: "Okay, there's one more. Let me see your notes . . ."

LYNN: "Uh, this is the best one."

JANE: "9:04pm."

KATHY: "We were technically closed."

LYNN: "Yeah, but we saw it was an 800 number and we were all cleaned up . . ."

KATHY: "And you thought, I wonder what he's got at 9:04pm?"

LYNN: "Yeah, we looked at each other and shrugged and called for him, 'Bobby! Sales call!' and we heard him drop the mop and come clomping up in his big Crocs."

KATHY: "That man does clomp."

JANE: "He settles in the stool and Lynn hands him the phone."

LYNN: "He looked happy and relaxed."

KATHY: "That goofy grin."

JANE: "Yeah, he winks at us first, like, Listen to this."

LYNN: "Like duh, Bobby's takes a deep breath, he's got the phone in his hand and I know it's a sales call and I'm going to go in the back and count the red onions?"

KATHY: "Your notes just say 'popsicles, mosquito insurance and what's this, Formica underwear?"

LYNN: "Formica underwear."

KATHY: "F. It looks like a B. There's nothing else, like the pen scratched off into the margin."

LYNN: "Sorry, we started laughing."

KATHY: "So he goes, 'Bard Earth Ca-fe.' What else? How does he go from Popsicles to mosquito insurance to the underwear?"

JANE: "*Formica* underwear."

KATHY: "Excuse me, *Formica* underwear. Yeah, I'm just curious."

LYNN: "It gets better. Go to the bathroom first then come back and you better sit down."

KATHY: "Is it bad?"

JANE: "Not bad. Funny, weird, Ripley's bizarro, random, but not bad. It's Bobby."

KATHY: "That's what makes me nervous."

～

It should be noted that "watching" Bobby (and listening to him) is all the girls *could* do . . . and maybe take notes for later.

In their words . . .

JANE: "He's like a big kid. But when Kathy leaves, we get nervous. She's like, the only one that can control him."

LYNN: "It's not like she controls him. It's like he tones it down a little when she's around."

JANE: "Yeah, but if she steps out . . ."

LYNN: "All bets are off."

～

Once, I decided as a test of myself more than anything, to leave the girls at the restaurant with Bobby and the Public for two whole days . . .

～

Day 1

JANE: "Oh God."

LYNN: "Where is he?"

JANE: "He's at a table with four women."

LYNN: "Oh God."

JANE: "No. Wait, it's okay. They're laughing."

LYNN: "Wait. Look he's repeating it."

JANE: "They're laughing again."

LYNN: "Okay. We're okay."

JANE: "Uh-oh."

LYNN: "What?"

JANE: "Door. 3-top. Looks like they're staying."

LYNN: "Uh-oh."

JANE: "It's only 6:00."

~

LYNN: "So, Kathy said we're supposed to keep an eye on him."

JANE: "Keep an eye on him? How?"

LYNN: "She wasn't specific, she just said, 'Keep an eye on him.'"

JANE: "Like she's worried."

LYNN: "Wouldn't you be? Bobby's like, the bull in the china shop."

JANE: "God, did he break something again? Bobby!"

BOBBY: *glass breaks somewhere and Bobby's voice is distant* "I didn't do it."

~

KATHY: "Full report."

LYNN: "Two words: Oompa Loompa."

KATHY: "God."

JANE: "It gets better."

KATHY: "How the jalapenos did he get on Oompa Loompas?"

LYNN: "We were talking about Willy Wonka . . ."

KATHY: "Why? Never mind. And?"

JANE: "He told someone we were your children. My name is Sunflower."

LYNN: "I'm Blueberry. So, no, I get it, Violet, Blueberries, Willy Wonka, Oompa Loompa."

KATHY: "BOBBY!"

~

Day 2

LYNN: "He was mellower today."

JANE: "Bobby? Yeah, he was."

LYNN: "Like maybe he does some of it for her?"

JANE: "I think he does it all for her."

~

And then there was the day Bobby, eager to have a green vegetable juice drink, decided to forego the formalities of washing the spinach bunches first, Let's not stand on formality, son.

He's scrupulous at the café, but this was at home and he "explained" that without the big cavernous vegetable sink and the big 5-gallon salad spinner, the task seemed daunting. "There was dishes in the sink..."

"But you're a dishwasher! Couldn't you have moved them into the dishwasher?" I asked rhetorically.

He hesitated, so I closed.

"So, you were just plain lazy," I said softly.

"You make it sound bad," he mumbled.

Spinach bunches that had enough dirt stuck to the base of each clump to start a small terrarium. Within hours he complained of nausea (big surprise). He'd brought it home with the "best of intentions," those three words that sit at the precipice of any foolish act. The girls commented that it was some of the dirtiest spinach they'd ever seen. "He didn't wash it? Didn't even rinse it, not a quick splash, didn't even hold it over the sink when he walked past, faking it, or run the water like some little kid in the bathroom, pretending to brush his teeth, wet the toothbrush and run the water a couple believable times?" And I'm like, "I take my eye off that man for 1 second..."

So, I banished him. "No soup for you, 1 day," I said sternly.

He mumbled something incoherently.

However, this presented me with a classic Kathy dilemma: How do you keep your eye on him, 15 miles away?

About mid-afternoon, I called and discovered he was feeling better . . . after spotting a Facebook status that, as I had come to expect, had not been written by me.

I called his phone, which he answered on the first ring, but he spoke in a croaky voice, not really able to put much into it:

BOBBY: "Bard Earth Ca-fe."

KATHY: "I don't like you not being here."

BOBBY: "You said, 'Stay home, we'll handle it,' but now you're worried, thinking, Maybe he's getting into trouble."

KATHY: "See, it's like you're psychic. I'm guessing you're still in your pajamas."

BOBBY: "They're lounge pants. Sales calls?"

KATHY: "Not a one. It's like they know you're not here."

BOBBY: "Maybe they're psychic, too."

~

And then, a little later, he must have been on the mend . . . I spotted this. Yes, sometimes I'd worry about him, so, like a Facebook thermometer, I'd circle up front, navigate to my profile page and hit the refresh button.

Gotcha, Hee-Haw.

KATHY: "I have to keep a Facebook eye on you. Here I'm picturing you laying on the couch and, Hello! We're talking."

B: "A Facebook eye? You just made that up."

K: "Okay, Mr. Inappropriatism."

B: "Mr. Inappropiatism! Love it. Can I switch from Bobby?"

K: "A lot of people would be sad to see Bobby go."

B: "Yeah, but it's like, 6 syllables."

K: "7."

B: [mouthing, ticking fingers] "I still get 6."

$\sim$

When I got home, we had another Talk. A talk that was 2 parts concern and 4 parts "You dumbell!"

Before he tumbled off to bed, he walked slowly into the bathroom through the little open doorway in our master bedroom and I lay in bed, listening to the sounds of him brushing his teeth.

I peeked around the corner to make sure he wasn't faking it.

Lord, I have to watch that man like a hawk.

$\sim$

Bobby alone with the girls was nerve-wracking enough for me to handle, but after his son Jimmy, a big kid just like Bobby, all smiles and never-serious, a chip off the old clompy block and, that boy, a natural on the phone, but, get this, he can play like 14 different instruments. Against my better judgment, we hire him on and him and Bobby are this force of goofiness to be reckoned with, finishing each other's sentences, but not always finishing the dishes.

~

Bobby's 23-year son Jimmy has joined our ranks as a waiter in training and while Bobby volunteered to train, I declined the offer, taking it upon myself:

KATHY: "Go seat those people."

JIMMY: "What's my motivation?"

KATHY: "Oh, yeah. You're serious, but casual, like they're old friends."

JIMMY: "But I don't know them."

KATHY: "Just go seat them." *sighs*

KATHY: "Here we go."

~

JIMMY: "Is there like, a dress code?"

KATHY: "For the customers?"

JIMMY: "No, for me. Like, can I wear tie dye shirts?"

KATHY: "Like the one you have on?"

JIMMY: "My dad says it's polite to ask."

KATHY: "Afterward?"

JIMMY: "He calls it, what is it Bobby?"

BOBBY: *in the distance but listening* "Retro-asking."

JIMMY: "That's it."

KATHY: "You call him Bobby too?"

JIMMY: "Not Bobby 2. He's technically Bobby 3. Just Bobby."

~

KATHY: "For the record, Jimmy, I'm not you're baby sitter."

BOBBY: "But you could have been. Ow!"

~

Jimmy's real name is Robert, but asked to be called Jimmy, so as not to be distracted when I'm yelling at Bobby.

KATHY: "Why did you name him Bobby too?"

BOBBY: "Technically he's Bobby 4, I'm Bobby 3. My dad was Bobby 2 and . . ."

KATHY: "I get it. No, why did you name him Robert also?"

BOBBY: "His last name's not Also, it's . . ."

KATHY: "Never mind."

JIMMY: "What'd I miss?"

KATHY: "Any hope of normal."

JIMMY: "Sweet!"

~

After a couple of weeks, I decided to test my metal again, take it up a notch. I left the dynamic duo, Alpha Dufus and his son to mind the store. They did a whole dinner shift alone. A patio full of people, a man and his son, an accordion . . . the Titanic Café sets sail, heading on a collision course for the iceberg lettuce.

~

BOBBY: "Did she really leave us here by ourselves for dinner?"

JIMMY: "I know, right."

BOBBY: "I don't know what to get into first."

JIMMY: "Trouble though, right?" *plays theme from Dragnet on accordion*

BOBBY: "See? She knew that I'd be so wound up that I couldn't decide and that I'd end up behaving."

JIMMY: "That's because she's WAY smarter than both of us."

~

JIMMY: "Do that again."

BOBBY: "You were Mr. Do That Again when you were, like three. Like under duck on the swing when you were little?"

JIMMY: "I loved that, it would almost feel like I was going over at the top, then you'd run under."

BOBBY: "And duck. Under duck."

JIMMY: "Under. Duck. Nice."

BOBBY: "Hey, can we stop at a park one the way home?"

JIMMY: "As long as you don't hurt your back. Maybe I should be the under ducker, Kathy'll be like, 'What happened to your head,' and there's my big shoe print on your back, and you're like, 'We were under ducking.'"

BOBBY: "Yeah, and, 'I was worried about you two in the restaurant and I didn't even think about you stopping on the way for a recess re-enactment.'"

JIMMY: "I love a good re-enactment. Let's get civil war costumes, then hit the swing set."

BOBBY: "See? It's like the old days."

∾

BOBBY: "Look at those spastic kids out there all hopped up on ice cream."

JIMMY: "An hour later they're crying and they don't even know why."

BOBBY: "Ice cream?" *Bobby hands him a dish with a spoon in it*

JIMMY: "What flavor?" *takes a bite* "Mint chocolate. Yes!"

BOBBY: "First we eat the ice cream . . ."

JIMMY: "Then maybe go outside, push each other into the bushes?"

BOBBY: "It's like you're reading my mind."

∾

After the park.

JIMMY: "That was fun!"

BOBBY: "The swings? I think I clipped your head with my shoes."

JIMMY: "That was nothing. What does your mammy say about head injuries again?"

BOBBY: "They build character?"

JIMMY: "See you can't remember either. It's from the . . . the . . ."

BOBBY: "Head injuries?"

JIMMY: "What are we talking about again?"

～

When Bobby got home from the café after a nail-biting diner with just him and Jimmy his son running the café, I learned that they were playing musical chairs . . . and tables. Apparently while Bobby was taking customer orders, Jimmy was following him playing the accordion. "Mood music," Bobby called it. They got huge tips.

～

For example, Bobby's squatting by a patio table like Hairy Yogi Berra, talking to them like he does, all Tennessee charm and hogwash and gentility and Jimmy's playing this fast, up tempo Italian sidewalk café music on the accordion. Bobby's taking an order from a man, his wife and little baseball-cap wearing 10 year old looking longingly at the troupe of little kids running around just outside the patio, pushing each other in the bushes, running, laughing, all hopped up on ice cream from next door.

So, the wife orders (Burrito)and the kid gets the Gee Mom Can I Really Have a Banana Split for Dinner dinner and Bobby gets to the man, and the guy's having a hard time making up his mind and Bobby cuts a hand to Jimmy and says, "Give me something a little slower . . . he's having a hard time deciding." And Jimmy pauses on the buttons and keys and squeezing the bellows on that big old dented beast strapped to his chest and says, "Like this?" and starts playing something slow and pretty and Bobby's like, "Yeah, that's good," and turns back to the guy and the whole patio's listening and watching and laughing.

Everyone having a good time.

Maybe those two hooligans can be trusted after all.

Bobby gets home, all happy and dusty, like they stopped at a park or something, I asked and he just waves the question off like a fly and says, "Open it, Happy Birthday!" and drops a little draw string bag on my chest under the covers.

He had got me a pair of earrings that our friend Tara Brisbine had made. Sweet!

So I say, "My turn," and he's like, "But I just had a birthday."

And I said, "And mine's not 'til the 16th of this month."

I told him to run downstairs and get that old 12-string of his.

He'd broke at least 4 strings on it, banging away, belting out songs, and one of the strings still hung there, trailing off behind the peg board on the finger print and sweaty fore arm marks, that string like a big 2-foot long errant nose hair that your grandpa won't clip because he's bald now and not willing to cut any hairs lose without a fight at 84.

He runs downstairs and like he knows what I've done, he goes right to where he keeps that guitar on the corner of the blue couch next to the birds and I hear the Rebel yell.

I had gotten tired of Kathy Holiday at about 2 in the afternoon and decided to surprise him by getting his 8-string polished and re-strung back up to a 12-string. The guy at the store laughed at the strings hanging off it and the weird middle-eastern sitar tuning Bobby'd cooked up and the music store guy re-strung it with these beautifully bright-sounding brass strings.

Couple more strings off that guitar and Bobby was heading toward it being one of those whiny Japanese kotos, the kind the Geisha girls play off on the side of the business men sipping tea from little cups, all demure smiles.

Bobby sitting on the edge of the bed, all smiles now, singing me to sleep.

A girl's gotta have a lullaby now and again and since all the dishes were done, I figured I'd put that hooligan to work.

A new set of strings and he's wrapped around my finger.

A new pair of earrings . . . they're nice.

But, I wrapped myself around his finger (the ring one on his left hand) five years ago and it had nothing to do with any presents . . .

:)

STUCK ON STUPID

BOBBY: "It's like I'm stuck on Stupid."

KATHY: "I thought you were going to get that fixed."

BOBBY: "Yeah, the guy's like, 'I think I know what the problem is.'"

KATHY: "And he's, what, like a doctor?"

BOBBY: "Not so much."

KATHY: "You banged your head on the vent hood, didn't you?"

BOBBY: "I think so."

KATHY: "You think so?"

BOBBY: "I might have."

KATHY "Uh-huh."

BOBBY: "Maybe I should go back, you know to the guy."

KATHY "Or we could get you a helmet."

BOBBY: "Sweet."

~

BOBBY: "What are you laughing about?"

KATHY: "Oh, I'm reading these statuses."

BOBBY: "Like, world events, 'China 1, USA 2,' like that?"

KATHY: "No idiot, Facebook."

BOBBY: "I knew what you meant."

KATHY: "People are starting to do screen play style."

BOBBY: "Like, *MAN: DOG:*?"

KATHY: "Well, there's not a lot of animals."

BOBBY: "It's like some sort of thespian explosion?"

KATHY: "Is that dangerous?"

BOBBY: "Now you're sounding like me."

KATHY: "That's depressing."

GUARD DOG

Last night, Bobby's got the back rear door of the car open, loading up, and some guy pulls in to the space next to us, mouthing something to Bobby about that open door. Bobby looms up next to the guy's window and growls, "Careful buddy, I bite." The guy's eyes getting big, the door locks clicking, him and his girlfriend staying in the car 'til we drove off.

~

On International Yarn Bombing Day, which is a day when people knit things and put them in unusual public places, like fun, non-property damaging graffiti, I posted this:

"Nothing adds to the fun like a tree wearing a sweater, worn here by our tree, The Hugging Tree. Stop by and pet the tree for good luck and happiness . . . Happy International Yarn Bombing Day from Borrowed Earth Café, in Downers Grove, IL USA."

So, me and two friends, Kathleen and Mary Beth (our friend with the beautiful therapy dogs, Maggie and Timmy), knitted little rectangles and fastened them to the trunk of the tree in front of the restaurant.

I love it!

I put a sign on the tree proclaiming it, "The Hugging Tree" and all day long, I watch young and old (mostly young) hug the tree.

That tree's gotta feel mighty good.

~

Bobby fell in love with the tree and sat out on the patio in the middle of one afternoon, slouched down in one of a pair of striped sling back canvas chairs we've got on the patio, watching all those people hug The Hugging Tree. And, to pass the time between hugs, I watched his hair cascading over the back of the chair. I could almost hear him typing, like he does. He got up once and mumbled something about the bushes, and I'm like, Tell me, and he pushed past me and sat at the stool behind the computer, Warped Walt Whitman.

~

But, if you look at the picture of the tree, all decked out with her colorful sweater, you see that low hedge trying to cover the storm grate nearby, and the bushes are like, "Look at Miss Modesty, got the sweater buttoned up all the way to her neck . . . what a prude!"

~

Kidding aside, he was like German shepherd, watching it.

~

Bobby slouches in a chair on the patio and surveys the passersby like a big dog on the porch . . . until he spies two young boys trying to get to Second Base with the Hugging Tree, sliding the yarn panels lewdly down the trunk of the tree, hoping to cop some trunk. He roars, "HEY, PUT THE SWEATER BACK ON THE TREE!" and they look back, get a good look at Alpha Dishwasher, comply and scurry off . . .

~

And, occasionally, we do have some unsavory characters come in . . .

. . . all I gotta do is whistle . . .

FULL MOON

My Gut, the only reliable source of portent, says silently that yesterday's Full Moon Fever Observance is still in full force and effect today as well. Call it a Farmer's Almanac hunch, a twitch, the part of us that hesitates at a darkened doorway, the keening sense that heightens when a bird suddenly crashes into the window dead as you type this . . . buckle up, Bobby!

ROCKY AND BUDDY

We are the mostly proud owners of two birds, a soft grey and white cockatiel named Rocky (who we may have incorrectly guessed to be a girl) and a Domesticated Quaker Parrot named Buddy (who we may have incorrectly guessed to be a boy).

I say incorrectly because even the squeaky adolescent boy at the pet store shrugged when we asked about determining gender.

"I dunno," he said helpfully.

We've looked on the Internet and apparently Squeaky's uncertainty is not uncommon.

Cockatiels and Quaker Parrots, like most birds of this sort, don't possess any helpful visible physical gender identifiers, just beak, feathers, eyes and feet—nothing to help with the male or female question mark, nothing to give you a clue as to whether to say, "Excuse me, sir," or "Excuse me, ma'am," (adding a tip of the hat) if'n you happen to bump into them in the hallway.

Unlike people and other species, no visual swinging parts you can glue a gender label on.

So, using the human propensity toward personification, we have assigned male and female qualities to them, fixed with our own stereotypes and prejudices, and enjoy allowing them the run of the house for several hours each morning and for a quick pet and a "Good night, you two," in evening . . .

Who knew they could type?

Apparently Danny.

I'm worried about him. All those characters clanging around in his head. I'd password protect my account . . . but, I usually can't wait to read what "they" have written.

Bless their hearts.

We love those birds.

Turns out, they think we suck.

Totally suck.

~

KATHY: "So they talk."

DANNY: "The birds."

KATHY: "Who else? They talk."

DANNY: "Like an old married couple."

KATHY: "Giving each other a hard time."

DANNY: "But it's like us vs. them. They get along 'long as they're nit picking us."

KATHY: "Like people."

DANNY: "Where do you think they got it?"

KATHY: "But it's not like a contest."

DANNY: "It's definitely not a contest."

KATHY: "Good. 'Cause I think they could take us."

ROCKY: "What happened?"

BUDDY: "I got shooed."

ROCKY: "We don't wear shoes . . ."

BUDDY: "Shooed. Shooed! Like, Get outa the way pigeon! Shooed."

ROCKY: "I got shushed."

BUDDY: "Shushed?"

ROCKY: "Like, yeah, I'm trying to watch something on YouTube and you're singing your song, knock it off, shushed."

BUDDY: "They suck."

ROCKY: "They totally, suck."

∾

ROCKY: "They're writing about us on Facebook again."

BUDDY: "What! Are you sure?"

ROCKY: "I'm sitting on his shoulder. He just typed shoulder."

BUDDY: "How did he spell it?"

ROCKY: "S-H-O-U-L-D-E-R."

BUDDY: "I wouldn't have guessed that. Is the u silent?"

ROCKY: "He just wrote that."

BUDDY: T-H-A-T?"

ROCKY: "No, keep up. What we're saying!"

BUDDY: "He doesn't understand us."

ROCKY: "No, bird brain, he does. Every single word. It's like he's a bird."

BUDDY: "Sure, look at that hair. I knew it."

ROCKY: "This sucks."

BUDDY: "This totally sucks."

~

BUDDY: "What're they doing now?"

ROCKY: "She's on . . ."

BUDDY: " . . . Facebook, I see it."

ROCKY: "Typing . . ."

BUDDY: " . . . what we're saying, yeah. Where's he?"

ROCKY: "On the porch. Got his . . ."

BUDDY: "Feet up. Laying down on the bench. IT'S A BENCH. YOU'RE SUPPOSED TO SIT, NOT LAY DOWN, BUM!"

ROCKY: "He could at least come in so I can poop on him."

BUDDY: "Not before me you don't."

~

ROCKY: "How do you do that?"

BUDDY: "What?"

ROCKY: "Hang there like that."

BUDDY: "I dunno. I just flew and was like, Wait, that's a door! and I saw the bar and was like, Okay, I have an option. I grabbed on and was like, Look at me, I'm clinging. I cling!"

ROCKY: "Clinging."

BUDDY: "Cling. To cling. Grasp, whatever. Try it."

ROCKY: "I'm scared."

BUDDY: "What, you're not gonna discover it by accident. I already paved that road for you. Yours will be a deliberate flight plan and landing."

ROCKY: "You talk like you worked at an airport."

BUDDY: "You don't know the first thing about me before we got here do you?"

ROCKY: "You never want to talk about it."

∾

BUDDY: "Ask away."

ROCKY: "So you worked in an airport?"

BUDDY: "Do I look like I can carry a suitcase, call someone over the loudspeaker, maybe process someone's tickets? What job is there for a bird? Work at the airport."

ROCKY: "But you •were• at an airport."

BUDDY: "So to speak."

ROCKY: "Cage of shame?"

BUDDY: "Cage of shame. You know, little bird's going to see Aunt Alice with the kid, you're all tucked in under the kid's feet in that little cage big as a shoebox."

ROCKY: "I hate that. I think mine is in the garage."

BUDDY: "Right on top of mine."

ROCKY: "They put a toy in."

BUDDY: "You got a toy? I got like three seeds, no water and they were like, 'Who's going on a plane?' and I'm thinking, What the heck's a plane?"

ROCKY: "Then they call you over, cooing like they do when they're trying to trick you, Nice bird, and wham, they shove you in there and you're like, Wait, this isn't a cage, I'm supposed to stay in here for how long?"

BUDDY: "Told you."

ROCKY: "What?"

BUDDY: "They suck."

ROCKY: "They totally suck."

~

ROCKY: "Jeez, stop making that repetitive screeching sound."

BUDDY: "What? This? REEEE-REEEEE-REEEEE-REEEEE!!!!"

ROCKY: "That's it."

BUDDY: "You don't like it?"

ROCKY: "Not really. Is that even a song?"

BUDDY: "REEEE-REEEEE-REEEEE-REEEEE!!!!"

ROCKY: "Shush."

BUDDY: "Shoe."

ROCKY: "How long 'til they come home?"

BUDDY: "10 hours. REEEE-REEEEE-REEEEE-REEEEE!!!!"

~

ROCKY: "10-letter word 'self-important person.'"

BUDDY: "Panjandrum. When's the mail man come?"

ROCKY: "1/2 hour. 9-letter word, 'excessive words.'"

BUDDY: "Logorrhea. Half-hour! There's the lady & the annoying dog. SCREEEEEECH!"

ROCKY: "My ear! 9-letters again, 'study of algae.'"

BUDDY: "Phycology. REEEEEEEEE!!!!!!!!!"

ROCKY: "Too loud! How do you know all these?"

BUDDY: "I watch Jeopardy, fool. REEEEEEEE!!!!!"

~

Not Really Empty Nesters

Our two youngest children, Adam and Stuart are starting to prepare to leave the nest.

Problem is, even after those two birds have flown, we'll still have two birds in the nest.

Messy, demanding birds that have reached their intellectual and functional peaks, hit them about 7 years ago . . . not getting any smarter, no hope for that. Maybe a little trick or two, or a bad habit or three.

But we're looking at at least 18 more years if Buddy the Domesticated Quaker Parrot hits the top of the actuary tables for his breed in captivity . . . our captivity, not his.

He got out about a year ago, flew right through an unrepaired screen flap at the bottom of your front storm door, Ffffffttttt! he was gone and up and out of sight.

I thought, Why don't they have an invisible fence for birds? Suddenly liking the idea of having a little collar on him and me with some little walkie talkie thing with a knob to turn up and a button to push, maybe sending him a little juice if he starts yacking when I'm on the phone or I catch him popping a squat on the couch cushions or up on the stack of towels.

ZZZZZzzzzt!!!

But I run outside after him, my real feelings there, I don't want to shrug and say, "Oh, wow, Mr. Annoying got away, too bad, boo." Closing the door and I can still hear his wings flapping away.

No, I tore after him hollering his name, BUDDY! BUDDY! and I see him 150 feet up, eclipsing the morning summer sun racing across the blue sky down to the end of the court, looking down at the little squares of the roofs of that U of town homes, all painted the same, and then, like a boomerang, he hooks a tight left turn and banks for return and descent, probably thinking, I don't even know where a

7-Eleven is around here let a alone a place to watch *Jeopardy!* later and he comes back and lands right on the top of the porch swing, panting practically, his little chest working like a bellows from probably the highest he'll ever fly in his little life.

I picked him up, my real feelings right there now, Buddy's Buddy, no many how many times I dragged the trash can over and changed the papers, spray and cleaned the crap off his cage bars, the banister, the towels, the top of the couch cushions or my shirts or the plug on the juicer or God, the top of the cabinets, and I'll guess I'll have to love him for the next 18 years, cupping him and pulling his head right up to my lips to shower him with kisses, him making that purring noise, like he's saying, "Yes, yes, yes, yes, that's the spot. Yes, yes, yes."

No, this nest isn't going to be empty for quite some time.

And I think I'm okay with that.

I think Buddy's made his decision too.

Raspberry Mang-go

KATHY: "Which cheese cake did you get?"

DANNY: "Raspberry Mango."

KATHY: "Say it with the Melodious Lady Voice."

DANNY: "Rasp-berry Mang-go!"

KATHY: "That's it."

BOBBY: "Can I answer the phone that way sometimes?"

DANNY: "With the Raspberry Mango Voice?"

BOBBY: "That's it."

KATHY: "Why not?"

~

BOBBY: "Can I be Mrs. Bobfire?"

DANNY: "Like the movie, but sneak Bobby's name in, right at the beginning, change it a little?"

BOBBY: "Bob-fire. Not Bobby. Yeah, what I'm thinking."

KATHY: "I like it, Mrs. Bobfire. Do the voice again."

BOBBY: "Rasp-berry Mang-go."

DANNY: "That sounded good."

KATHY: "Do it again."

BOBBY: "Rasp-berry Mang-go,"

~

JANE: "Do the voice again!"

BOBBY: "Rasp-berry Mang-go! Your turn."

JANE: "Rasp-berry Mang-go!"

LYNN: "Rasp-berry Mang-go!"

KATHY: "Rasp-berry Mang-go!"

DANNY: "Rasp-berry Mang-go!"

BOBBY: "That wasn't right."

DANNY: "What?"

KATHY: "Not even close."

Exactly Frank

KATHY: "So the accountant, he's doing laconic?"

DANNY: "La who? No, see he's sitting there, half asleep, 60-something years old and all hunched over in his little numbers world, not much of a conversationalist."

KATHY: "Laconic. He's feeding you the dry economical lines, asking about categories, you're looking at your watch thinking, Here we go."

DANNY: Yeah, but let me back up. I get there and he's out front with our folder tucked under his arm . . ."

KATHY: "I can see him. He's in, what, a little dark blue golf shirt?"

DANNY: "Green."

KATHY: "Yeah, and he's got the khakis on, the loafers and he's got that little smile, like, You're late."

DANNY: "I'm five minutes early . . ."

KATHY: "Which gets him there 10 minutes early, otherwise he can't give you the look."

DANNY: "So we're inside and I'm thinking, This guy's not gonna say a word and what do I usually do? Start yammering away, try carrying both ends, him sitting there with the categories."

KATHY: "And you're thinking the yammering's a bust."

DANNY: "A total bust. He doesn't talk and I'm trying to do both sides of the conversation, help him out a little, keep me from getting out a coloring book, waiting for the next fastball at my head about a category. I got a category: Boring. Who's an accountant anyway?"

KATHY: "Not every accountant's Frank."

DANNY: "Yeah, the guy's good. We didn't have Frank, what, I'd be in some cubicle . . ."

KATHY: "Crabbier than you already are."

DANNY: "Right. And you're telling some lady wants copper handles it's an upgrade from the one's in the model home and she's gonna have to pay extra and she's like, "Here, Ill give you a roll of pennies, it's copper, not gold.""

KATHY: "So did you try it?"

DANNY: "What, the yammering? No, I'm thinking, four hours, I better put on my thinking cap."

KATHY: "Your rasta hat?"

DANNY: "The white one with the red, yellow, green stripe. Yeah, helps me think and I decided to turn it around."

KATHY: "Not say word one. Make him uncomfortable. You're the cigar store Indian, your tall, but you don't move, back by the walk-in humidor."

DANNY: "Big Chief Bobby. Folded my arms and everything. Pretended that hat was a war bonnet."

KATHY: "Frank get squirmy?"

DANNY: "No, he doesn't look like he cares, but he starts asking about the family. Pretty soon I'm hearing about his grand daughter. I dunno, maybe he's got this little tricycle he lets her ride in the living room, it scuffs the floor, but Frank's like, 'Who cares? She looks cute.'"

KATHY: "I can see it. He's sitting in his Lazy Boy, got the ball game on and a sleepy eye on her, riding in circles. Grandpa Frank."

DANNY: "And I'm thinking, if it was just me talking, I'd pick something else."

KATHY: "Like he turned it around on you again, like, You're late and now you're stupid."

DANNY: "But not mean about it, just telling it like it is."

KATHY: "Frank."

DANNY: "Exactly. Frank."

LATE FOR GRADUATION

"Part of the secret of success in life is to eat what you like and let the food fight it out inside."

—*Mark Twain*

We went to our son's high school graduation yesterday, made a wrong turn and got him there an unrespectable 15 minutes late, and to our relief, we saw the throngs of kids, moseying in, la-di-dah, walking like they were in no particular hurry . . .

Problem was, I grabbed a take-out container on the way out, take a little food for the road, a snack to tide us over while they're reading off 1,183 names, pop out in the hallway, hunker down on one of those curvy modern couches they had up by the entrance, those names still echoing from the auditorium's open doors, keeping an ear peeled for our kid's name.

I told Danny later that it had the same heft as the identical take out box with the Calzones, but it turns out it was half a strawberry cheesecake, now all smashed up in broken bits, stuck obscenely to every part of the inside of the container's compartments, not lookin' so purdy now.

With a stoic acceptance, he looked at it, and held his hand out, like, Gimme, and I closed the lid and handed it to him grimly, no food for Kathy for 4 hours. Danny's blood sugar, a thing to watch, watch it plummet, him all crabby and tired like some little kid, didn't get lunch or breakfast, his body feeding on itself like it does, whittle him down to a size 2 just in time for swimsuit season.

He slid the box carefully in his little olive drab messenger bag and we saddled up and herded inside with the rest of the parents and late arrivals.

About two hours and 400-some names to go, Danny's on his third trip out to the lobby café. Each time he comes back and sits next to me, I'm looking for little crumbs in his dreads or dusting the front of his patchy hoodie, stuck there in the corduroy, faux dandruff or something.

And, mercifully, those little trips kept him from crashing; I sucked down a snuck-in kombucha (Mystic Mang-go! again with the Mang-go!) and willed my body to not snack on itself. Then, Danny, all happy, got his agave buzz on, all those strawberries shoring up his reserves, maybe getting a little glow in his cheeks, maybe now able to give Bobby a run for the money. Maybe I could just fatten him up and send him back to the dishroom, let Bobby out of the cage, Mr. Seat & Greet, saying things to the customers not in the Waiter Training Manual, no sir.

After Danny gets home, sure, he ate his Calzone, and 3 more, if you're counting. Put away a big salad, thank you, yeah, I'll have another, throw a little avocado on, sprinkle it with dulse, call it a meal.

For 3 people.

Named Danny.

Then, I can't believe it, he jumps up, "Hey, I still got that strawberry shortcake!" Runs upstairs, lifts the flap on the messenger bag and comes down like he found a prize, gonna eat me some more.

Right out of the box. Got my Calzone fork right here, let's not stand on ceremony, no need to get some little baby dessert fork.

Getting all fancy.

Scrapping it off the bottom, the sides and the top, the peaks and valleys of the compartment, gonna get it all.

Half a strawberry shortcake.

Oh my.

Next morning, Mr. Shortcake not feeling so good.

Pound of almond pulp and two cups of cashews and a dozen strawberries starting a little war down in Danny's basement, a little turf war, a sometimes noisy, disturbing, uncomfortable, often embarrassing, visceral battle engaged in all over the world each day by sorry food combiners who overfill themselves with ingredients which disappear from view and thrash it out inside to determine, just for the day, who will be king of the colon . . .

All those nuts.

Look at him, walking a little slower.

A little less pep in the step.

The jokes, a little slow. Come on, keep up, son.

His mind, maybe a little preoccupied with that unforgiving woman that lives in us all, the sovereign queen of gastrointestinal distress, Indie . . . Indie Gestion.

KATHY: "Don't we tell our customers it's not good to overeat?"

DANNY: "Mix it up, don't have to much of the one thing."

KATHY: "No pressure to finish the plate."

DANNY: "All those nutrients, filling you up, sending the Leptin flare up from the stomach, Whoa pardner, we're good, stop eatin.'"

KATHY: "Push away from the table."

DANNY: "Not one more bite."

KATHY: "It's like we're talking to ourselves."

DANNY: "And we're speaking German, can't understand a word."

KATHY: "Untrainable."

DANNY: "The dumb kids."

KATHY: "Back of the classroom, talking and goofing around, getting dirty looks from the teacher."

DANNY: "That was you, wasn't it?"

KATHY: "It was."

DANNY: "We got in a lot of trouble back then."

KATHY: "We were just kids."

DANNY: "Having fun, though."

KATHY: "More than our share."

DANNY: "Making up for the dour kids."

KATHY: "The book worms."

DANNY: "Eyes front."

KATHY: "Got my finger on the words, following along."

DANNY: "Lips moving. And we're in the back."

KATHY: "Corner farthest from the door, got the view of the whole room."

DANNY: "Like the catcher."

KATHY: "Squatting behind the plate. Fingers making signals."

DANNY: "Just the one finger really."

KATHY: "We haven't changed a bit."

DANNY: "No need to."

KATHY: "Are we in the front now?"

DANNY: "So to speak. But it's like we're in the back too, still gettin' in trouble."

KATHY: "Because we're bored."

DANNY: "More like we're philosophers."

KATHY: "And comedians."

DANNY: "I always wanted to be a comedian."

KATHY: "See how that works?"

DANNY: "I never thought I'd marry the girl I was goofing around with."

KATHY: "It's like it was meant to be."

"Bard Earth Ca-fe"

KATHY: "Ugh, my feet . . ."

DANNY: "Everything's done. Go sit in the car. I'll finish mopping."

KATHY: "Thanks."

DANNY: "Call if you think of something else to bring home."

5 minutes later

BOBBY: "Bard Earth Ca-fe."

KATHY: "Tell Danny to bring home a cupcake."

BOBBY: "Danny's not here . . ."

KATHY: "Hush."

VISITING THE SCENE OF THE CRIME

Last night, we visited the scene of the crime, our private think tank, refuge, meditation center, musical stage, breakfast nook, lunch spot, outdoor café, family therapy office, park, vista, garden . . .

The place where we first "cooked" the idea of opening a restaurant.

I know I wrote on our website that it happened when we were driving to a raw food restaurant in the city—true, the idea popped in that little beige Toyota Corolla, Why don't we just open our own place? It was said, for sure, I was there, here we were just going to, some place on a Friday night and it's an back-busting 90-minute trip, all to have a quick meal and get back in the car and go home, crazy yeah, we thought, why are we driving this far for something to eat which we could make at home, the age old conundrum and here we're stupid enough to decide the best solution to the problem is to open our own restaurant.

Consider people who would do that.

Like a guy who takes his family to the zoo. Afterwards, he doesn't turn around in the van in the parking lot after and say, Hey, I'm thinking we could get some animals, maybe put up some pens in the house and the backyard, I don't know, I'm thinking an elephant and a donkey at least, they get along, right? Save us all this driving. We can charge a little money. Whadaya say kids, who wants to open our VERY OWN ZOO?

Not normal people.

Not even close.

These are masochists.

People who sit on a porch, have a little conversation, arrange some food pretty on a plate . . .

. . . Say, that tastes good, ma'am, you say it's raw?

. . . Food you bring it and pass around on plates, then, everybody eats, there's a lot of talking and laughing and Danny says things that I want him to publish, him not getting around to it just yet, still content leaking it out in little bits on Facebook, in email, a shotgun approach more, not wadding it into a single cartridge, shoot it into a book, get some legs on all those words . . .

You run a couple courses out, the people looking up from the bench there or a lawn chair, wherever they find themselves. Hey look, Danny's handing me another plate of food, and I'm laughing about something or another and everyone's having a good time.

So, you're thinking, Why not just spend the whole day doing this?

Two or three times a month, have someone over for the weekend, Sit down, we made something we think you'll like . . . it's not enough.

Sure there's cleaning and dishes.

A little extra work.

But it's worth it.

Sitting out on that porch, having a grand ole time.

You're like this entertainment glutton, I wanna do the people / food thing all day long, let's stop screwing around with the day jobs, Danny, you're not getting any younger, and I have had my fill of sitting in front of a computer, writing out specs, listening to some lady go on about the cabinet handles, Should I get the brass one with the thing on it or do you like this one, looks like a spoon?

All those nights, sitting out on that porch, laughing, eating, swatting mosquitoes and talking about things you thought you were going to say if you ever get around to seeing someone to talk to about things you don't usually bring up but boy it feels good, like sighing, finally letting it out in the air, not so big and scary now, traveling up into the night 1000 feet beyond the porch, settling in with the clouds and scattering out amongst the stars, taking a long ride to the end of the Universe, a little speck now really, putting it in a better perspective maybe, that speck, then that big endless thing that doesn't have a fence, an end of the Universe wall.

Finally, you get there at the base of the wall and stand and look at it, sure, says it right there, END OF THE UNIVERSE.

And you start wondering what's on the other side of that wall.

The place where your imagination ends and it feels a little scary.

So, you find a ladder.

Carry it over and put it up against the end of the Universe wall.

CLUNK!

And you look up and take that first step up, a little two-handed pull up.

And another.

And another.

Pretty soon, you're up top. You swing your legs over and sit up top.

You see absolute Nothingness.

It's not dark and it's not white.

It's clear.

Nothing to see.

And it's quiet.

Nothing to hear.

No refrigerator hum or car noise in the distance.

No little bird on your shoulder, working a seed and watching you type.

No noise at all.

So quiet, you don't even think about talking.

Nothing to see, nothing to hear, nothing to say . . .

And then, nothing to think about.

You're just right here, wherever you are right now.

You close your eyes and a little smile plays on your lips and you don't ever remember feeling this relaxed and happy.

Then, even that thought drifts away and you're just in this Nothingness and you're not the least bit concerned, just sitting there on top of the wall, sucking it up.

And you realize that there's nowhere else to go.

No one to become.

You're already who you are ever going to be and who you've always been and it has nothing to do with your history, your story, all the things you've thought, felt and had happen to you.

All your accomplishments.

And all that you didn't accomplish.

It doesn't mean anything.

It never did, you just now getting that.

And that's okay.

There's no reason to become somebody; that would mean you aren't already something terrific.

A person, taking breaths in and out.

Each moment precious.

Just as it comes.

Not filtered through the past.

Not held up against someone's "story" and judged, compared, criticized, feared, worried about, grieved over, dismissed as nonsenses or any million other distractions.

This is the peaceful place you slip into when you finally get to sleep.

When you go out side and take in a breath and feel the sun on your face and close your eyes and smile.

Pure feeling without thoughts or words attached.

This great big feeling that's nothing to feel . . .

. . . nothing to feel but good.

The Greatest Treasure in Life is Found in the Place You are Most Afraid to Go . . .

DANNY: "You're a good writer, too. Why don't we put something you wrote in the book?"

KATHY: "A recipe?"

DANNY: "Don't start with the recipes again. No, I'm thinking . . ."

KATHY: "The thing I wrote on Mother's Day?"

DANNY: "That's my girl."

KATHY: "You wrote that."

DANNY: "No, you told me the story, in little pieces over seven years. The picture? Well, I've looked at that 100's of times. I can close my eyes and tell you what I see."

KATHY: "Has it been seven years?"

DANNY: "My math, not Bobby's."

KATHY: "Yeah, otherwise with the finger counting. Wow, seven years. Wait, seven. Isn't that what you got on your ACT in Math? One less than the guessing monkey holding the pencil with the rubber grip, making sure his fingers hold it right, filling in the circles. Okay, I started something in a message to someone on Facebook."

DANNY: "And you got up from the chair in the kitchen and asked me to read it, and I said, Can I add something? And you're like, Go ahead. But all those details are your words. I just added a little House Dressing. But then you got the big idea to post it on Mother's Day. You know, I think that monkey got lucky. Maybe he wasn't high . . ."

KATHY: "The Mother's Day thing, yeah, that was big. It still makes me a little nervous, thinkin' about it. Hey, I like that, House Dressing."

DANNY: "Yeah, you were scared, but you did it anyway. Go Oklahoma. Yes, the *green sauce*."

KATHY: "I love when people say that, *[with southern accent]* 'What's the green sauce, ma'am?'"

DANNY: "Nice Bobby voice. More like the secret sauce."

KATHY: "So, you're thinking, If you put it on Facebook for 2,000 of your Friends to read, why not put it in a book? That makes me nervous."

DANNY: "You said I make you nervous."

KATHY: "Yeah, when I leave you alone. No, not that kind of nervous. Scary feelings nervous."

DANNY: "Scary feelings nervous? Is that a sentence?"

KATHY: "Listen to you, Mr. Fragment. Scary feelings nervous. You know what I mean."

DANNY: "So, I can put the Mother's Day thing in?"

KATHY: "Knock yourself out."

DANNY: "Are you really my girl?"

So here it is, the thing I am most afraid to write about. But, there's been this little voice in my head saying, Share your story, someone is waiting to hear it, don't be scared . . . close eyes, deep breath, push send . . .

Here goes.

The places life takes you.

It's been over 12 years since my mom passed away. Her death was a rebirth for me and in a weird way, a final gift from her.

Would I be here in this place if my mom were still alive? Would I have had the courage to make the changes I've made in my life or take the risks I've taken if she were still alive?

I ask myself these questions at times.

My Mom and I had what one would call a "turbulent" relationship; lots of shared mother/daughter time; some of it good, but lots of it bad. There was fighting, controlling, co-dependent dysfunctional family stuff, periods of silence and withdrawal, awkwardness and then we'd be back again, pretending everything was okay.

She would get in these dark moods and she would get mad at me for the littlest things and I felt like I was walking on eggshells at times.

I have two brothers, but neither of them had the relationship I had with my mom. I felt like she gave me a part of herself that a mother only can give to a daughter and we shared these wonderful moments. I remember lying on the bed watching her fold laundry and having these wonderful talks . . .

And then, something small, like leaving a cup by the sink or a drawer partly open would set her off and it was like a big storm had suddenly rolled in.

I have a picture I cherish: Me and my Mom sitting on an ugly flowered green sofa, she's got this slim white and blue wide striped pants on, the big colorful belt, the fitted t-shirt just right on her slender frame, her hair pulled back. I'm a little slumped over to one side and I've got this yellow long sleeve t-shirt on, a puff of brown frizzy shoulder length hair, my buck front teeth arranged into this big goofy grin and I'm looking up at my Mom like I'm looking into the center of the whole universe. She's got her arm around me and you can see the slightest hint of a smile.

She's looking down at me with so much love I still get emotional looking at that picture.

That's me and my Mom and at the center of our universe, beneath all the swirling planets and stars and beauty and cruelty and kindness, the aching confusion, the fights and the tension and then the blessed relief when the silence ended and we carried on until the next time.

All of it, the sweetness, the drama, the tension and the reconciliations, all of it made up the world I knew as a child and then as an adult.

IT all started in my teens.

As the years went by the relationship became more strained, guarded, distant, unpredictable and absolutely frustrating and painful.

I know my mom's parents forced her little sister's care on her and she was denied a lot of the enjoyment of being a teenager . . . and maybe when I became a teenager, all that hurt and resentment smoldering inside her came up to the surface. Maybe unable to forgive her own parents, who were, no doubt, victims of victims of victims. That strain and dysfunction became like a family heirloom passed down in the family like some horrible knick knack that sits on the end table in every living room.

Maybe when I got to the age of the hurt little girl inside her, that monster of anger, sorrow and pain was awakened and when she saw my life and compared it to hers, she was mad. Maybe in order to forgive her mom, she had to become her. Without a little sister to take care of, my mom grounded me, keeping me from going out a life like the one she'd been denied. My friends joked that I was always grounded. It was like, looking back, my mom wanted me to suffer the longing and separation from a normal social life that she'd suffered. She was kept under house arrest, apart from a teenage life outside the home, saddled with the care of her younger sister. With no sister to care for, my mom created impossibly complex and random rules and infractions that I could never follow (and I doubt she could either) which resulted in my own house arrest.

They say you can forgive someone sympathetically, using your heart and reason to let go the wrong another does to you.

Or you can hold onto the resentment and anger, not forgiving and the hurt sows itself like a seed in your heart. Later, the body begging for release, you begin to act out those same qualities.

Now, you are presented with another opportunity to forgive. This time, your forgiveness is empathetic. You have become what you could not forgive . . . and so, in order to forgive yourself, you must forgive them . . . and maybe you start to see that this business is trickier than you thought when you were little. Not so much a matter of selectively being nice or cruel at all, but something deeper and more complicated, tied up in our own past and present.

I remember about a year before my mom died, I was still living in the UK, married to an Englishman I'd met in my home town, with two small boys. I was all grown up and out on my own (had been since 18 when I moved out to get away from *IT*). My parents were visiting and tension was high and the house became too small. I needed to remove myself from the house and it's constricting feeling.

I left my husband and boys to entertain my mom and dad for a while and drove over to my best friend's house to take a few minutes to breathe, have a cup of tea and talk to an understanding friend.

It was there, sitting on my friend Kathy's sofa that my life began to really transform. I said to her, "I don't know what it is, but this I do know: whatever needs to be fixed between me and my mom cannot be fixed until she heals something within herself."

It was there with Kathy, her dog Kissy and a cup of tea that I became at peace with the fact that my Mom was my mom and there was nothing I could do to change the situation, no reason to be angry about it, it just was and there in that moment I made peace with who I was, who she was, our faults, differences and love for each other. I also in many ways said goodbye to her.

A person can't love anyone unless they love themselves first. I didn't understand this until a few years later. What I also did not know was that my mom was suffering from depression and had been for so many years.

In 1998, a year later, I got a phone call from my brother in Tulsa. I was sitting at the dining room table in my home in Sussex, England, the boys were playing in the next room and the boys' father was out running errands. "Kathy, Dad just called. Mom is dead. She'd been missing for two days and they just found her. She took an overdose of pills, no note, no hint, no warning. Dad didn't want to call you until he knew where she was . . . you being so far away and everything. I'm leaving for Colorado today and I'll see you there."

Life in that moment changed forever.

Suicide is still such a taboo subject and often leaves families feeling ashamed and holding a sense of guilt and responsibility.

First, the questions come. How did I not know? I should have seen the signs . . . I could have done something.

Then, comes the anger . . . and more questions. How could she? What about me? And finally, getting to it:

That was selfish.

Not really understanding how they could do this, so you start from your own selfish place—how this is affecting you—and paradoxically, from your own selfish place you see their final act as selfish.

Trying to find a reason for something so unreasonable.

Support from family and friends, when someone in your inner circle commits suicide is one thing: awkward.

Cancer, heart attacks, tragic car crashes . . . these are much more acceptable forms of death.

Like there's this unwritten pecking order of acceptable deaths, all stacked up . . . down at the bottom: Suicide.

Don't do it. Don't talk about it.

Someone tells you that there mom has died, gosh, I'm so sorry.

She committed suicide?

Excuse me, I just remembered somewhere else I need to be.

When a loved one dies of suicide it becomes something like a contagious disease, something best not talked about or mentioned for fear that they might catch it too.

A shame. An embarrassment.

Your mom kills herself and people start looking at you like you have a bomb strapped to your chest . . .

And after all the dust settles and you think you can breathe again even though this new bigger *IT* some times at the oddest moments still can sneak up behind you and tap you on the shoulder and you turn to ice inside, a hand reaches in and grips your heart too tight and squeezes and all the air hisses out of you and the grief is suddenly overwhelming like it just happened.

And there you are, looking up at her with that big grin on your face, at the center of universe for the little girl in you . . . and now she's not there again and you feel yourself suddenly deflate into an awful hollowness that hurts deep in your bones.

But as time goes by, the whole thing feels like that awful moment in your sleep, when your terror is at it's worst, that moment when suddenly you find that you are awakening.

In her life, I think the one think my Mom felt good about, the thing that gave her joy, was being the teacher.

She was a good one.

What she couldn't give me, her own daughter, she was able to give to others.

I think her own childhood waged war in her and at home, when she was being my mom, all those demons she tried to suppress would come out.

Some how, at school, her own reason prevailed and she gave those kids her best.

So, my Mom the teacher . . . what final lesson did she leave for me?

If I want her best, I needed to understand what she was trying to teach me.

I believed she loved me the best she could and no matter what, I have that picture to remind me that her own failings as a mother, as my own failings as a mother, weigh more heavily on a mother's heart. The child longs for the return of the feeling of basking in her mother's love . . . but even later, the mother may carry the shadow of guilt in her own heart. Forgiven by her daughter, but unable to forgive herself maybe.

What we are when we are little, still inside, demanding a reckoning, the voice of reason though, growing softer and softer beneath our own pain.

Was I willing to learn from this or simply go on and like her, pretend everything is fine on the outside, when inside? I wasn't happy and the struggle to hold all that in was becoming greater than my fear of actually doing something to change things?

Everything was not fine and perfect and it seems like a whole lot of people in my life were also pretending that everything was fine and perfect. In the year 2000, we moved back to America, back to a land where pretending everything is fine and perfect is practiced even more. I went along pretending and playing the game for another year and then decided, I didn't want to play anymore.

I wanted to learn from my mom, accept her final gift, and make her proud. My life was not what I wanted, and I admitted to myself an awful truth: I was in unhappy, verbally abusive, co-dependent marriage.

My life? Just an extension of my childhood and teen years now.

Something I created . . .

I found someone who would continue to treat me the way I felt I deserved to be treated, creating an interplay of love and anger and silence and the quiet slip back into pretending, no one ever talking about what they are really feeling. So I spent the bulk of my time feeling afraid and noticed that my sons' father and I were finding more reasons to avoid each other. Spending more time outside the home. Noticing that feeling of dread inside when I heard heard his car pull in the garage. Him probably doing the same.

The house like a powder keg.

All of it.

What was I teaching my boys about relationships?

I knew somewhere deep inside of me that if I didn't make some changes, I was going to end up like my mom. Not that I would also commit suicide in the classic way, but in a much more acceptable way, get cancer, die of a heart attack . . . acceptable deaths and ones that can be caused and grown by fear, unhappiness and stress.

But, when it was the worst, I did think about taking my life and this was after she was gone . . .

God help me . . . maybe I had to get that low to understand the place she must have found herself.

But I was given just enough strength to turn away from that awful Door.

Today, I realize that my mom loved me as best she could. She was the best parent she could be with what tools she had. She made the greatest sacrifice and left me the ultimate gift. Do I wish there was another way? Do I wish my mom was here today to see my beautiful boys grow up, meet my wonderful new husband, visit our restaurant, eat our food, get a hug.

Of course I do, but would I be here?

Would I be in this place had her own tragic end not awakened me from a bad dream . . .

I wonder . . .

~

DANNY: "Wow. I love you."

KATHY: "Hush."

EARNEST WAKENER'S SECRET

"Science says we are 75% water and 25% soluble matter, but maybe I'm neither the water or the soluble matter or a man who lives and dies . . . maybe I exist in the Space in and around the water and the soluble matter . . . in the field of energy which is the canvas upon which what I see exists, hearing myself say, Hello! You were sleeping, I didn't want to wake you . . ."—Earnest Wakener

Our friend, poet and philosopher, Earnest Wakener told me that every time he feels really good, first thing, he wants to share that good feeling, spread it around.

He said, "One day I woke up and thought of something, something wonderful, and I felt really happy—I just had to tell someone.

"So, I went to work. I smiled at everyone I saw. I did everything I could to be kind and I said yes to each task that presented itself, doing them without hesitation. I tried to help each person I encountered.

"Sometimes, as the day went on, I would just feel this calm, happy peace settle over me and I'd take a breath in and out and this little smile would play across my lips. I remember making a lot of people laugh.

"It was like being in on this wonderful secret. Like there was this joy bubbling up from a fountain deep inside me."

He paused, and smiled to himself, nodding a little like he was right back there, remembering that moment, feeling that fountain inside him again, then he handed me a plate of food he'd prepared for me while we were talking.

'Here you go," he said. "Enjoy.

It was delicious!

"Wow," I said, "What's in this?"

"Fresh salad greens, romaine lettuce, kale, fennel, a little dill, red onions, sprouts, some sea vegetables, hemp seed oil, avocado chunks, sliced tomato . . ." he said, pointing at each thing as he spoke.

"Good?" he asked.

I nodded.

I looked at the plate and took another bite. The food seemed to glow with something from Earnest himself, that joy he was talking about and was trying to share. With each bite, I could feel something, small at first, but then growing, a feeling, a good one, spreading inside me . . .

"So who did you tell that day?" I asked.

He was watching me and I looked into his eyes, twinkling now and suddenly, a little thin pool rimmed up under his eyes, almost ready to spill out into tears and he pressed his lips together and his chin quivered.

"I told everyone," he said in a hoarse voice.

"Tell me." I said expectantly.

He pointed his chin at my plate.

"I just did," he said in a whisper.

ENOUGH

> *"commitment is emptying all your pockets prying your fingers loose from all the things you've convinced yourself are okay to hold on to when you really know they're really not commitment isn't a hard forward motion of the body it's a gentle one-by-one letting go and an honest ear to the voice inside that never lies"*—*Danonymous*

You know, someone talked to us seriously yesterday about Franchising (and I use the capital F deliberately) . . . serious talk, earnest tones, leaned forward, I Mean Business, Pardner.

"Have you thought about Franchising . . . ?"

Not a question, but a statement

Like they're turning over the 53rd card in the deck . . .

A card they bet you never thought existed.

The King of Wallets . . . .

. . . depicted as a stern-faced sovereignty, topped with a black men's fedora hat set at a jaunty angle, winking lewdly at you, two-dimensionally, on the slick card face. He's got a fistful of dollars in one hand and he appears to be reaching into someone's pocket with the other. He's in a black $2,200 fitted suit, fitted around a belly betraying an insatiable appetite for more . . . that winking eye squinting around a fat cigar clinched in his teeth . . .

The Modern Pirate . . .

Not sailing around in a ship to loot, pillage and plunder.

No, this King drives a black H2 Hummer with a grill that looks like a grinning chrome set of shark's teeth, the vanity plate tells it all:

GIMME

A Taker all the way.

We nod as if we're interested, like we always do . . .

. . . until they finish The Pitch . . .

Then we tell them politely that one is Enough.

Enough.

A nearly extinct idea in the Era of More . . . unless it's preceded by the word not.

Not enough.

More.

Gimme.

Maybe this Jesus, when he talked about Daily Bread, meant Enough. Just for the day.

Not a bread factory.

Enough to keep me going.

Enough for my family.

Not a franchise on stuff or a stockpile to last for 100 generations of Me and Mine, but Enough.

Enough to keep a modest, non-leaking roof over my head, pay for groceries and have a little in the bank in case the car needs to be fixed.

Just enough.

Enough so we can focus on serving other people without being worried or distracted.

Enough so we learn to trust that the daily bread will show up if we keep doing what feels right and true for ourselves in our situation without feeling like the King of Wallets, playing a game that we can't stop playing . . . the Quest for More Than Enough.

Trying to fill the hunger that is never satisfied.

But just being happy with Enough.

And feeling satisfied and content.

Enjoying what you already have and who you already are, right now, not putting those feelings off until the future, a future that you hope contains a sense of accomplishment for something that might never come.

Feeling good . . .

Right here.

Right where you are.

Right who you are.

Right now.

SILENCE

"A man has to learn that he cannot command things, but that he can command himself; that he cannot coerce the wills of others, but that he can mold and master his own will: and things serve him who serves Truth; people seek guidance of him who is master of himself."—James Allen

"Teachers open the door. You enter by yourself."—Chinese proverb

"Like a silent messenger bearing inward, the food stole into my very essence and spoke in a quiet whisper: I love you."—Danny Living

KATHY: "Hello. Did you just sign that?"

DANNY: "James Allen or Chinese Proverb? Yeah, I'm thinking of changing my name. Do you like Kathy Allen or Kathy Proverb?"

KATHY: "How about Kathy Living? Look, I've given you free reign up until now. It says, dash Danny Living. The poem one."

DANNY: "Coulda been Bobby, forged my name, used the computer when I was away like he does. So, rein me in, like I'm a horse? Does this mean you're still riding?"

KATHY: "So to speak. Reign, not rein or rain. It's a homonym. Let's just say I'm walking with you down the Path. I'm thinking just a few recipes."

DANNY: "It all sounds like rain. So, we throw a bone to the people we've been putting off for 3 years and nearly 300 pages. The people who say, 'When ya' gonna have a recipe book?' Or the publisher's like, 'Uh, I need 15 more pages and you get a refrigerator magnet or you're like, I'm sick of searching Older Posts, all that copying and pasting, let's throw in a few recipes for ballast, keep the book from floating off.'"

KATHY: "Did someone ask that question?"

DANNY: "'When ya' gonna have a book?' Ha! 1000 times."

KATHY: "So now we are gonna have recipes."

DANNY: "How about one more chapter on silence. Then we do the recipes. The recipes, though, it's like, in the Appendix. The thing they can take out and you still live."

KATHY: "More like the tonsils . . . don't put it down there."

DANNY: "I get your logic, I think. The appendix is down there and the tonsils are in the back. Like, the back of the book. In the mouth, 'cause it's a food place, but in the back, hanging there all useless and waiting to get infected, poor kid gets all that ice cream. Keep 'em above the belt, up by the mouth. Stay away from down there. Got it."

KATHY: "See, now you're trying to make tonsils sound bad."

DANNY: "I still have mine. Wanna see? Wait, so, free reign?"

KATHY: "I'll pass on the tonsil check. Okay Pony Boy. One more chapter. Then it's recipe time."

DANNY: "Pony Boy?"

KATHY: "Okie talk."

BOBBY: "Shoot, why'nt you say we was down South?"

KATHY: "Yeah, but we're in the library. You know, the big building with the books you avoid."

BOBBY: "Like the plague."

KATHY: "Give it wide berth."

BOBBY: "A city block's what I prefer. Got me a Kindle. Who needs the library?"

~

After many years of trying to tell people about being vegetarian, vegan, raw and not getting anywhere, except for apparently offending someone or making them uncomfortable or upset, we came to the conclusion that talking about food was nearly useless.

It didn't work.

We tell people who take our classes, come to our restaurant or any of the vegan/vegetarian people in our personal lives who tell us their own experiences of trying to share their lifestyle with the non-vegan/vegetarian people in their lives (including friends, families and co-workers) that the best way to promote being vegan, vegetarian or even raw . . . is to say nothing.

You mean, don't say anything?

Yes, you heard me.

It breaks down like this: Your pie hole is an ineffectual tool to try and get someone else to change what's going in their pie hole.

You would be surprised how difficult it can be for a well-meaning person to simply observe the people in their lives—what they do, including what food choices they make—and simply accept those people as they are, where they are, including the food choices they make—even if you know that the choices they are making are hurting them, animals or the Planet.

After all, who are we?

Who appoints us our brother's (and sister's) keeper?

I think the original use of that came when God was looking for Abel, knowing he was in a shallow grave over next to the rhododendrons the whole time, checking in with Cain, a guy whose foot was trying to brush twigs over the bloody club or whatever and he says to God, "Am I my brother's keeper?"

Keeper. Like the people tasked with feeding the animals at the zoo.

Most of the animals in your life on two legs can feed themselves without a lecture.

Food is such a personal choice. In fact, a person's food choices are so uniquely personal that when you try and *tell* someone about why you make *your* food choices it is nearly impossible to not offend them . . . even if they ask.

"So, why are you vegan?"

Our first impulse is to inhale deeply, arrange our thoughts and launch into The Case for the Vegan Diet, which includes snippets from our own story, citations from nutritional authorities, quotes from books, all delivered in a oratory worthy of a pulpit.

Absolutely, totally, worthless and ineffective.

What makes us so sure?

Well, four years of hard, front-line, first-hand data.

Seeing husbands dragged in by the ear, sitting there with folded arms, "I ain't eatin' salad," the thought bubble, the wife going on about nutrition and diet and health and he's thinking, "What'd I do? You're all on the muscle."

The meal fraught with tension.

The guy doesn't have a chance.

He likes the food and it's like admitting she's right if he says so. So he doesn't. He's a jerk that doesn't care about himself, not quite as good as her.

Sure, he's got a little gut, but do you mean I can't have a burger once in a while?

Slow down.

Food is such an important part of our lives, physical and social, that when we try and inform someone about their food choices we can invariably hurt them, because what they hear is that if you disapprove of the food I eat, you disapprove of me.

It's impossible to reject something a person eats, which biologically becomes part of their physical form following digestion (even if it goes to fat cells on their butt) and not imply that you are rejecting a part of them.

The most powerful way to reach people is to say nothing at all. Just lead by silent example.

Bring a dish to your next family event and challenge yourself to do something different, and don't tell anyone that it is raw, vegan or vegetarian. Don't say a word, just set it down on the buffet and take your seat, son.

No need to sound the vegetarian trumpet: TA-DAH. "Attention everyone, if I could have your attention. This dish, right here, is a fine example of organic goodness. All the digestive enzymes have been carefully preserved and the nutrients, by God, they're still intact. You'll notice an increase in your vitality even while you're chewing it."

If you've already established a pattern of showing up and pointing to your dish and announcing it's vegan/vegetarianess and ethical qualities, be patient, as it might take months or years for your family and friends to "forget" your earlier (well-meaning) attempts to "help" them and "educate" them.

Just show up with food and serve people.

This is not advice or suggestions but simply our experiences.

We serve and encounter hundreds of people in a day, at times, and so we've had far more experience than we would have had if we'd simply not opened a restaurant. All these 1000's of people, coming from different walks of "food life" have shown us what approach is most effective.

I know this sounds funny and counterintuitive, but we really think that, absent commentary by the human serving it, the food itself silently goes into the person and talks to them at some level that we don't understand.

Many people will eat at the restaurant over and over and suddenly tell us that they're reading The China Study and that they're eating more vegetables, fruits, nuts and seeds and less animals products all on their own. Those people who have the self-discovery that's not prompted by an already vegetarian / vegan person's talking to them or convincing them of something seem to "stick" or stay in the food choice category of non-animal products.

That's what you want, isn't it?

So, Einstein said that the definition of insanity is trying the same thing over and over and expecting a different result. Not to imply that anyone is crazy here, but I think what Einstein meant is, try different things until you discover something that works, rather than repeating the same method over and over.

We've found that saying nothing and simply serving the food works.

As much as we can see ourselves feeling a sense of accomplishment and pride in "converting" someone through our words, it seems that that method is least effective—and if the "goal" is to see more people embracing a vegan diet, then we say, use the tool that works best.

Food served silently.

"Hey, I made brownies for everyone!"

Or better yet, set them down and say nothing

Every time you're tempted to say something, take a bite and trust the food.

Probably the biggest gift we got from the restaurant was this discovery.

I wish I could say that it happened in the first week.

It didn't.

It took some time before we noticed that the self-discovery / silent food service thing was the secret.

We've shared "the secret" with many people in the restaurant who were trying to help family and friends and we've heard that those people had similar positive results when they stopped talking about the food and their beliefs.

Since they agreed the goal was to have those people in their lives consider a change, they decided to try the way we discovered.

Know though that in some cases, there will be those who may never try it.

Most of our family circle is comprised of omnivores—including three of our four children—and we say nothing.

No one is a "better" person than the next person solely based on diet alone.

What makes us unique is our uniqueness—stop trying to get everyone to be just like you. How boring would that be?

Goodness is a product of our service and our ability to receive and give love freely, in our opinion, without sprinkling in our own "stuff."

Which means loving people where they're at . . . and ourselves too. It's easy to get distracted from your own Path if you've made it your job to be Mapquest for everyone else, Here, let me tell you how to get there.

We're all already here, Magellan.

They know how we eat—and we know how they eat.

Someone told us once that when we try to convince people of something, it means that we ourselves are not convinced. He said, "When you are sure of something, you will no longer need to tell people about it."

Food is magnetic, meaning, the more you eat of something, the more your body will crave it.

We both remember our first taste of coffee. We both agree we thought it to be nasty, bitter stuff. "What's all the grown-up fuss about?" we wondered.

Later, we drank it every day and loved the taste.

The more we ate raw vegan food, the more coffee started to taste nasty and bitter.

What happened?

We remember that when we were little, our parents cut up our meat in tiny little pieces. We remember that we didn't like it—too chewy and not very good.

Later, we ate meat all the time.

The more vegetables and fruit we ate, the more meat started to lose its appeal.

What happened?

The food, we think, must do something to your bio-chemistry.

The more you eat meat or drink coffee, for instance, the more you'll acquire a taste for it.

Taste, acquired or otherwise, seems more to do with the body than the brain.

Bobby always uses his Uncle Jed as an example. His uncle has diabetes.

We ask this question at our class: Do you think that when the doctor told him that it was his diet of processed food, pizza, sweets and beer that contributes to his diet that his uncle said "You're kidding?"

He knows all that but continues to eat all that.

Maybe Bobby's uncle will outlive us all. So, who are we to point and say, "Hey, don't eat that!"

It is, after all, his choice.

I think Bobby's aunt and family tell him to not eat this and not eat that because they care about him.

So, in a weird way (think about it), they've trained him. If Bobby's uncle wants to know if the family cares about him, all he has to do is reach for a cookie.

Can you see that?

In a weird way, if he starts eating healthy, he risks losing all the attention, even if it's for something he's doing that's harmful.

Or maybe he's tried healthy and the way he's eating suits him just fine, Y'all can have your salad, I'm happy with a sandwich.

Which is perfectly okay.

People's reasons for doing things can be complicated, but they're their reasons and we say, respect them.

Silence it truly the best.

We have many people come into the café.

Some are raw and most are not. Most are omnivores. Once in awhile, someone will go over to the hamburger place next store to get their kid a burger and fries and bring it back to Borrowed Earth to eat it with the rest of the family who is eating raw. We smile and say nothing. 95% of the time the kid or person who was eating the cooked food will try something off their mom's plate or order dessert and then come back for another visit and eat our food and skip the burger and fries next door.

Try eating the way you are quietly—and say nothing. See if you don't see a little more peace in your life, which is all we are really looking for anyway.

DISEASE DUCK, DUCK, GOOSE!

I've read that 75% of people would rather die than change their diet.

Take their chances with their current lifestyle vs. try something new requiring energy in a new direction—worried about friend and family friction.

So, they coast along, hoping not to get tagged in a game I call, *Disease Duck, Duck, Goose!*

Holding their breath as the disease circles them and all the people in their lives . . .

Duck, duck, duck, duck..

Hoping not to get tagged, have to get up and run in a circle, not sure if they can beat that disease and get back to where they'd been. Not wanting to be the goose.

SHOULD WE PUT RECIPES IN THE BOOK?

Cultural Anthropologist and plastic turtle collector Rudy Wakening calls this the Age of Culinary Darwinism. "People eating fast food, drinking soda and not reading ingredient labels are dragging their knuckles," he says in a somber baritone.

KATHY: "When are we gonna put in the recipes? I thought you said next."

DANNY: "Soon."

KATHY: "What things should we put in?"

DANNY: "Breakfasty, Lunchy and Dinnery or more Deserty?"

KATHY: "Can't you use the regular words?"

DANNY: "Now you're reining me in again."

Wouldn't It Be Nice?

Okay, that's the first line of a Beach Boys song, but stay with me.

Imagine living in a place where you breathe clean air, drink clean water and live in a temperate climate, which allowed year-round access to fruits, vegetables, nuts and seeds, organically grown, right outside your sustainable, eco-friendly hut . . .

[Soft, relaxing Hawaiian music begins to play]

The only work we'd do is to take care of our families and ourselves. Education would consist of learning to identify plants that are edible, food preparation, environmental care, story telling, singing, musical instruments, empathetic listening, yoga, meditation and play.

When was the last time you played?

You'd live in small community of friendly happy people. Everyone sings and laughs and dances and is happy to be alive. People are quick with a smile and always willing to stop for a hug and or to invite you over for a delicious meal.

People would walk outside barefoot and select what they wanted to eat: fresh, organic produce from their local environment, available when they were hungry. There would be enough variety to fill people with all the vitamins and minerals they needed to live to be 120-plus years, disease-free and with all their teeth and not a gray hair in sight.

Stress . . . does not exist.

[Abrupt sound of scratching needle across a record album]

Okay, enough dreaming.

In the world we live in, I think we need to do the best we can.

Since this is about food, let's focus on the food. It's our hope that the fact that you're reading still means that you're maybe thinking about supplementing your weekly food choices with something different . . . maybe try some foods that are relatively simple to prepare, foods that'll keep for a few days in the refrigerator and give you a wide variety of options for getting plenty of tasty, easy-to-make food in your stomach.

Variety is the Spice of Life

Plan at least two trips to the grocery store each week, and try and buy different foods as the seasons change—man, don't get stuck in that rut of buying the same thing every time. For example, instead of purchasing the apples and pineapple that you enjoyed earlier in the week, reach for oranges and peaches.

Explore your store's produce section and pick up things that you have never seen before. That weird-looking fruit or the vegetable with a name you can't pronounce may become your new favorite raw food ingredient. Pick up a small amount of unknown foods, and search the Internet for recipe ideas you can add to your daily diet.

Include a wide variety of green leafy vegetables in your diet, as they are possibly the most important sources of vitamins, minerals and even protein in your diet. Instead of choosing the same lettuce, experiment with various kinds. Additionally, this is a great time to try some of those leafy greens you've always turned your nose up at, like bok choy, kale, chard or simple spinach.

Before You Shop, A Word About Bug Spray, Chemical Preservatives and the Legion of Unpronounceable Words on the Labels . . .

100+ years ago, there wasn't a war on drugs; there was a war on bugs.

Chemical companies developed products to sell to farmers and agricultural corporations that could be applied to crops. The idea was to spray the crops with something that would kill the bugs and any bug eggs.

I think the prevailing logic was that the residue would either evaporate or wash away, leaving the plants unharmed and ready for human consumption, but farmers would see an increased crop yield, as the crops would not be lost to bugs.

And it seemed that big companies went on a soulless, profit-only quest to make food last forever.

Preservatives became the word of the day.

These engineers and scientists were tasked with making things like bread last.

I can hear them, "Guys, don't think bread. Think Egyptian Pharaoh."

No one thought too much about any dangers associated with the use of these chemicals.

"Better living through chemistry," became the slogan.

Culinary embalming is what is was and is.

And it's like *we* know it's bad, but until *they* admit it, Oops, sorry, that's prolly not a good idea to eat that. But they don't, so we keep eatin' it.

I remember reading about someone who wasn't going to quit smoking until the tobacco companies admitted that smoking caused cancer. She died knowing it was bad for her but some crazy part of her brain held to the end to the belief that cigarettes still being allowed to be sold by the government meant that someone still felt that they were somehow, in some way, still okay to smoke.

Maybe not thinking that a multi-billion dollar industry might have a say in any attempts to have the plug pulled on it.

Holding on to the crazy idea that consumer safety was some kind of over-arching moral compass, some standard that trumped any industry's ability to influence legislation, governmental controls or news media reporting. I suggested that maybe, while in theory a good idea, this consumer safety litmus test, but in practice, not practiced.

And some people say, "But the government wouldn't do that."

Uh-huh.

And so as we started swallowing plants that, turns out, contained the residue of those pesticides and herbicidal cocktails. Unknown to us, the residue of those poisonous chemicals began to store itself in our fatty tissues, and since those chemicals also leached into the water supply and contaminated grazing fields, the animals we were eating also began to store these chemical residues in their fatty tissues.

In American history, books have often been the change insurgents for social reforms and evolution.

For example, according to Wikipedia:

Common Sense is a pamphlet written by Thomas Paine. It was first published anonymously on January 10, 1776, during the American Revolution. Common Sense, signed, "Written by an Englishman," became an immediate success. In relation to the population of the Colonies at that time, it had the largest sale and circulation of any book in American history. Common Sense presented the American colonists with an argument for freedom from British rule at a time when the question of independence was still undecided. Paine wrote and reasoned in a style that common people understood; forgoing the philosophy and Latin references used by Enlightenment era writers, Paine structured Common Sense like a sermon and relied on Biblical references to make his case to the people. Historian Gordon S. Wood described Common Sense as, "the most incendiary and popular pamphlet of the entire revolutionary era."

About 10 years before the Civil War, Harriet Beecher Stowe's *Uncle Tom's Cabin* caused a stir in the Northern States, leading to a widespread opposition to slavery.

And in 1962, Rachel Carson, a respected author and a former marine biologist with the U.S. Fish and Wildlife Service published *Silent Spring*, which exposed the hazards of the pesticide DDT

Carson questioned the wisdom of our uninformed trust and faith in the chemical industry, helping pave the way for the coming environmental movement, and like Paine and Stowe's books, *Silent Spring* caused a stir, got people to thinkin'. . .

. . . for themselves.

Now, half a century later, Carson would likely have something to say about all those chemicals, synthetics and preservatives in the food supply.

And I'm sure Thomas Paine and Harriet Beecher Stowe would have said, "Yeah, I think I'll shop organic . . . you can keep your tomatoes and stuff steeped in bug spray, your frankenfood, your Dolly the sheeps.

Gimme real food, or give me death, to borrow a Patrick Henryism.

Genetically Modified foods.

Cloned animals.

Bug spray food, the residues, all gooey in our fat.

No thanks, Pardner.

I found this on the Internet (but with no attribution). Some guy says he received this in an email.

I think it tells the story:

The year 1900: Cancer caused only 3 out 100 deaths in the US. Breast cancer was basically unheard of.

—Food manufacturers began developing "better living through chemistry" products like artificial sweeteners (saccharin), taste additives (MSG), partially hydrogenated vegetable shortening and margarine.

—Refined white sugar (acid and fat on a spoon) replaced molasses as the leading sweetener in the American diet.

1911: A grain-milling process was discovered that strips away the germ and outer layers of wheat grain (where the nutrients are). The result: Nutrient-poor, acid-creating white bread and refined white flour.

1921: General Mills invented a character named Betty Crocker to convince Americans to eat more processed foods (and increase the company's stock value).

1935: Only one case of cancer had been reported in the last 50 years by the Inuit (EsLynno) people of Alaska and Canada. After they began eating processed foods, their cancer rate exploded until it equaled that of the US by the 1970's.

1938: From now until 1990, the average male sperm count will drop by nearly half, and testicular cancer will triple.

1949: After being unheard of 49 years ago, the breast cancer rate is now 58 out of every 100,000 women.

1950: From now to the year 2000, the overall cancer rate will go up 55%. (Lung cancer due to smoking is only 1/4 of that.) Breast and colon cancer will go up 60%, brain cancer 80% and childhood cancer will increase 20%.

1970: Americans spend $6 billion on fast food. By 2001, that will skyrocket to $110 billion.

1971: The US Congress declares its "War on Cancer" which has done virtually nothing to stop the growing rates of cancer in the US in the next 30+ years.

—The US Department of Agriculture wrote "An Evaluation of Research in the US on Human Nutrition; Report No. 2, Benefits From Nutrition Research" which blamed the lack of nutrients in the American diet for most major health problems. That report was banned from public view for 21 years, reportedly at the insistence of the processed food industry.

1973: From now to 1991, prostate cancer will go up 126%.

1982: Teenage boys drink twice as much milk as soda. By 2002, they will be drinking twice as much soda as milk.

1990: From now to 2005, over 120,000 new processed foods will be developed to join the 320,000 processed foods already on the store shelves.

2000: Cancer is now the cause of 20 out of 100 of all deaths in the US, compared to just 3 out of 100 in 1900.

2001: Americans spend $110 billion a year on fast food. Every single day, 1 out of 4 Americans eats at least one meal in a fast food restaurant.

2005: Breast cancer, which was extremely rare back in 1900 and only affected 58 out of 100,000 women in 1949, now strikes 1 in 3 women in the US. That means that in just 55 short years, it has gone up 568 times what it was.

History speaks for itself. If you want to be alive into your golden years and stay pain and disease-free, stay the hell away from processed foods of any kind. That includes boxed, bagged, canned or jarred foods, fast food, soda and bottled sweetened drinks.

Jack La Lanne (who is 93, but looks about 70) has an easy rule. Here it is: "If man made it, don't eat it."

～

Someone wrote to us once and said, "I have all this non-organic food, what should I do with it?"

Meaning, now I know.

Here's what we said:

"Now that I know . . ." we always say.

Will it kill you? Well, as we mentioned, we have eaten our share of non-organic in the past . . . but once we knew, well, then we did things different.

Pretend all of it has a skull and cross bones on it. We don't hesitate to throw away spoiled milk or something that will harm us . . .

Usually, when people think about this, they might find that it's money fear underneath the feeling . . . and maybe not feeling that they're worth the extra money.

Someone asked me how, as a single mom (back then), I could afford *Whole Foods* grocery bills. And I replied, "Do you have a car payment?" And they said yes, they did. I said, "Well, I consider my body my Mercedes Benz . . ."

I promise in the long run you will eat less food, spend less money on health care . . . as long as changes in diet and lifestyle include a change of heart . . .

Will it kill you to throw it away and start fresh?

Well, if you have a little clutch of fear about the money, let me share with you something we said about that feeling of fear that accompanies any decision . . . kind of like as you stand at the fork in the road, "Should I do this . . . or that?" when you think about one of the decision options and you feel a little something, call it what you want . . . apprehension, nervousness . . . whatever.

Think of this "feeling" connected with mentally moving yourself toward one of the two directions, in this case, the apprehensive feeling you get when contemplating throwing away the toxic stuff and going out and buying organic. When you think about this direction, maybe voices tell you that you're wasting money, that you can't afford it, whatever and then you get this feeling, boom, in your guts . . . let me tell you something about fear and the bodily energy that accompanies it.

It's just energy. Period.

The thoughts before and after the feeling are results of mental habits and conditioning and maybe our parents or other characters in our story.

Maybe underneath the thoughts we assign to the feeling, just the "energy" we feel, that's ours to use.

Meanwhile, back to cancer.

I haven't mentioned heart disease, diabetes, infant mortality, rates of autism or any of the other diseases you can play *Disease Duck, Duck, Goose!* with.

(I love ending a sentence with with <—or putting with twice . . . sorry Ms. Steinkamp, my ambivalent senior year in high school English teacher, I ain't re-writing and the best thing about modern composition on a computer is the Ignore and Add to Dictionary features. Ain't might not be in your dictionary, but I've added it to mine, along with a whole collection of grammatical inappropriatisms—like the word inappropriatisms, which I made up, just now, to thumb my nose at convention and renew my applause each and every time the Airplane of Rebellion touches down at the Authority Airport. Lastly, though you encouraged my writing, along with a host of others, I have not added your name to my dictionary. Steinkamp will forever appear with a red squiggle in my electronic text windows, as a reminder to myself: Forget convention and write how you talk.)

PSYCHOLOGY VS. BIOLOGY

> *"When my old body hurts I try and remember to let go of my old hurts."*—Guy Dunyoga

> *"Before you take to your lips the smallest drought of medicine, first search heart and soul. Then, laugh, sing, walk, play and give of yourself to another."*—Guy Dunyoga

Often, the first time someone comes in and they tell you they want to eat better, this food, the stuff they just ate, that they really liked, that tastes really good . . . this food has somehow made them mentally consider what they're eating now and suddenly, they're telling us, who don't really know them, just a couple people who put something they asked for off the menu or a Special, maybe a dessert, on a plate or put it in a take out container, and they open up a little and we hear those words:

I should eat like this more.

And we aren't thinking they mean here, goodie gumdrops! Another customer.

That's okay too, but we know they're talking more about what's going on outside our place.

Back it home or at work or eating out or on the road.

When they're in charge.

Picking things out at the grocery store, off a menu somewhere else, or grabbing something out of the refrigerator or pantry to stick in their mouth and eat.

Stuff they've been eating for years.

Now, they tell us that want to eat differently. Something they've given thought to for any number of reasons and now, here, standing by the cash register or sitting at a table looking up at us, taking their order, clearing a plate, saying hello or goodbye, in an earnest tone, they say, "I want to eat better."

We've given a lot of thought to this.

And we'd like to tell you what seems to work for those people who eat and leave and begin to make changes . . . and eventually they overcome the desire to eat the things that they've eaten for years.

We call it Psychology vs. Biology.

Rule Number 1: You can only change Biology with Biology.

Rule Number 2: You can't fight Biology with Psychology.

Stick with me for a minute . . .

Eating is something that the body demands of us.

You can go 3-4 weeks without food and not die. People have done it.

Give 'em water and air . . . they might not be happy, but they survive.

Lifeboats, plane crashes, hunger strikes, fasts—people have done it.

They survive to tell the tale, skinnier and a lot worse for the wear and tear, but they live.

Take away the water, and, 3 days later, they dry up and blow away.

Take away the air, and, unless you're a Guinness Book of Record holder, you're looking at 2-3 minutes.

But, back to the food.

The 3-4 weeks you can survive without seems to be the same interval that it takes for biological change to occur.

By that I mean, preferences and cravings.

Cravings as simple as I Need to Eat Now, I'm Hungry, or as complex and specific as Dang, Those Fries Smell Good, Think I'll Supersize It and Eat It In the Van on the Way to Pick Up Bobby from Piano Lessons, Pull Over Now.

(Not that Bobby—he's a guitar man, man.)

Those cravings come from things you've eaten before, which trigger memories, either from seeing it, thinking about it, or smelling it.

In order to create new cravings, you can't get rid of the memories and triggers you have with mental determination.

That's psychology.

Most people will tell you that their will power is the problem.

Will power is a mental struggle to make yourself do something physical.

In the case of food, it's what you employ to help you NOT do something physical, which is eat something you decided you shouldn't any more.

Eventually, they tell us, their will "fails" them and they cave in to the craving.

Of course they do.

Psychology doesn't work against biology, which is what drives the Craving / Preference Bus.

In other words, the Body is the driver, not the Mind.

In order to change the Body, just start feeding it more of what you want.

And eat a lot of it.

If you're hungry at 9:00am, eat 5 bananas. You heard me.

All of them.

Cool Hand Luke had his 50 eggs.

You've got yer bananas.

5 of them.

Or something else, but eat 'til you're full.

Leaving a lot of room with that one banana you eat to be "disciplined" opens the door for some unwanted guests.

Your Body says, "Uh, I'm still hungry."

Then, it triggers cravings.

Cravings for things you decided to give up . . .

. . . But how can you give them up when you still want them.

Hard, isn't it?

The good news is that the more meals you have of the "new" food, not little tiny snacks, though that's a start, but big, fill your stomach meals, even if it's a meal of bananas to start, you'll start to create new cravings.

And, magically, in just about 3-4 weeks, you start to notice that the Body is craving more things from the "new" category.

It's really that simple.

Eventually, and be patient here, things like fries will start to smell, well, not so good.

You'll think, "Hey, I like fries," but the smell will betray something else.

That's your body saying, "I don't want that."

Any more.

But, you could douse them with ketchup and force yourself and eventually, your body would go back to Like from Dislike.

It's just a matter of repetition and quantity and time.

The Body is trained to like certain foods and dislike others through repetition.

Eat and repeat.

And wait.

:)

Biology works.

Leave psychology out.

And enjoy the food!

LAST DIALOGUE (PROMISE)

KATHY: "So, that's a book? Most of that was silly."

DANNY: "But some of it's serious. I sneak serious in while people are laughing."

KATHY: "When they're not paying attention. See, people thinking they're just laughing . . ."

DANNY: "..but that's just the distraction, isn't it?"

Okay One More, But Then You Have to Turn Off the Light

BOBBY: "Are you two gonna kiss now?"

KATHY: "Hush."

GUY: "Maybe we could do yoga."

EARNEST: "Or we could all meditate."

RUDY: "Maybe we could visualize ourselves in Maui."

DANNY: "Kathy, Rudy can have my kiss. Not on the forehead like he's 5, come on, a good one."

ROCKY: "This book sucks."

BUDDY: "It totally sucks."

KATHY: "Shush."

APPENDIX:
BREAKFAST, LUNCH, DINNER & DESSERT
RECIPES, PLUS, SOME THINGS TO PONDER

KATHY: "Appendix?"

DANNY: "Tonsils sounded weird."

KATHY: "What would your English teacher Ms. Steinkamp say?"

DANNY: "Somehow, I think she would like this book secretly, but hand it back all marked up in red."

KATHY: "Forget convention?"

DANNY: "Are you really my girl?"

KATHY: "Yeah, and I'm afraid I am. Okay, so we're finally gonna share some recipes, but maybe we should give them a little back story, not just push 'em into the kitchen. Throw in some, whadaya call it, 'Things to Ponder.'"

DANNY: "Ponder, listen to you. Who's pushing? Want me to lay some more inappropriatisms on 'em?"

KATHY: "But we're eventually gonna see a recipe appear, you know, Name, List of Ingredients, Instructions, right?"

DANNY: "Can I sprinkle in some inappropriatisms?"

KATHY: "I've given up trying to tame you."

~

So, you're thinking, okay, I'll try eating a little more of the uncooked organic stuff.

But, God, where do I start?

How about breakfast? No sense putting it off.

Want simple? Man, go to the store and get some organic bananas. No, not one. Get 'em all, a whole bunch.

Now, start eating and don't stop 'til your full.

When you get hungry, eat more. Don't leave that half empty stomach to your imagination, 'cause we both know that when you get hungry, if drinking a glass or two of good pure water doesn't help, you need food again. Sorry, that bloody stomach is a relentless taskmaster.

Man, eat 'til your full. Satisfied. No more, I'm good.

You can mix that up with different fruits, but don't get too fruity on me. You'll get all sugar buzzed out. Fruit is still sugar. Man, you're gonna have to mix it up a little. Have some salad, some nuts, some seeds. Having small little meals more often'll keep the beast in check rather than those long stretches, let yourself get all spaced out and jittery and you start looking like Danny after pulling three non-stop hours behind salad bar during the dinner rush.

Whole Foods carries raw snacks. Get some and try 'em. I'll give you this easy yogurt recipe that'll hook you right up, cut out the middle man and his plastic cup with the lid and the expiration date, get you in the kitchen, Pardner. Plus, Danny's got a million smoothie recipes, but I'll give you one to start with. Once you get the general idea and take the lid of the notion that you are gonna drink an 8 oz glass and be like, Now what? 20 minutes later. We're gonna make 'em big so you last 'til lunch.

Promise.

Don't go all Raw Rambo on me, either, man, you know, get all hung up in what we call The Purchasing Phase, which can really be just a huge distraction, if you look at.

We all know the kinda guy that watches a golf game on tv, hack, there's nothing else on and it's perfect snoozing backdrop, that announcer's voice like a sweet lullaby, but sweet cherries! them guys look cool, all golfy and faux fly in their fitted pants, the golf shirts and the hats pulled down low. All those people clapping.

Hey, you decide to take up golf.

Forget borrowing or renting clubs, man, you go out with your Visa in your teeth and head to a pro-shop and walk out with a set of Ping clubs, the best shoes the guy had in back, four outfits, a couple gloves, five dozen Titlest balls and a Visa bill that will require at least three mail interceptions.

"You spent how much?" your wife will say.

Don't be that guy.

Start slow.

Just start eating more organic unprocessed, uncooked, fruits, veggies, nuts and seeds.

Don't worry about the "other" food.

You heard me.

The turtle wins the race.

Use the equipment you have, unless you have no knife or cutting board or blender.

Start small and use what you have.

Reward yourself in intervals of 3-6 months with gear. We always suggest this order: Vitamix blender, biggest food processor you can afford, like the Cuisinart 11—or better, the 14-cup model, 9-tray Excalibur dehydrator with the 24-hour timer (man, don't get that little Excalibur—we did that, "Perfect for small kitchens!" but turns out it's like an Easy Bake Oven—you go through all the trouble of making cookies or crackers or tortillas, you want enough to eat off for a few days, not provide a snack for Malibu Barbie and Ken, sitting all casual out back next to the camper, Skipper frolicking around the yard with a plastic dog), then, go get your Omega Juicer.

But spread it out. Take your time. Remember the goober with the Visa at the pro-shop.

Don't be that guy.

KITCHEN SET UP AND RECIPES

Blenders, Juicers, Food Processors . . . Oh My

A blender is an essential tool for any kitchen. When we first started making smoothies for breakfast, we used a lot of frozen fruit. While we'd both heard of Vita-Mix blenders, there was no way we could justify the cost: Almost $400!

Our parents had those metal base, glass pitcher Osterizers and those things lasted 30 years. I bet they bought them with S&H Green Stamps too.

You can imagine our shock when we saw the Vitamix price tag.

So, over the course of the next two years, we went through three blenders, each progressively more expensive, in search of the best blender shy of the Vita-Mix. The daily smoothies proved too difficult for any conventional blender. We realized, when we totted up how much we'd spent on cheap blenders, that we'd already bought a Vita-Mix. So, when our last cheap blender's motor burned out, we bought a Vita-Mix.

In our restaurant, we tell people that if they're only going to get one piece of equipment, get a Vita-Mix.

You'll have it forever. It's a great piece of equipment and is virtually indestructible!

When you are finished using the Vita-Mix, it is very easy to clean. Just add water and a few drops of dishing washing liquid. Place it back on its base and switch to low. Let the machine do the work.

After 30-45 seconds, rinse and you are ready for the next use. It's that simple.

The Vita-Mix comes complete with a recipe book and information on how to maximize its use. This is a pricey machine, but well worth the money.

We searched around on the Internet and found some for under $400 on Amazon.com. A few weeks ago, we saw the 5200 (with the variable speed) knob at Costco. Shop around! There's a code you can get from our website that'll get you free shipping, if you want.

But, all Vita-Mix applause aside, if you have a blender, try it and if you can get some mileage out of it, do so. If, down the road, you decide to upgrade: Get a Vita-Mix!

Kitchen Equipment

You probably already have some equipment in your kitchen, knives, cutting boards, peeler, etc., but here's a list of some things:

—8-inch chef's knife

—Serrated (tomato) knife

—Kitchen scissors

—Knife sharpener

—Salad Spinner

—Measuring cups

—Measuring spoons

—Spatulas

—Garlic press

—Colander

—Springform pan

—Squeeze bottles

—Storage containers

—Large metal mixing bowl (9-quarts or more)

—Nut milk bag

—Cutting board

—Mandoline slicer

A great resource for equipment: www.webstaurantstore.com.

Stocking Your Kitchen

Refrigerator

Try as much as you can to get organic produce! We shop at *Whole Foods*. They can have reasonably priced organic (I know, can you believe it?) produce. Here's some examples:

—Romaine lettuce

—Kale

—Cabbage

—Cucumbers

—Celery

—Red Bell Peppers

—Carrots

—Zucchini

—Parsley

—Fresh herbs (basil, dill, cilantro)

—Green Onions

—Red/Yellow Onions

—Garlic

—Seasonal fresh ripe fruit

—Ripe avocados

—Fresh ginger

—Lemons

—Oranges

—Miso (light)

—Nuts (almonds, walnuts, pecans, pine nuts, cashews).

—Seeds (sunflower, sesame, pumpkin, flax)

Kathy and Danny's nuts and seeds shopping tip: www.nutsonline. com

Freezer

We keep our 1-gallon Ziploc bags filled with frozen bananas we've peeled and stored as well as all our frozen fruit in the freezer.

Pantry

This is just a partial list, and, by all means, with any of the above-mentioned stuff, don't feel that you need to go out and buy everything at once. Ease into it. Get only what you need, and then, see if you need more.

—Extra Virgin Olive Oil (First Cold Pressed)

—Vanilla Extract

—Dried Fruits (raisins, dates, goji berries)

—Grade B Maple Syrup

—Agave Nectar

—Celtic sea salt

—Herbs and Spices: onion powder, garlic powder, cayenne pepper, black peppercorns, dill, basil, oregano, Italian seasoning, cinnamon, nutmeg)

—Nama Shoyu (Shopping tip: www.naturalzing.com)

—Braggs Apple Cider Vinegar

—Sprouting Seeds (e.g., alfalfa, broccoli, chick peas . . . .)

Breakfast

Almond Milk

(makes 3 cups)

Some of the recipes in here will call for almond milk, so here's the recipe.

—1 cup whole, raw almonds, soaked 8-12 hours, drained and rinsed (about 1 ½ cups after soaking)

—3 cups water

—4 pitted dates

—½ teaspoon vanilla extract, optional

Blend all the ingredients until they are smooth and creamy. To separate the "milk" from the almond skins and pulp, squeeze the blended mixture through a paint thinner bag, nut milk bag or cheesecloth. It also makes a great drink, by itself or in a smoothie.

See, we ain't telling you to stop drinking milk, but, why not try some from the Vitamix cow?

Green Smoothies

—2 frozen bananas

—1 cup of fruit (e.g., apple, pear, pineapple, mango)

—1 small handful of leafy greens (e.g., kale, spinach, cilantro, parsley)

—Fill the blender about two-thirds of the way up to the top of the "stuff" in the blender with water

—1 tablespoon of coconut oil

—½ teaspoon of cinnamon

—a pinch of cayenne pepper (wash your hands after pinching, trust me, I've done the eye thing more than once, ouch!)

Blend until smooth. If this proves to only last in your stomach for an hour or so, tomorrow, double everything. Get yourself one of those Mason jars with a screw top lid, the canning jar kind. Fill that up and carry it around with you.

Keep mixing up the greens you use. When you get bananas, get those spotty ripe ones, those are best. Chuck 'em in a gallon ziplock freezer bag.

If the idea of putting leafy greens sounds nasty, just put a few leaves in at first. Spinach and cilantro are good mild greens to get you going. Try working up to more green and less fruit.

But take your time about it. No hurry t'all.

I think the queen of green smoothies is indisputably Victoria Boutenko, the author of *Raw Family*, *12 Steps to Raw Foods* and *Green for Life*, all of which have stories and recipes that will help you. Her two children have written a book containing delicious raw food recipes called *Eating without Heating*. Visit Victoria's site at www. rawfamily.com

Pecan Yogurt

Makes 3 cups or about 2 servings, but don't feel guilty if you eat it all yourself. We have a more expansive view of portion sizes. Hey, the Pringles can describes a serving size as, like 11 chips, but we all know that once the top's off, you're headed to the bottom and you'll drink the dust and crumbs. No shame, Pardner. For me, it's healthier to eat both portions of the Pecan Yogurt vs. 11 Pringles, right?

—1 large apple

—5 large ripe organic strawberries or other seasonal berries

—2 1/2 cups coconut milk (Coconut milk made from the blended water and meat of a young Thai coconut. To open it up, look on YouTube and look for the shave and chop method. Go ahead and bypass the shirtless raw food guru demos where the guy's holding the coconut at eye level and then whacks it mid-air with his machete on the set of his home-based internet tv show for "insiders"—the milk is made by pouring the water into a blender, then using the edge of a sturdy spoon to scrape the meat off the inside . . . blend the water and meat quickly and voila! You've got milk.)

—½ cup shelled raw pecans

—½ teaspoon vanilla extract

—¼ teaspoon of salt

—¼ teaspoon of cinnamon

Wash, core and chop the apple. Wash and remove the tops from the strawberries. Place the fruit and all other ingredients in a blender. Blend to a consistency—chunky or smooth, we don't care and we promise to never to stop and be like, "Good Lord, this is way too chunky, Pardner." Taste and adjust salt, cinnamon and vanilla, if needed. Pour yogurt on top of a bowl of fruit or pour into two bowls and top with fresh organic strawberries, pecans and a sprinkle of cinnamon. Did you put the whole thing in the bowl? Forget the two portions, chief. It's all for you. It's all good.

Lunch

First, let's throw out the rulebook. We have eaten a salad for lunch or a whole watermelon (that was Danny; an 8-pounder and boy was he sorry). You know how we feel about convention. You could drink those green smoothies a couple pages back in the middle of the afternoon and no one would throw you in jail, but here's some yummy favorites for when your stomach says, "Gimme somethin' with a little more oomph, Kathy."

Hummus

Nothing nicer than having a little hummus to dip stuff in or you could just blob a little on a salad. Call it the Hummus Blob.

—1/2 cup hulled sesame seeds

—1/2 inch of ginger

—1 clove of garlic

—1/4 cup olive oil

—1/2 tablespoon cumin

—1/2 tablespoon salt

—1/2 teaspoon pepper

—1/2 teaspoon agave nectar

—2 tablespoons lemon juice

Put all the ingredients in a blender and fill the blender to the 2 1/2-cup mark with water and run 'er on high 'til everything looks smooth, usually for at least a minute. Stop the blender and add 2 cups of raw cashews that have been soaked for at least 6 hours. I deliberately didn't put how many servings, 'cause I trust you to divvy up the lucre. Tell you what, you put this down on the buffet and no one will know there ain't chick peas in it.

Spring Onion "Cheese"

The easiest cheesiest spread ever! Serve in a piece of Napa cabbage, a collard wrap or romaine lettuce leaf with some sprouts!

—3 cups sunflower seeds, soaked for 2-4 hours

—2 lemons, juiced

—1/3 cup olive oil

—1 bunch of green onions

—1 tablespoon sea salt

Put the sunflower seeds and salt in a food processor and run it until it's a fine meal. Meal, as in corn meal, a texture. Don't think I meant the meal, as in the whole meal. Then add lemon juice and olive oil. Process again until smooth and scrape off the sides as necessary. Add a little water slowly at this stage to keep the mixture rolling. Process until smooth, but still thick. At the end, add the green onions (everything but the roots!) until the onions are little pieces. Allow to stand for 30 minutes.

Thai Vegetable Soup

—2 red bell peppers (minus the "hat" and the seeds, rinse the insides)

—½ tablespoon Himalayan salt

—3 carrots

—¾ cup cashews

—3 small radishes bulbs

—2 cups water

—1 tablespoon curry powder

—¾ cup almond milk (the almond milk recipe is back in the "Breakfast" section)

—1/2 tablespoon nama shoyu

—½ tablespoon jalapeno pepper

—1 green onion

Blend all the ingredients until creamy in your blender. You can run it a little longer to make it warm, but don't cook it! Yes, a Vitamix can cook.

Sweet Potato Corn Chowder Soup

—4 cups of fresh corn kernels (if you can find a farmer growing fresh organic corn, please call us . . . usually you're safest bet is frozen organic corn that's been thawed . . . but frozen veggies are blanched, which means they're not TECHNICALLY raw, but TECHNICALLY raw is sometimes tough to do. But just steer clear of "conventional" corn.)

—2 cups of almond milk (refer back to the "Breakfast" section for the almond milk recipe)

—1 avocado

—1 peeled and chopped sweet potato, cut in ice cube-sized chunks

—1 cup of water

—1 teaspoon of cumin

—1 teaspoon of paprika

—½ a jalapeno pepper (seeds or no seeds or some seeds, dependin' on yer taste fer fire)

—1 tablespoon of minced onion

—½ teaspoon of salt

Blend all the ingredients together.

Guacomole

—3 medium avocados

—1 cup chopped green onions

—1 bunch cilantro, stems removed

—1 cup chopped tomatoes

—½ teaspoon salt

—4 cloves peeled garlic

—2 tablespoons olive oil

Combine all the ingredients in a mixing bowl. This is another salad blobber, or, I won't tell, just get yourself a spoon and hunker down at the kitchen table with the bowl. What did we say about convention again? Oh yeah.

Kale Salad

I love Kale for more reasons than a person can tell here. People ask what you're favorite this or that is, and, very often, it just means, "Help, I'm having a hard time pickin'." But, outside the café, it's just you and me and you ask me, I'm probably gonna tell you that the one thing that's traveled along the trail of change that's made up our travel West, the thing we stop and make along the way, it would be this. I know you're supposed to vary your greens and all that, but, there's something about Kale . . .

First time Bobby saw me chopping some to put in some soup (before we started eatin' raw), he goes, "Hey, that's the stuff they used to garnish the fruit plates with . . . can you eat that?" Yeah, genius. That goes for Parsley too.

—1 bunch of Kale, washed and soaked for 15 minutes in luke warm water

—2 tablespoons of olive oil

—2 tablespoons of lemon juice

—2 cups of shredded cabbage

—¼ cup of hulled hemp seed

—½ teaspoon salt

Strip the kale off the stems and stack the leaves, roll them in a big cigar, a real Phatty (you know, like you're back in your dorm room hunched over a Pink Floyd album, everyone around like, "Hurry dude, let's get comfortably numb before Comfortably Numb comes on and you're like, Chill, you're wrecking my concentration) then chop that stogie into thin strips or shred in the food processor using the shredding blade. Shred the cabbage old school by chasing it around the cutting board until you're like, Yeah, I could chew it now. Put the shredded cabbage and the shredded kale in a mixing bowl. Add the olive oil, lemon juice, salt and massage thoroughly. Now add the hemp seed and serve. Keep in an airtight container.

Swiss Chard Salad

—1 bunch of Swiss Chard, washed and soaked for 15 minutes in cold water

—2 tablespoons of olive oil

—2 tablespoons of lemon juice

—½ cup shredded coconut

—½ teaspoon salt

Strip the Swiss Chard off the stems and roll and do the choppie stogie thing described above (you remember, the Pink Floyd album . . . no? my, we *were* studying hard at school, weren't we?) or shred in the food processor using the shredding blade. Add the shredded Swiss Chard, olive oil, lemon juice, and salt to a mixing bowl and massage thoroughly. Now add the shredded coconut and serve. Keep in an airtight container.

Find It Salad

Super Chef used to make something he called "Find It Salad," meaning, I scrounged around in the 'fridge and here's what I'm thinkin'. . .

Forget convention. Why does everything have to be an exact recipe? I bet a lot of great soups and dishes were the result of taking what was on hand and getting creative.

That's what we're talkin' about.

So, you're scanning down, Hey, Kathy, where's the ingredients?

Here's where I take you by the hand and say, "Go over to the 'fridge and open it. See, there's a couple leaves a kale, some chard, a little spinach, a carrot, hey, an onion, a quarter of one, but what can I make with that? Got some lemon juice, a tomato, some sprouts, a little cucumber . . ."

Getting' it?

Put it in a bowl, put some olive oil or whatever on it. Maybe flax seed or hemp seed oil. Or one of the Blob brothers: Spring Onion, Hummus . . . any of that left in a container? Put that in too, if you like.

Or not.

It's up to you. It's your Find It Salad.

Dinner

Spinach Borscht Soup

—1½ quarts of pure water (no, you can't go dip a pot in the retention pond)

—1 lb of spinach

—1 cup of chopped onion

—2 tsp of Himalayan salt

—1/3 cup of lemon juice or Bragg's Apple Cider Vinegar

—¼ cup of agave nectar

—1 cucumber

—1 tablespoon of olive oil

Blend all the ingredients. Pour in a bowl and garnish (if you want) with avocado pieces, tomato and cucumber or anything else you got hanging around, some vegetable in the back of the drawer raising it's hand, "Pick me! Pick me!"

Super Chef, a dyed-in-the-Communist-wool Russian, used to make this dynamite beet borscht soup. We asked him if borscht, which to our ear seemed a foreign word, one not in the American dictionary that was wedged between the Mark Twain books in Bobby's parent's breakfront bookcase. We asked if it was Russian for beets and he said that was a different word and while borscht is traditionally made with beet juice, he said it's origin is rooted in a story, which I'll let Bobby tell.

"Once upon a time, there was this king, and man, that guy was mean. Decides in the middle of winter that he wants fresh soup, "SOUP NOW!" he shouted. The cook's thinking, Dude, we got no veggies, it's winter, but, he worries he'll get beheaded or sent to work at the equivalent to a Medieval Russian Walmart, a worse fate, greeting villagers who pull up in the market in the horse-drawn carts, a little blue Medieval smock with a name tag on it, having to act all happy and thank you for shopping at Medieval Russian Walmarty. So, in a panic, he runs out with a bowl to all the neighbors, "Dude, give me anything you got, I need a Find It Soup or I'm headless, or worse, the next greeter at Russian Medieval Walmart." Knowing that he'd be better off beheaded, but not wanting to express their opinion, they decide to help the guy out. All of the people all disappeared and rummaged in their root cellars and came back with what they had, and probably, a lot of beets, which he juiced down using some ancient blender operated by animals turning great mill wheels, walking in circles, pushing the handles.

So, Super Chef says that it don't mean beets so much as it means *borrowed*.

After he told the story and we scooted back from the edge of our chairs, that chef, nearly a Medieval Russian Walmart greeter (whew, that was close), and Super Chef said we could change the name of the restaurant to Borscht Earth Café.

We did the girl thing.

We said we'd get back to him.

Kathy's dad and his wife were in from outa town once and his wife, who carries a Yiddish-to-English dictionary in her clutch purse, said that her grandma said that spinach borscht, not beet, was the schnizzle.

So Kathy looked up some "cooked" versions and tweaked away until she came up with what you see up above, several inches above my bizarre back story."

Quiche

Crust

—2 cups dry walnuts

—2 tablespoons olive oil

Pulse the walnuts down, then drizzle in the olive oil. Press the crust into a pie pan or tart pan.

Filling

—2 bunches of spinach

—6 medium-sized carrots

Wash and chop the spinach. Pulse the carrots to a fine texture or finely chop them.

Yella Cheese

—1 cup of water

—1 cup of lemon juice (Tip: cut the covers of a half-dozen or so lemons and put them in the blender separately, add a little water, just enough to get those naked lemons down by the blades a tiny bath, so once you hit the ON switch those lemons start moving and blending to liquid, otherwise, they'll bounce around on those blades—keep the juice in a separate container and use it for recipes, or squirt a little in a glass of water, impress your guests, Say, Bobby, is there lemon in this water? and you can say, "Heck, I made it myself.")

—4 cloves of peeled garlic

—3 teaspoons of turmeric

—2 teaspoons of sea salt or Himalayan salt (my money's on the Himalayan for taste)

—3 cups of dry raw cashews

Blend all that up, then get your spatula and shovel it all in a small mixing bowl.

Now add the yella cheese to the spinach/ carrot mixture and combine in a mixing bowl and use a spatula to put it in pie pan or tart pan. Chill and serve.

Note: You can use the yella cheese as a salad topping too.

Falafel

You'd be surprise how many people pronounce this FAL-UH-FELL, accent on the first syllable. But, you have to start somewhere and Bobby always is more pleased with a customer who proudly botches the word and hands him the menu. "Is that how you say it?" they ask and he usually says, "I liked the way you said it," not giving anything away. The pointers? He usually tries to get them to try to take a stab at pronouncing it and twists his mouth into a wry smile, like, not even close.

—3 cups pistachios (which have soaked about 6 hours)

—2 chopped green onions

—1 cup of chopped carrots

—3 chopped celery stalks

—2 cloves of peeled garlic

—½ bunch of finely chopped cilantro

—½ bunch of finely chopped parsley

—1 ½ teaspoon salt

—2 tablespoons cumin

—¼ cup falafel seasoning (frontiercoop.com)

Grind the carrots and the pistachios in the food processor first. Then, chuck everything else in. Shoot for a batter that's mixed well, but leave it just a little coarse.

Use a small ice cream scooper and scoop them onto the teflex sheets of a dehydrator and dehydrate for about 24 hours. You want these babies to be a little dry on the outside. At about the 8-hour mark, you should be able to take them off the teflex sheets and dry directly on the racks, allowing for air to flow underneath these little guys.

Usually, I'll get about 20 out of a batch, depending on how big my balls are . . .

BOBBY: "Say that again?"

KATHY: "What are you doing here? Out!"

BOBBY: "What? Ow!"

Earth Burger

—2 cups of walnuts

—1 pound of carrots

—1 medium red onion

—2 tablespoons oil

—3 Tbsp poultry seasoning

—1 tablespoon of dill spice

Put the walnuts in the food processor and grind it to powder, but don't go overboard, man, you gotta watch it. If you see the nuts starting to glue to the sides down at the bottom, you've gone overboard. But don't panic, Danny does this all the time—goes overboard. Hey, let's put out a recipe book and he does this whole crazy Facebook thing, the recipes turning into a tonsil, er, I mean appendix. He's the writer; I'm the chef, although I'm working on him. Lord, that boy's a project.

See, I'm hearing you say, Hey, Bobby, it's hard to follow a recipe when there's all the silliness, but what's making food without fun? You laugh the whole time you make something, all that fun and feel good's gonna stick to that food. Don't be surprised if someone takes a bite and ends up chuckling. Shhh! It'll be our secret.

Okay, now that you've got yer nuts ground, dump 'em in a mixing bowl. Now, dump everything else in the food processor BUT the red onion. Run the food processor now with everything else (tell me you left the onion out) a little more than you did the nuts and then spatula all that stuff into the bowl with the nuts.

Peel off the onion skin (I had to say that, sorry, you never know) and then chop the onion small and even if some tears flow, you can still feel good. Go ahead and do the Alice Brady thing, "Darned onions," and wipe your eyes.

Note: At the restaurant, we say "Darned onions."

You're like, uh-huh.

Fried Green Beans

—1lb fresh green beans

—2 cups ground almonds (place almonds in food processor or blender and process until finely ground, careful not to over process)

—1/8 cup coconut oil

—1 tsp Himalayan pink or sea salt

—1 tsp ground black pepper

—1 tsp garlic powder

Combine ground almonds with salt, black pepper and garlic powder in a small bowl. Put coconut oil in a small bowl. Roll green beans in coconut oil and then in almond flour mixture and lay on dehydrator sheet.

Dehydrate 2-3 hours. 105 degrees.

Ranch Dressing

—3/4 cup cashews

—2 teaspoons lemon juice

—1 Tablespoon olive oil

—1/2 teaspoon Himalayan or sea salt

—1/2 teaspoon onion powder

—1/2 teaspoon garlic powder

—1 Tablespoon fresh minced dill or 1/2 teaspoon dried dill weed

—1/2 teaspoon Italian seasoning

—1 basil leaf

—1 Tablespoon minced parsley

Blend the cashews, lemon juice, olive oil, salt, onion powder, garlic powder in a blender until smooth and creamy. You may need to add a little water if it is to thick.

Place the contents of the blender in a bowl.

Stir in the dill, Italian seasoning, basil leaf and parsley.

Store in an airtight container in the refrigerator.

Dip the green beans in the ranch dressing and eat!

Pasta Marinara

Marinara sauce

—2 cups of diced tomatos

—1 red, orange or yellow bell pepper

—1 cup sun-dried tomatoes (soak 'em a couple hours in warm water, then drain off the water and chop 'em up)

—¼ cup olive oil

—2 cloves garlic, peeled and crushed

—1 teaspoon salt

—Pinch of cayenne pepper

—2 tablespoons minced fresh basil or tsp dried

—2 tablespoons minced fresh oregano or 2 tsp dried

Put all the ingredient in a food processor and let 'er run 'til it's chunky or smooth, however you like yer sauce.

Noodles

—6 zucchini (you don't have to peel it, 'less you're chicken to eat green noodles, or wait, I know, you're trying to trick someone . . . okay, peel away . . . we been tricking people for years)

Magically turn the zucchini into noodles using a vegetable peeler or spiral slicer.

Now, put yer noodles in a big mixing bowl and cover with sauce, then stir it up 'til it's as saucy as you like.

Desserts

Enough already. Let's talk about dessert.

First, any time of the day is good.

You heard me.

Join the Dessert Mile High Club. Heard of this Mile High Club? We're not proposing you try and eat dessert under a blanket on a plane. We're saying, hey, you don't have to eat in a certain order, breakfast foods for breakfast, lunch for lunch, dinner for dinner, like you're worried about decorum, all OCD and kooky, maybe like Danny, one of those people that subdivides their plate, eating each thing separately, in a specific, obsessive order, trying to do a TV Dinner Re-enactment. Napkin all tucked into their shirt. Sitting up straight, all Emily Posty, pinkie out, all those confusing dessert and salad forks and gear all around your plate like you're getting ready for major food surgery.

Goodness.

Man, loosen up.

Get over that Fear of Dessert Flying, to morph a metaphor.

"TRUCK STOP LOVE Pudding"

—2 ripe avocados

—1 cup of Grade B Maple Syrup (No, you can't use Aunt Jemima, pin head)

—½ cup of raw cacao (raw chocolate) powder

Throw it all in the blender and tell me that you took the skin off the avocados and took out the pits. Wait, never mind, go ahead and turn on the blender . . . I want to hear this.

~

DANNY: "Didn't we, like, eat this every night for a year?"

KATHY: "God, don't put that in the book."

DANNY: "I wouldn't do that to you."

Strawberry Rhubarb Pie

Crust

—1 1/2 cups of dry walnuts

—1 cup of shredded dried coconut

—¼ teaspoon salt

½ cup of unsoaked Medjool dates

Place the walnuts, coconut and salt in a food processor fitted with the S blade and process until coarsely ground. Add the dates and process until the mixture resembles coarse crumb and start shtickin' together. Don't over do it, Hoss.

Filling

—4 cups of fresh or, if you use frozen, thawed and well-drained, strawberries

—2 stalks of fresh rhubarb, chopped

—¾ cup pitted Medjool dates, soaked

—¼ cup of agave nectar

—1 tablespoon fresh lemon juice

Put the crust into a pie plate or tart pan. Press gently, but firmly with your palm to get the bottom and then use your fingers and thumb in a kind of pinching motion along the edge where the bottom meets the sides and then, up the sides of the pan. The goal is a thin layer, maybe around a quarter inch. The crust is really just to keep the filling off the bottom, give you something to get the pie lifter under. You don't want to take a bite and be like, wow, this is like walnut stew! Just a little taste, an accent. Don't get all mopey if it happens though. We've done it too. Danny's first pie looked like a geological cross-section of the earth, the crusty layer, the dominating feature of the landscape. I said, "Are you gonna eat that?" and he says, "I'm afraid to . . ."

That man has a history of punishing his stomach. I gotta watch him like a hawk.

Place the crust in the freezer for 15 minutes.

Now place 2 cups of the strawberries, the chopped rhubarb, the dates and lemon juice in a blender and process until smooth. Transfer to a mixing bowl and now add the remaining strawberries, and mix well. Remove the crust from the freezer. Pour the strawberry / rhubarb filling into it and press down with a rubber spatula.

Pop it in the freezer and take out to thaw for about 10 minutes before serving. You can refrigerate thereafter . . . if there's any left.

Vanilla Ice Cream

—2 cups almonds, soaked 6-8 hours

—2 cups water

—1 ½ cups cashews, soaked 4 hours

—2 ¼ teaspoons of psyllium powder (yes, the stuff that makes you move down there, intestinally speaking—don't panic)

—1 cup agave nectar

—1 vanilla bean, scraped

—1 ½ teaspoons vanilla extract

—1 pinch Himalayan salt

Blend the soaked almonds with water to make a thick cream. Strain the mixture through a nut milk bag or a one-gallon paint mesh paint strainer bag from a hardware store. Blend the almond cream with the soaked cashews and other remaining ingredients until smooth and creamy. Pour the blender mixture into a shallow square or rectangular container and cover tightly. Freeze for 24 hours or until starts to set up. If the ice cream is too hard when you take it out of the freezer, let it thaw for 10 minutes before scooping or try setting your ice cream scoop in a bowl of hot water. (It's hard to be patient—we know.)

I remember the first time we made this, we were on the couch watching tv and Danny keeps filling up my water glass, which led to many trips to the bathroom. Mr. Polite, I discovered, was using my trips to the bathroom to sneak into the freezer and skim off the corners and the next day he's like, "Wow, look how it sunk in around the sides." Well, I can spot a spoon scrape as well as any mom and I've read enough of his prose to recognize fiction.

"Don't talk to me like I'm some salesperson on the phone, Mr. Helpful Water Refiller," I scolded.

BONUS RECIPE

Chocolate Cheese Cake

Okay, you've been good boys and girls. Who wants cheesecake?

Crust

—2 1/2 cups walnuts, soaked and dried

—1 cup dates, soaked and pitted

Filling

—3 cups cashews, soak 2 hrs / drain

—1 cup agave

—1 cup coconut oil, liquefied, which means it has to be over 72 degrees, otherwise it looks like a jar o' lard

—1/2 cup lemon juice

—2 tablespoons vanilla extract

—2 tablespoons psyllium powder (again, don't panic)

—1/2 cup cacao (raw chocolate powder)

Crust: Put the walnuts and dates in the food processor and process until it begins to stick together. Press the crust mixture evenly in the bottom of a 9-inch spring form pan.

Filling: Place the soaked and drained cashews in the food processor along with the date paste and coconut oil and process until smooth. Add remaining ingredients and puree until smooth and creamy—note, put coconut oil in last! Also, whenever anyone's made this and it didn't turn out right, the usual culprit is under processing the filling. Turn that thing on and let it run, dad.

Assembly: Place the filling in the crust and spread it evenly. As a final step, I usually pick up the pan an inch off the counter and tap it on the counter once or twice to get it even. Chill for 2-3 hours before serving. This will last about 2 weeks if refrigerated and covered with plastic wrap between servings—if it can last that long—we usually polish it off well before the thing has a ghost of a chance to head below the Spoilage Mason Dixon Line!

TONSILS

KATHY: "You have a section called Tonsils?"

DANNY: "Happy?"

KATHY: "You're right . . ."

DANNY: "Say that again."

KATHY: "Seriously, tonsils looks funny. Take it out."

DANNY: "I will. Promise."

KATHY: "I think you also said the last dialog was the last dialog."

DANNY: "Where did I say that?"

KATHY: "In the last dialog."

～

I'm picturing some guy in a bookstore, starting from the back going, "Tonsils?"

And quickly putting it back . . . or maybe pausing, he's thinking, What kind of people have a section called Tonsils?

Surviving the Holidays, Social Situations and Other People

Whenever the holidays are approaching, I can visualize the buffet at my Aunt's house, festooned with turkey, stuffing, mash potatoes, gravy, corn glistening with butter, a glass tray with cranberries fanned out, a bean casserole, pumpkin pie and more.

I imagine walking in, kissing my Aunt—her commenting how long my hair is, touching my beard cautiously and telling me I'm beginning to look A LOT like Willie Nelson's Little Brother. Behind my back, I've smuggled in some contraband raw food: a couple delicious appetizers and desserts that no one will know are raw, because I won't tell them about the grievous lack of oven time.

I ease over to the buffet and set them on the end, still facing my Aunt, commenting on her latest Hummel statue, a little cherubic boy in a business suit with a brief case and an umbrella over his shoulder and a bemused look on his face. There's another little boy who's lying face down on the ground and the kid with the umbrella and the brief case and the look has a triumphant foot on his back, the kid on the ground's face all scrunched up in pain. There's a little inscription on the base in the front in quotes, umbrella kid saying, "Outa my way or I go right over you."

Auntie tells me its Number 54, called Corporate Climber.

I slide the contraband raw food behind my back next to the bowl of chopped liver and Saltine Crackers, my glass plates gently clinking against the pebbled glass chopped liver bowl.

While we've been upfront with Auntie about raw food, but she's still a little skeptical and we think it best to avoid the splashy front hall inspection and recital of the ingredients and preparation.

We even have thought of strapping some food to my cousin (another guest of Auntie's Thanksgiving Feast) and have him mule some in for us.

Kathy and I will have some raw friendly eats for people to try. The other possibility involved each of us filling our plates and volunteering to go sit at the Kiddie Table and feeding her dog Dumpling the contents of our plates. Dumpling, 17 years old and legally blind, will appreciate us, though for the next few days, poor Uncle Lenny will spend an additional hour in the back yard wondering if a horse got into the back yard and left the sizable deposits likely to exit Dumpling's lower GI.

Remember, shush.

The food has it's own voice and can sing acapella without any help from you.

It's just another Voice.

All the food needs is your hands and your heart.

And your Silence.

PRACTICING DISTRACTION

Maybe meditation isn't some elusive discipline reserved for the avatars. What if it's as simple as practicing distraction?

Merriam Dictionary definition of *DISTRACTION*

1 the act of distracting or the state of being distracted; especially: mental confusion <driven to distraction>

2 something that distracts; especially: amusement <a harmless distraction>

Distraction. I used to think of it as definition 1, something to take my attention away from something else and, the mental confusion, but I think I've had it wrong. Maybe it's 2. Not the first part, the "something that distracts part;" the second part of 2, which says, "especially amusement," and the real gold at the end: "Harmless" as in you're safe, don't worry, nothing's going to happen, relax, breathe, get comfortable. And then, just so you don't forget, the word again, repeated so you remember: distraction.

Prayin's cool, especially if you're smiling.

Avatars are known as people of prayer.

Prayer. A person's conscious attempt to reach out and touch the finger of God.

We say pray, not all dour, sending out *those* kinda vibes.

Think about a dog.

A dog's happy when you're happy. You know how their tail starts thumpin', you get that little lift in your voice that they tune in to, their eyes light up and they lift their head and just look at you, like they're staring at the only thing that tops a walk and dinner AND up on the bed? Laughter, the best medicine, some times, is the best first thing to try . . .

I look at each day, which is all any of us get, like a Laugh Ladder, the kinda thing you lean up against a wall with a clunk. The only way up is to climb each thing that I experience each day, seeing if I can find the humor in it, rung-by-rung, experience-by-experience, like scenes in a movie. By the end of the day, see how high I go.

Give it a try.

Maybe even picture yourself up there, sitting on the top, top of the Universe, on top of a wall, a clear view extends as far as the eye can see, nothing to distract you.

Your mind, settling down, everything relaxing, but you're alert, a little hiss of air going in and out of you like it does, but now, that hiss coming into focus and the movie changes, you're up there, and you're alone, but you're not scared, because there's Nothing up here. No things. Nothing to see, nothing to hear; quiet, except all you're hearing's that air, going in and out.

Pure silence, minus the breathing, still slow, but a couple big ones in and out, almost like a relaxed sigh—that underwater scuba diver quiet, everything out of hearing but the air tank noise, a little louder than you're used to, but you're not really used to it because you don't usually pay attention, distracted by all the things, the experiences, looking for the humor in them, the good part really, not really stuck on the past or thinking about what's next, that looking back or ahead, hey, they'll get that air noise off the soundtrack faster than anything.

But back up on the wall, the wall up at the top of the Universe.

Boy, close those eyes, there's nothing to see anyway, might as well look inside, really feel the way your body feels, that air going in and out and now, the heart beat.

Hey, how often do you hear this without a stethoscope?

It's a simple song, that repeated thud, but now that you're up here, sitting with your eyes closed, that ladder behind you, the base of it, those two wooden feet, pressed into the Earth, the last couple rungs, just over your shoulder behind you, this top of the wall wide enough to sit on comfortably. A comfortable seat. Somewhere to sit without any distractions.

Just these words and that air noise and the heartbeat feeling, the steady thud in your chest sending tiny waves out, a little vibration, like sonar waves traveling outward in the ocean inside us, bouncing against the bones and finally the skin, maybe even shaking the hairs on us, so little we don't see it, but it's happening, sending all these waves out into the moisture in the air all over the world, those waves extending all over out to the edge of the atmosphere around the Earth, but not before every human being on the planet feels, whether they know it our not, your beating heart. A heart that speeds up when you're happy, or speeds up a dog's heart, when it gets the signal from you, a look, when your eyes touch, and then the thud, the wave, reaching out between you, whether you're in the same room our anywhere on Earth. Nobody hides from anyone's love.

Everyone feels everyone else when they're alive, not just the people they touch.

We just sent you love.

You're reading, yeah, and we hope the words made you smile, but how we felt when we wrote them, like we were sitting up there on the wall, one of us on each side of you, three ladders up against the wall, wide enough to sit on comfortably up there, looking out into the clear view of Nothing, No Sound, No Distractions, hearing your breath go in and out, the thud of your heart, when you think about it, always feeling the thud of everyone else's, that those sonar waves traveling out from us, across the water in the air, the moisture, humidity, whatever. We live in water when we're inside our mother and we live in water outside our mother and then, we are entrusted to the care of the Earth Mother, that womb of water we all share, just less now, most of it under us in the oceans, seas, lakes, rivers, ponds, and puddles, that drop on the counter next to a glass.

That water that we write our intentions and feelings on, the water inside us, the water around us, is the Ocean of Air we all swim in, and if we listen closely, we hear the air, going in and out, the air filled with water, filled with feelings and intentions of everyone else on the Planet at once. In and out. In and out. All our hearts beating together in some symphony, if we listen.

Those six billion plus thuds we feel, if we really feel, the gentle pat, like the kind we give a dog on the head, or when we rub its chest. A dog. A pet. Petting. We all love to pet a dog, but every moment we're alive we're all petting each other, just a gentle pat, like the kind we give a dog, right on his chest, thud, thud, thud, these wonderful creatures who capture our hearts, looking right at us telling us the secret, you're looking at it all wrong, you've got it backwards: You're not separate, you're all one, all of your hearts beating, in this giant Ocean of Moist Air, this womb we all share.

We come from Nowhere and pass through the portal, our mother, from a place where we did not breathe to a place that we do and come into Now, the present, and we climb the rungs of the ladder in our life until we reach the top, and we climb into the next womb and go on to the next Life, a place where we don't breathe air.

And the place we go is a wonder beyond our dreams, a place where everyone is connected, where, if they're quiet, the can feel each other, everyone, all at once, just being together.

Nowhere to go, nothing to say, nothing to even think about, nothing to feel . . .

. . . but good.

Hey, maybe if we think about it, we're already there, we just need to be conscious of it, to be careful not to be distracted. Distract. Off track. Derailed. That train. Gliding along the track just fine all by itself if we let it.

Maybe when you're happy when you look at a dog, he wags his tail, not because he's happy for the reason you think he is.

He wags his tail to tell you that you've got it backwards.

He's smiling in the front, but waving from the back, like, look at it backwards.

He's happy because you're happy but mostly because you've got it right. He's wagging to praise you for being happy.

You're prayer, to touch God, has been answered.

By the dog.

Ever wonder who's behind those eyes?

:) :)

:) :)

:) :)

:) :)

:) :)

:) :)

YOU CAN TEACH A DOG . . .
AND MAYBE THE DOG
CAN TEACH YOU

I wish, with a little kid's heart, the one inside me still, that everyone in the world reads this and feels happy, even if it's just for that moment when they finish and wonder who's really watching them. In every language . . . and for those moments, whether they come in clumps or one at a time or for 1000 years, and that moment when someone smiles, they send a little pulse of something wonderful, like a deliberately placed pat on a dog's chest, thud, thud, thud. Touching the dog's heart, and he wags his tail, telling you, yes, yes, the heart, when you pet my heart you are petting everyone's. We are everyone at once, this moment, if you will.

Look down at the bottom, no, not there, THERE. See the smilie face?

That's for you.

We put it one the cover once, and at the bottom of every page and on the last page, if you look, it's the last thing you'll see.

Remember.

Re-member. Become a member. Remember we're all in the womb together . . .

See you up on the wall.

We want the spot right next to you, one of us on each side of you. We'll each hold your hand, we'll close our eyes and smile.

Nothing to do but feel good.

I'm not talking about later, Pardner, I'm talking about right now or any time you want.

We'll be there.

You're the Pardner we were looking for all long. How are you?

We have this crazy idea.

We wrote something down on a piece of paper with a date on it.

We wanted to open a restaurant called Borrowed Earth Café.

We want everyone to eat there.

Starting with you.

Kathy makes food. Danny puts it on a plate. Danny hands you plate. There's the plate, a knife and a fork and a real honest white cloth napkin, but we don't think you'll miss a crumb.

We're thinking about puttin' something a little extra in the food, something people don't see, but we aren't going to tell them. It's a secret.

YOU: *chewing* "I think you got something here. When can we start?"

US: "How about right now?"

YOU: "So were Pardners, right?"

US: "Pardners. Shake."

hands shake

YOU: "So Pardner, now tell me the secret."

DANNY & KATHY: *nodding toward plate* "We just did."

The Art of Thinking

All the great avatars have taught, narrating from the lens of their own experience, having visited the Realms of Dreams, touched the Void, the Center of the outward spiraling Universe. They tell us that the only real point of power is there and Here, in the the Present Moment, capital P, capital M, and that the past and future hold no power over us.

That we are bound to history or destiny with our own cords of unconscious thought, cords that can get all knotted and tangled with the rest of the things in the washing machine of our minds.

We look at creation, ours and those of others, and we use the dictionary of our own history to define. And those words we choose trigger feelings and emotions. Those thoughts, like potent electricity, sending vibrations into us that we *feel*. Feeling, feelings, *feeling* those thoughts rippling across the water in us . . . 75% of us, or so I'm told, that water then, that 75 some percent of us, the most substantial thing in a human body.

Our real brain, if you will, not the organ behind our eyes or the wires leading in and out of it, but the whole thing, the whole body maybe.

Our mind, the screen we type the words on, the screen we see when we close our eyes and watch old movies, the old ones, our past, the place where we see and imagine and direct new ones, before we see them Out There, in our future.

These avatars tell us of an Enchanted Realm of Dreams.

A place within and the path to a seat, maybe up on the wall at the top of the Universe, to a point of power, a place where thoughts begin and end, that center of the outward spiraling Universe, a place to send and receive love.

The Void.

A place of Silence. A place of Peace and Contentment. A place where thinking is unnecessary.

The beginning of Creation, a place to create, for the artist.

The clean kitchen, the blank canvas, the tilled garden, the first clean page of the notebook, the musical instrument ready to be played.

Ready for the artist.

An artist, someone who draws from their past creations, those they can see and those they remember, and from the creations of others which inspire them.

Someone who creates.

Using creations to create again.

A new recipe, a painting, a garden, a poem or a book or even just a little piece of paper that you imagine tearing off and setting down next to someone, a piece of paper that says, "I love you."

Now that's art!

The artist, the creater, creates.

The definer, the person with the dictionary, does not.

The artist, is seated amongst the avatars, past and present and future, avatars who sit up on the wall at the top of the Universe.

Seated at the center of the Universe Within that spirals inexorably outward and at the moment before creation, the place from which they all begin and end . . .

One hand, holding a knife poised over a cutting board, a paintbrush, a seed (but where to put it?), a pencil (but what to write?), a musical instrument (but what to play?).

At that moment, we hold in one hand the tool in the Present Moment, that knife, the brush, the seed, the pencil, the musical instrument . . .

The other hand? It's touching the Void, the finger of God . . .

Ready?

And we seize the threads of our thoughts and bind them to the loom and we begin to weave . . .

—Artie and Constance Weaver (aka, Danny & Kathy Living)

BORROWED EARTH CAFE☺

"That in whom reside all beings and Who resides in all beings, Who is the Giver of graces to all, the Supreme Soul of the Universe, the Limitless Being—I am that."—Amritbindu Upanishad

So all 6 billion plus of us, in some ways, we're spinning around in some giant washing machine, getting bound together like a load of clothes, getting all knotted up in the spin cycle, and then a big hand opens the door, takes us out and gently unknots us and we all go out of the wet place into a warm dry one and we all get fluffed, folded and put away, like clothes to be worn another day at another time.

And then the next load goes in together . . .

All clothes from the same closet, going in to the wash and the dryer, different clothes in different combinations at different times, but they all come and go out of that same closet, a closet without a door now, someone named Kathy, taking off the hinges . . .

"You're out now, mister . . . miss . . ."

This is Danny talking, I've been talking the whole time, hiding behind Kathy's voice.

She's just another Voice.

She's you and me.

The big Mother Blanket, not on us, around us. We hung one up on the wall to see right when you come in so you'll remember.

Remember?

We're all writing now, hugging, laughing more . . . able to be who we are without reservations . . . you don't need reservations at Borrowed Earth Café, it's just you, but you'll be eating with the rest of us.

That Kathy, she's watching though. She sees and feels everything and once the bell rings on the door and you're inside, for that time that you're here with us, she'll be watching you, making sure you're okay and that you leave feeling good and satisfied, maybe with something to think about or just feeling better than when you walked in . . .

It's our mission . . .

She watches you, even if you clomp around in the café like Bobby, but she looks at you with love, and that love beckons like the warm of the sun that rises in the East and settles over the horizon in the West.

Get in your wagon, or maybe the balloon, see where it takes you, but enjoy the scenery, high five the birds, meet that bolder version of you along the way, but still see those tiny miracles that illuminate around you like fireflies on a summer night, especially those tiny yellow glows that light the faces of the other children so you can see the real miracles . . .

The other kids illuminated in the night.

But do stop in for a bite.

It's Simply the Best Food on the Planet, just like the sign just to the right of the front door says.

Don't miss the signs.

But also connected by threads of thought, threads we place on the loom, like the Weavers, Artie and Constance.

Use those threads to weave your loom, make a blanket to put around yourself or better, for someone else to wrap around them or you can hang it up on the wall to look at and remember . . .

And we're also able to send love to everyone else in the womb; there's no where we can hide in the whole womb, we're always feeling each other, the breath and the heart beat and the vibrations rippling out and rippling in a spiral.

Traveling outward and inward, rippling through the water.

In and out.

In and out.

Thud thud.

Thud thud.

Ripple in, ripple out.

Ripple out, ripple in.

The black line and the white one.

Which do you see?

They're both there.

Be gentle in the washing machine, we're all in it together.

Be creative with the loom, keep your finger on the finger of God, and make something beautiful, all of the threads, at first separate, become one. And, when the blanket's done, the threads become the blanket and they're all in it together.

Be kind in the womb, we're all in it together.

And take care of the restaurant. After you leave, someone else will come and we'll feed them too.

When you sit in here, it's not your seat and table, you're just borrowing it.

You didn't inherit it from the last person, you're just borrowing from the next person.

So, let's leave it nice.

Don't leave a mess.

But while you're here, be nice, have fun, enjoy the food and the laughs, smile to the other people, but pay attention, sometimes we sneak serious in when you're distracted.

It just means we love you . . . all of you.

We'll see all of you up on the top of the Wall.

Even if we don't say it, it's there in the food, in the joke, in this Borrowed Earth Café ☺

So, Who Wrote This?

That's the question, isn't it?

Was it Kathy Living, born Kathleen Brodsky, the oldest daughter of Arnold and Meryl Brodsky?

Or was it Kathy's husband Danny Living, born Robert Porter, the illegitimate son of a 17-year-old girl? Was it Danny, who at three weeks old was adopted by the Morans, who took Robert home to raise and filed papers and went to court and legally changed Robert Porter's name to Daniel Moran?

But how did he go from Daniel Moran to Danny Living?

Living, is that really your name?

Here's the backstory.

When Daniel Moran went off to Loras College in Dubuque, Iowa to go school, after those two years of spending his summer job money on booze and drugs and life and going through the motions of school until he had to figure out what to do with his life, after those few solid months of beer for breakfast, lunch, dinner and dessert, he decided that he'd had enough Iowa. His little brother PJ had enrolled at Columbia College in Chicago and he decided that after sharing a room with PJ all those years, he would go to school with him, not really knowing where else to go and not ready to grow up and start grinding away at his soul full time in a job he didn't really like just yet, he signed up for classes at Columbia, not too long after he sent that flare up in the backyard behind the basketball net and had his first real conversation with God . . .

Borrowed Earth Café ☺

He took classes in writing and studied poetry and read other writer's works.

He sat in circles with other kids who wanted to learn to write and his teachers helped encourage him.

And he went to practice the martial arts with an almost religious zeal that probably surprised everyone including his parents and brother and sister.

Like some obsession or quest undertaken by someone heading to some destination different than anything he'd imagined as a kid for himself.

The slow kid, the turtle, the kid who got picked on, who was now going to martial arts or karate as everyone else called it every day and practicing at home in the basement. He was riding his bike or driving the family's little yellow Honda Civic 4-speed or later the 2-door brown Ford Escort and then his 1973 blue AMC Hornet and then his silver Oldsmobile Cutlas or when that broke, his black Jeep CJ7 or his blue Chevy Cavalier with the broken seat that hurt his back or the wonderful car he called The Boat: the smoke gray 4-door 1986 Crown Victoria with the black vinyl top and a front seat you could really get comfortable on, a car that in 1998 was hit from behind while it was stopped at a red light by a man driving 45 mph in a blue Chrysler Grand Caravan, a man on the phone who didn't see the cars were stopped or the red light and didn't see the back of that Crown Victoria and Dan Moran's head just over the top of the head rest looming up on him suddenly, so he didn't brake, just slammed into him, no skid marks the police report showed, no squeal of brakes. Dan and that man in the van, just a mile from where Dan Moran, Dan, as most called him then except those who knew him as a child or who just liked to put a Y on the end, called him Danny.

Dan suddenly looked up and saw the grill of the van in the rear view mirror and then ¼ second later felt that horrible impact and heard the big crash and felt his chest (he wasn't buckled) slam into the steering wheel and his left knee crash into the dashboard down at the bottom, his neck whip forward, sending him and The Boat (which saved his life, that big boat of a wonderful car) plowing into the back of the black Jeep Cherokee in front of him and then when he hit the Jeep, his neck snapped back, bouncing off the head rest.

In a daze, he got out of The Boat, everyone looking now, everything in slow motion, the details a little fuzzy, the shock and anger and confusion all churning in his head, the girl in traffic, someone it later turned out he worked with rolling her window down and her mouth moving, "Are you okay?" and then looking at the front of The Boat (not too bad) and then the back (not too good) and then going back to the van, the driver, a 40-something year old man with glasses in a business suit still talking on the phone, all excited now, climbing out of the van, talking in some language Dan didn't understand, putting his hand over the phone saying, "You stopped too fast and I couldn't stop . . ." already trying to turn it around.

He was more upset about The Boat (The Boat!) then the man's lie and he went back and closed the door on the Crown Victoria and waited for the police. And then, the waves of nausea and the dull ache in his back and neck, a singing pain in his chest and deep in his left hip that would keep him from sleeping more than a few hours and popping over the counter anti-inflamatory tablets like Tic Tacs, as many as 14 a day, when it was bad.

A dull constant pain that was like someone twisting you too far or pressing too hard with an extended middle knuckle, like Sister Mathilda. A pain that kept him awake, that made sitting, standing or anything a low-grade agony.

A pain that distracted was the beginning of the lingering end of his marriage to the girl he met his senior year in college, a girl he recognized that first day in class that last semester who looked like the girl from the coffee shop across from the karate school he drove to everyday back when he was still driving his parent's Ford escort.

A pain that came after he sold his own karate school and resigned himself to a corporate life.

A pain that came before he started cutting all that hair off every two weeks, all those little pieces of him falling to the floor in a shower to be swept up and thrown away or later, folded up in that newspaper on the floor in the basement.

A pain that frightened him, as it seemed to never go completely away and which could be aggravated by a moment's lapse in his posture, sleeping more than an hour in one position, sitting in the car for a few minutes, walking, standing . . . there was no escape.

Like being cooked in a pain crucible at a low steady temperature.

Walking in the middle of the night and going downstairs to sleep on the couch, which became a nightly ritual, reading, listening to the same song 1000 times, a 43-second little chant of something he didn't understand but seemed to distract him from the pain, which never left.

His sense of purpose lost, now it was just the grind at his soul, the corporate games and politics and the climbing, Outa my way!

And maybe that pain was more than just the car accident.

A lot more.

He watched himself and his kids' mom drift farther apart. Like it was happening to someone else . . . just watching it happen now.

She didn't know how to live with his pain and neither did he.

Two years later, someone gave him some yoga tapes for Christmas, which seemed cruel, yoga for a guy who could hardly touch his ankles, let alone his toes. A guy who had logged 1000's of miles on the road and 10,000 in karate schools, other people's and later his own. A guy who went from being a lazy turtle to an obsessed rabbit and then back to being a turtle, but now a turtle who was pulling his stiff neck and sore legs and arms into some shell of pain and grief, his life and purpose seemed lost beyond the joy of his children, who also probably looked at that pillow on the couch and heard those footsteps, maybe, walking slowly down the steps from their parent's room to the sofa some nights, or the front door open and close in the middle of the night while their father wandered the streets in the dark.

Maybe not lost, but certainly lost his way.

Then those yoga tapes, sure, he promised he'd watch then try it but thinking, No.

Then being surprised to find that few minutes of relief after a quarter-hearted attempt to follow along with the tv, laying there at the end on his back in the family room, everyone still asleep upstairs, the tape clicking off and slipping into a relaxed sleep for the first time in two years. And wakening up and noticing that the pain was gone . . . even for those few minutes, it was like having his body pinned down by an elephant's foot hard and then, the foot lifts for a few minutes and it's the most wonderful relief . . . and though it doesn't last, he does it again the next day, and yes, it happens again at the end for a few minutes, and then each day, with the same obsessive discipline he put into karate, he puts into yoga.

And the relief, the no pain, starts to last longer and longer.

"Within six months," he writes on a piece of paper, remembering the other piece of paper, "I was able to wake up and bend forward and press my forehead to my shins in the May of 2000, five months after starting yoga," and sure enough, it happened.

Something he couldn't do *before* the accident.

And then, it seemed as suddenly as it had come, the pain left, it's work done.

And, not satisfied with just being a student, he wanted to share and he thought about what it would be like to teach.

After a sour family vacation in Florida, fate intervened.

His kids' mom, who used to take turns driving with him the whole 24-hour drive they'd make to to visit her parents in Naples, Florida, this trip home, was unable to keep up her end.

So, feeling angry, he drove the whole way. He set his CD player on repeat 1, locking on some song that matched his mood and drove almost the whole way without relief.

Maybe feeling guilty and knowing the tax the drive could have put on his barely mended body, she suggested he go to a local gym and take a hot yoga class, sweat out the drive.

So he drove up to the gym and to his disappointment, found out the teacher hadn't showed.

The women and Dan, all standing around by the desk where greeted by the owner who said the teacher couldn't come, but asked if anyone would like to lead a class. Everyone looked at their shoes, but Dan.

"I'll do it," he said.

He stood up front and took the women with their colored mats through a shorter version of what he himself did every day now. Having graduated from the tapes, he'd gone on to a grueling 90-minute routine of 72 postures, but he cut out the middle sequence and proceeded slowly, explaining with the barest of words the beauty of the practice.

After he left, the women thanked hm and he walked out feeling better than he when he'd taught karate.

Which was lucky for Danny.

The next day, the owner called him and offered him a job. No training or teacher experience other than what he'd learned himself and maybe helped by all those years in karate, teaching, explaining, connecting with people who knew pain, not the people bullied by other kids or trying to work out the ghosts of their past, to feel safe again. No this was different, but it was somehow the same.

He said yes.

A few months later, he met Kathy and they became friends, practicing together a couple times a week and attending each other's classes when they could.

After that trip back from Florida, he had tried to get his kids' mom to consider taking their considerable savings and buy a property in Florida, their own. She didn't like the idea of the long distance between them and what they owned and so he looked into a local investment and found a condo for sale right across the street behind the grocery store where Andy would work as a cashier. She shocked him by saying yes but even more when she suggested he move there.

Alone.

She said he could live there, their relationship being more like a brother and sister who didn't like each other now.

In Florida, a few months back, after a vicious fight, one of his kids had said to him, "I always thought if you two got divorced I would hate you both, but now I think I would understand."

But he loved them, those two who were the only people in the world related to him by blood, in whom he could see his own features and maybe the features of that 17-year old girl and the idea of not seeing them every day, being in the house they slept . . . those thoughts caused a hollow pressure in his chest that pressed outward.

And now, just two months later, his kids' mom says, "You move out, we'll stay here."

Move out.

Go live alone.

It was the last shoe to drop.

He found a little apartment in town next to the church he'd stumbled into 14 years earlier when his daughter was first born. An apartment next to a church he'd walked into all those years before and gone into a confessional and told a man in a black outfit everything he'd ever done that he'd been afraid or ashamed to tell aloud.

He'd written them down and read the list, his voice choked with emotion.

Face to face.

He walked out in the sun and felt the world had been lifted from him and felt once again the finger of God on him, more a feeling than a word, but a comfort and peace he couldn't articulate but was as palpable as the heat.

After he signed the lease, but a few days before he left, he sat on the floor of the sewing room of the house behind his son and daughter, who sat at a folding table in front of the family computer, talking and typing, he on the floor behind them studying their backs, his heart aching to tell them.

And their laughter made him happy and suddenly, it was like an assurance, they would be okay.

He knew too that if he didn't leave, they would only live in a house electrified by the tension of two people who had loved each other, than drifted apart until the gulf was so wide you couldn't even see across it, didn't know how to get back and it kept widening into a bitterness.

They would be themselves, yes, but all those years of being in that house of pain, the arguments, the silences, the angry outbursts, the together but alone living, everyone off in the four corners of the house, the uncomfortable dinners, all of it . . . he worried that they would repeat it, like some horrible knick-knack, the heirloom of dysfunction, dry hollow loveless bitter existence.

It happened.

And it was no one's fault, but everyone ate from that same sad plate, wishing it was the way it had been, but searching for when it had been that way, little moments and big moments, all of them grow farther apart under the same roof.

And so he felt he had to have the courage to do what turned out to be the hardest thing he'd ever done in his life. He left the two people who he loved more than anyone else in the whole world.

But he wrote on a piece of paper, "My kids turned out okay."

A piece of paper he didn't put on the mirror in his bathorrom but that he stuck on the mirror behind his eyes.

And he trusted that the God who flew to him that night in the backyard behind that basketball net on the pole on the gravel mound on his parent's driveway, the God or feeling that flooded him outside that church in Naperville after confession, the God he'd prayed to as a child, the Angel of God, would protect them.

And he felt a flood of relief and suddenly a yoga pose that had eluded him, laying on the floor on his back, he pulled both ankles behind his neck, one crossed over the other and lifted up his lower back and linked his curled fingers together.

It was a foot closer than he'd been the day before. He hadn't even had a shower or warmed up, but he was bathed in some deep contentment that opened some door in his body all the way and allowed him to let something big go, like it had suddenly left and flew away.

He asked his daughter to get the camera, on that folded table in a little dock by the computer and the kids turned around, whoa, and she took the picture.

CLICK.

He felt it a proof of something that had shifted in him, a foot in one day.

In a yoga practice that had seen changes measured in millimeters, 12 inches was like leaping across a chasm in one easy step.

He took it as an answer.

The next night, he lay in bed next to his wife, her back to him and maybe sensing a change in him, she began to argue. About nothing and everything, and as was her habit in fights, when there was nothing left to argue about, logical or illogical, she pulled out the club that she'd hit him with a hundred times before, the club that she knew hurt him more than any other.

"Fine! Let's get a divorce," she said for the hundred and first time.

Usually he would not say anthing or say, "Fine, call a lawyer," and they would drift to separate corners and pretend nothing had happened.

This time he said calmly, "Tomorrow I'm not coming home from work and I'm not coming back until I have my own place."

She probably thought he was kidding, but should have known this man didn't kid.

He joked, he laughed, but when he spoke calmly like that, he was telling you what was going to happen. Business like.

If he said he was going to do something, all you did was look at your watch or the calendar, thinking that you must never say yes and do no.

That you must keep your word.

Which was what had kept him here, that first promise to her, but this was hurting everyone.

Slowly.

Another crucible.

It was no one's fault.

So the next day, when he was due home, he never came, never called.

And he wished he had said something to his children before, sparing them the agony of wondering where their father had gone.

Three days later, he came home after seeing a therapist and put some clothes and his guitars in the back of that white Chevy pickup and drove to his apartment.

A tiny little single room place that had been a corner deli that had been converted into an apartment. The meat locker had been turned into a bathroom and a partitioned room the bedroom, a tiny kitchenette and a little room for a yoga mat.

But no kids.

And then, the most surprising thing of all happened . . .

One day he said to Kathy, "I wish I could just meet someone like you . . . ." thinking, hey, yeah, have things in common.

Opposites attract maybe, but do you have similar interests? Danny loved reading, running, watching movies, playing the guitar, writing, and just sitting around talking with people, having people over for dinner. He and his kids' mom had had this attraction and had enjoyed each other's company, sure, but she loved to draw, to garden, go for short, gentle bike rides and make arts and crafts. So, when they weren't working, they had doggedly pursued, in those few hours of leisure, the things that each loved to do . . . which, unfortunately weren't the same things . . . and what little time they'd had together they each agreed to squander on personally preferred leisure activities, separately.

Never thinking, duh, we're not enjoying our lives together. We're enjoying them apart. Together, aside from the shared love of the children, became together, but alone, really.

It had been sad. He really had loved her; they just didn't have a lot in common, and ultimately, he remembered as a kid imagining spending his whole day with his wife to be, of course they would love the same activities.

Of course.

Duh.

But the grown up Dan forgot that simple childhood idea and the wisdom attached to it.

Duh.

But he thought, maybe it's possible.

You see that husband and wife at 80 still holding hands or running a bakery or playing cards together or walking together or sitting side by side at a coffee shops reading together all the time and the answer's staring back at you.

Together. Not together alone. Together together.

Like you wanted to all along.

Not work at all. *Work* at your relationship. It shouldn't feel like a job.

It should be fun. Like play.

Is it unrealistic to want to pack as much fun into a day as possible?

Is it childish to pursue happiness by being with someone you love, who you love to be with, who loves you back and not only do they want to be with you right now, and later too, they enjoy the same things you do.

Unrealistic pie-in-the-sky sappy movie poppycock, right?

So he said that, "I wish I could meet someone like you."

Then drove away. Didn't think anything of it.

Apparently, this wasn't something to noodle.

More of a visceral reaction to those words.

After just a few miles, an incredible pressure pushed out on his chest and he stopped the car and tried to breathe deeply and slowly.

He feared all the stress of what was happening had given him a heart attack and as he sat there in the truck trying to stop his racing heart, a sudden realization hit him.

I wish I could meet someone like you.

There it was.

Oh no, he thought, I love Kathy.

And that thought wouldn't go away.

His rationale mind kicked in:

It's too soon.

And then, What, am I supposed to do forget that just happened to me?

What if she lookd at this guy with his nub of hair growing out now and said, "I don't think so," or "You're not even divorced," or worse, "I don't feel that way."

Two years later, the dating and the slow introduction to the family, the serious dating . . . maybe then . . .

But this was happening right now all of a sudden and it had hit him like a roundhouse kick in the chest.

What about convention?

Forget it.

He dialed her number and in an act that felt like running wildly off a cliff, no pinwheeling arms, no safety net, just jump.

He closed his eyes, he didn't want to look.

He breathed slowly in and out, there was that pressure again, but it felt good, and his heart quickened and his voice sounded shakey.

Hi, she said. What's up?

Uh, I wanted to tell you something.

Okay, what is it?

He took a breath and said it.

I love you.

Then he waited for what seemed eternity, but she answered right away in a rush.

I love you too.

He should have stayed in his apartment and done the conventional thing. Date for a few years then maybe move in together and then maybe get married.

Forget it.

But, that pesky heart.

It seemed every time he was away from her, that pesky heart of his would kick in.

And the pressure.

This is crazy.

Like getting married when you're 22.

This is crazy.

Like opening a karate school.

This is crazy

But, the bar drops in your lap, the car starts with a jolt (you're already in) so keep your arms and legs inside the car for 66 years together.

So, without consulting even so much as his horoscope and knowing from experience that a man who doesn't trust his gut will soon break his own heart, he said to her the next day, "I don't want to be without you."

She lit up.

"You could just stay here," she offered.

And so he moved in and abandoned the apartment.

But not everyone in his life understood what had happened and maybe thought about convention.

And a gulf opened up in some places that still make him sad, but he was done ignoring what his gut and heart said. He'd gotten off the path doing that and knew that igoring your heart causes pain and grief that later turns into the spot on your lung, right behind your sad, deflated heart.

At first they were gonna just be boyfriend and girlfriend, forget convention. But later the idea of being married felt right and he said he wanted to get married.

The idea of being married felt right, but now they each had children with different last names, but they liked the idea of sharing a name.

His last name was Moran, a name his kids' mom had always hated.

At the final divorce hearing, the judge offered to change his kids' mom's name back to her maiden name and Dan waited to hear her say something like, "I always hated the name Moran" or something and then agree, yes, change it back. But, to his surprise, his kids' mom said, "No, I'll stay Moran."

He almost fell over.

So when they decided to marry, Dan and Kathy, Kathy said she didn't really want to be the second Mrs. Moran. However, she did like the idea of having the same last name so she said, Yeah, it would be okay. Moran, just a name, but the idea of being the second Mrs. Moran . . .

And also thinking about her two boys, who bore their father's last name, MacFadyen.

Two children would be the Morans and it seemed to leave her boys out of something and Dan didn't want them left out of anything.

They were his kids now, in many regards, as they were estranged from their father.

They decided to pick a new name. Before the raw food or anything a friend had stayed with them, a friend from Naples. She had worked with Kathy as a Mary Kay director in the UK and had spent a wonderful week with the two of them, going to yoga, eating their food and doing a lot of soulful, honest talking. At the end of the week, the astute business woman, now, like Kathy, having moved into the realty game, said, "You two are in the wrong business. Dan, with your IT and you, Kathy, with the custom homes. You should start a business sharing your way of living."

A year later, Dan and Kathy arranged a yoga trip with their friend David Williams and took 10 people to a little place in the jungle in Mexico. Dan's friend from his IT job helped him make a website where people could sign up called Danny and Kathy Living dot org.

Danny and Kathy Living.

It sounded more like their name.

So when they decided to pick a new last name to share, they picked that.

While he was at it, he changed his name from the proper Daniel, to Danny.

The name his brother PJ, the star in his childhood night sky, the little kid on the back of the bike, in the next bed and now a million emotional miles and 7 years of silence apart, the name he called him.

The name his sister called him when they were little.

When he was little, back when he wasn't hiding from himself.

Danny Living.

It fit.

But back to the boys, it was more than their last name that concerned Dan.

49 years ago, some girl who was not physically, emotionally or mentally ready or able to take care of Robert, Daniel, Danny, Dan stepped aside and let someone else do the job.

After he met Kathy and learned about their dad, he thought, Hey this is my chance to pay it forward, do what someone else did, made a sacrifice, let someone else do what, for whatever reasons, they just couldn't.

It wasn't because his birth mother didn't love him; she just didn't have the tools in her toolbox to build a kid beyond the reproduction part.

The real parenting, The Work, well, she hoped that someone else she probably would never know could do it.

That was her hope, but it was something that must have been hard. Not seeing or knowing the person, the people, her kid, or the stewards of that kid, the person (s) that would take care of him.

He always tells people he has four kids, because, if nothing else, he's here, and maybe all they might look and say he did was keep Kathy from worrying about them, "They're okay, put the phone down," he would say 1000's of times. Know this: For every phone call or text they would get, there were at least three that they didn't get and he took full responsibility for being the one saying, "They're fine. They're okay. They'll be home. They're smart."

And little by little, she's become willing to trust that.

So, if nothing else, he can say he helped with that.

And if nothing else, this man loved their mother fiercely, but in a way different than there father had, who rarely, even when he lived in the house, was home. A man who worked away from home for weeks and months and who lived in his own world overshadowed with an abusive childhood that maybe resulted in him, unable to control himself, protected his children by pushing them away, but because his intelligence was keen enough to recognize maybe that he didn't have all the tools in his toolbox that he would need.

Not his fault or anyone's. Just how it worked out.

Which was lucky for Dan. As hard as it was being away from his kids, who's mother didn't always respect the boundaries between kids and adults and who spread some of her grief and suffering around, with no one else she wanted to reach out to. And when Dan's kids would see him and return to her, it brought back all the fresh pain.

He said the thing that he couldn't bear to say, but he said it any way. "If, in order to survive, you have to not see me as much, I'll understand."

They had given him their understanding about the divorce and now it was his turn to pay it back, pay it forward, even if it meant a sacrifice.

The Biggest Sacrifice. Trusting your kids will be okay, without you.

Their comfort traded for his broken heart. His daughter was 14 and his son 16, now working as a cashier at the grocery in front of the condo his mom suggested he move to, still stay married, keep the paycheck deposited in the shared account, but living separately.

The grief of not seeing your own children is soothed some by having someone else's to care for.

To look after, even if it's just a hand on their mother's arm reaching into her purse for a phone.

Or to just be there.

Solid, sort of, a little worse for the wear and tear, but someone who walked around the house, laughed, cried, played guitar sitting on the edge of their mom's bed, singing to her.

He would never claim to be their father; that would always be the man who lived halfway across the country who didn't call or send for them or come to visit.

Not because their father didn't love them but, in his way, because he did.

To protect his kids.

A sacrifice.

Seven years after the run off the cliff, the I Love You call, after moving in, Dan saw their father, sat behind him in court, sat right behind him, heard him talk.

They'd never met.

Then, in the hall Kathy's lawyer walked up to Dan and said, "Where's Kathy?"

Dan was standing in front of her with arms folded and his hair wild and who'd deliberately put on a white shirt (peace) with a peace symbol drawn over the grey scale earth (whole foods, 18.95, but man, t's oganic cotton and soft as silk).

Danny told her to stand behind him and not look at the boys' father.

She was terrified.

Waves of fear rooted in her past experiences with their father, the moods, the illogical arguments, the weird behavior, and yes, the temper and the physical intimidation when he got really mad and out of control. And later, the shove up against the wall.

Danny could feel it all and he was the Shield.

The rottweiler, Kathy calls him, "My Rottie."

But Danny fixed his happiest smile on his face because he wanted Adam and Stuart's father to see, finally, who was the Steward of Stuart and Adam.

And Danny wanted him not to worry, except that maybe he was modeling hippy, worse case scenario.

He did that for his sons, Adam and Stuart.

He could have been an jerk, a hard guy, the mean stare, the sent aggression, but, for their sake and because he knew they loved their father, and even with their hurt and grief and confusion as to his distance and silence, they wouldn't want him to suffer, even if his on suffering was thinking, THAT's my Steward of Adam and Stuart.

While Danny can never be their father and thinks some of the legal parts of adoption is just a moneymaker, he adopted those two seven years ago, be sure of it.

He insists that Adam and Stuart call him Danny or Dan like his own son and daughter do.

Always though, all their dad.

Danny.

Living.

But Who Am I Really?

When someone asks us, "Who are you?'

What do you say?

~

You pause and then you tell the truth or maybe you add some things that are not true, but you start to tell a story.

You are a name, from a place, who was born on a day, who has a family and friends, and maybe a job, and a place you live, with a spouse, a partner, kids, pets (maybe a turtle named Wistful), a place filled with things that you own, with a car, maybe a bike you ride in the warm months, a garage, and a pogo stick you bounce up and down on in that garage under your house, dressed as a big yellow bird, wearing oversized ridiculous orange rubber bird feet, feet balanced on that pogo stick's crossbar, right above the squeaky metal spring tube, fitted in the thick black rubber cup. You've got a big yellow bird head on, your smiling face coming out of the hole in the front below the big orange beak, the yellow feathers springing in a gentle waving gesture as you bounce,

SQUEAK-CHUNK

SQUEAK-CHUNK

SQUEAK-CHUNK

Borrowed Earth Café ☺

You teased those feathers up with a big goofy pocket comb a foot long with three-inch teeth. Those teased yellow feathers waving nearly touching the ceiling.

You're in the garage of your place below the turtle named Wistful and the possessions, including the clothes you wear and your wallet and checkbook and financial portfolio showing your net worth.

There's a stub from your last paycheck on the dresser from the job you don't really like, but it's the job that helps you keep all this stuff, buy all your food, save for what's on your grocery list and wish list too.

Maybe a bigger TV or a frog costume, a green rubber one, with WAY better hands and feet, maybe ride around in here on a red unicycle with a sheepskin padded seat cover and a fake Mickey Mantle rookie baseball card clipped on the fork with a clothes pin so it makes that noise like someone shuffling the biggest deck of cards in the world when you ride in a circle in here. Maybe you can learn to juggle three rubber balls: red, yellow, blue.

Maybe throw together a little routine, get a webcam in here, you riding in a circle in the green frog suit, on the red unicycle with the sheepskin seat cover, juggling the red, yellow, and blue balls, winking as you go by the camera, like, Check it out. Maybe get some YouTube subscribers, "$9.95 a month, watch the guy in the frog suit, he juggles and rides in his suburban garage AND pogo sticks in a big yellow bird costume, his feathers almost touching the ceiling, all his stuff up above him . . . help him get more, supported by viewers like you!"

Maybe mic the garage too so people can hear that card whackety-whacking on the spokes . . .

" . . . whackety, whackety, whackety . . ."

Watching you ride in circles.

Maybe quit your day job someday.

Your plan.

Make a little extra money and have fun at the same time.

So you're bouncing up and down, no higher than a couple inches, not in the frog suit yet, back in the yellow bird suit.

Bouncing up and down on that pogo stick.

SQUEAK-CHUNK

SQUEAK-CHUNK

SQUEAK-CHUNK

You're a person from a place with a job and people or no people, pets or no pets (okay, maybe a turtle named Wistful in a terrarium about THAT high, sitting on your dresser next to your wallet), and you're bouncing up and down in a little space, your garage, and out there, outside your house high above, all the way up in the sky past where it's light into the starry dark and then farther still 'til there's no stars, just dark, traveling up, up, up, you on your pogo stick in your yellow bird suit, a trillion miles below, still bouncing in your garage . . .

SQUEAK-CHUNK

SQUEAK-CHUNK

SQUEAK-CHUNK

. . . and part of you WAY up here traveling fast and farther away and the other part of you WAY down there.

And I ask you, my little yellow pogo-sticking bird in the garage, bouncing up and down, if this is who you are, this guy, whether you're on a pogo stick now in the yellow bird suit with the big orange rubber feet and the yellow feathers and the head with the beak with your face peeking out, on your pogo stick, bouncing up and down, thinking about your frog suit and your unicycle and your YouTube fans, all 1,000,000 of them, riding in a circle, that fake Mickey Mantle rookie card clipped to the fork whackety-whacking, your Wistful turtle in there, I ask you this: Mr. I Am This, who points to his chest, meaning everything in the meat suit under the costume, under the underwear, the naked you and everything inside the naked you, my dear Wistful turtle, if this is who you are, then who will you be when you die?

What, of all this, what's in the meat suit, will survive?

The meat suit, okay, you know what's going to come of that—it'll go in the ground in some shady plot with a modest flat stone engraved with your name, the year you were born, a dash and the year you died and maybe some sentiment like, "He made a million people laugh."

But what about your memories?

Do those come with too? After all, when you wonder who you are, you sift through all those memories, those thoughts, those experiences and you try and think of who you are, based on where you've been, and maybe what you hope to be someday, what you know and believe to be you.

What happens to your story, your hopes, and your dreams, your memories? Your identity, which comes from your story, your experiences?

All your thoughts, the good, the bad, the ugly . . . aren't they stored somewhere, hopefully not on the terminally ill hard drive, or in that spot on your back that hurts on the lower left by your hip that you've come to suspect has something to do with 'money fear' and 'lack' after you read *You Can Heal Your Life* by Louise Hay.

Do those thoughts and memories and ability to feel, to feel anger, fear, hate, grief, worry, anxiety, sorrow but also love, happiness, relief, hope and gratitude, do those thoughts and feelings you feel in the meat suit, and which require the meat suit to feel, are they gone too?

Stored on that hard drive the salesman told you he couldn't guarantee the life of?

This, all that you know as me, what you think you are, will it all be lost?

If so, you think, What can I do so that I am remembered?

So maybe you just have children and hope that they tell their children about you and their children tell their children and their children tell their children about the man in the garage with the yellow bird suit on the pogo stick with the job and the house and the stuff and the turtle named Wistful, who bounced up and down and then who got the frog suit and who really made things happen.

But eventually, your story will stop being told because everyone who told it will die too.

Somewhere down the train line, all the riders you knew will get off at their stops.

They may ride for a few seconds or for a hundred years in a continuation of riders for a thousand years, but you will eventually be forgotten.

Gone.

The head stone blurred from five hundred years of rain and snow, fog and wind and sun. The cemetery records yellowed and illegible—the old guy leaning on the shovel, removes his grey ball cap and wipes his forehead with a rag from his back pocket, replaces his cap and shakes his head saying, "Sorry, don't rightly know who's buried there."

Poof! It's like you never existed.

So you decide to build big or little things, maybe invent something or do really good thing or destroy things, big or little, maybe do bad things, but in either case you hope that your fame or infamy will spread, scattering in a million little pieces everywhere people record things, newspapers, books, emails, hard drives, pictures, movies or in a million Google searches, printed, shellacked and framed and mounted over the mantels of a million fireplaces.

But a thousand years from now, all of that will be gone too and you will be forgotten.

So your meat suit, with your memories imprinted on it and everyone else who knew you and everything that was recorded will be gone. Buried, composted, evaporated, sent up into the atmosphere, burned up by the sun, the gases and fine particles left of you scattering out in a million tiny pieces to eventually bounce of the wall at the end of the Universe and fall back down after a million year journey up and away and then back down.

And it's like the whole thing never happened.

You came, you saw, you grew, you bought, you bounced in your yellow bird suit until your knees gave out, then you retired, sold the house and the pogo stick and gave away the bird suit to your grandson Timmy. You moved in a home with your kids, relatives or friends or family until they got tired of changing you, feeding you, bathing you, propping you up by the window to stare quietly out of and then you went to a home where other people did those things for you and then an ambulance took you to a hospital and the life in you leaked out through a big or tiny hole, then your thoughts slowed down suddenly like a car hitting a concrete pole at 75 miles per hour or slowed and stopped like a ball rolling down a gentle hill.

And your eyes slowly shut or they scrunched shut or the stared until they were sightless and the air in you hissed out slowly or in a cough and it was all over.

Gone.

And sooner or later, forgotten.

Like you never existed.

Time, on the train, going and going, new passengers getting on and off fast or going for a 100-year ride, if things go their way, they pace themselves, eat right, spread a lot of love and service around, or not, just be that lucky fool who races through life, smoking, drinking and eating crap, out for themselves, who cares about everyone else?

Eventually, every ride, slow or fast, long or short, the dark hooded man with the scythe who collects tickets on the train announces your stop. Stands next to you so you don't miss it and helps you off. Whether you're standing, sitting or holding the pole, or you got lucky and have a window seat, with a nice girl or guy next to you, snack and a drink on your lap, feet up 'cause there's no one across from you. Man you thought you could ride forever.

But you can't, you don't get to and something inside you knows it's coming.

Who you say you are and think you are and who I say I am and who I think I am, who I believe myself to be, none of it lasts.

You and everyone, every place and everything you know are headed for the Big Compost heap, destined to become air borne particles and gases to be burned by the sun and sent flying outward like a shower from an exploding bottle rocket, in a zillion little pieces to bounce off the wall at the end of the Universe.

But what if you've just got it backwards?

What if the real you isn't this, the meat suit, the memories, the name and the place you were born and the things you bought, including the library in your name and the Wikipedia entry chronicling your fame or infamy, fortune, deeds, words and known associates?

What if you are not this, but that?

Not all that's in there, but all that, which is out there?

All those tiny pieces of things that go up to bounce off the wall at the end of the Universe and float around and then rain back down to Earth again and become part of something that lives, even if it's a particle that an apple tree root sucks up and moves up into the apple on the top branch, which falls down and is picked up and eaten by some kid. And you become part of that tree, then part of the apple and part of the kid, who grows up to be King. But the kid who becomes King, the tree and the apple will die and then you're back out in the Universe headed to bounce off the wall and float, then sink back down.

Up and down.

Up and down.

Up and down.

And it's like your still on the pogo stick, minus the yellow-feathered bird suit and the garage.

This is way, way bigger now, but it's still up and down and it's like you're not really going any where, but hey, can you get THIS on YouTube? These big trillion year bounces up and down, maybe speed it WAY up, edit it down, no one able to download the file or have time to watch the original, that would take forever to load.

But then all this will die to, the Universe and all that's in it.

All that's spiraling out of the Nothingness. The Void.

The guys on pogo sticks and everything else that is this.

What survives?

What happens to all of it after it dies?

All that is in the space, that has come from the Void?

The Void.

Nothing. No thing.

The emptiness and silence and and place with no things to taste, touch, smell, see or hear with your senses.

Non-sense.

No-thing.

No vibrations.

All that is not.

That.

Maybe none of us is *this* really, *this*, which doesn't survive, can never survive, which comes and goes back from whence it came.

This, the realm of all that is and then is not.

That, all that which is not this and never will be.

The Void.

That.

Not *this*, but *That.*

Maybe we're really *That.*

And *That* never dies.

Maybe all those words that are written, those that many say are "inspired," maybe those words don't come from them, from this, they come from *That*.

Inspired. Spire as in church that you see. An outward, upward spire. An edifice we build outside that we stand under that points up. A place we go in, beneath a spire, that is outside us that points, like a finger up, out there, to remind us of a power outside us.

Like some big distraction built with the intention to connect to something outside, far away and shiny, but that directs our attention away from the real source of power completely in the other direction.

Maybe we have it backwards.

Inspired. In spire. The place or church or kingdom within that we do not build but which is built within us that is always with us and is the place from which we come and to whence we go.

The real us.

A place we go to remind us of a power inside us.

A power that never dies.

A power that is real and that survives without need for thoughts or memories.

It needs no past or future.

It exists Now and Forever.

Maybe I am not *this*, a notion that has an end, but *That*, not a notion at all but a Presence without end.

I am not *this*, I am *That*.

And these words that I say, written over four weeks, collected from Facebook and typed as fast as I could to keep up with what felt like something pouring from a faucet.

Anything that made you feel good and made your eyes fill with tears of joy, that was *That*.

Anything that was omitted or wrong, that was *this*; the unreal impermanent me.

Maybe I didn't write this at all, maybe at some level I know that, about *That*, which is why I hide behind other people, not wanting to put my own name on it. It feels like stealing, to say, I wrote this.

Maybe *That* did and *this*, me, just typed . . .

Mostly, all I've ever known is *this*. Maybe, if I forget all I've ever known, I can know *That*.

~

THIS: I am grateful. Thank you. I love you.

THAT: *You're always welcome.*

☺